CITY AND COUNTRY

CONTRIBUTIONS IN
AMERICAN HISTORY

SERIES EDITOR
STANLEY I. KUTLER
University of Wisconsin

CITY AND COUNTRY

Rural Responses to Urbanization in the 1920s

Don S. Kirschner

CONTRIBUTIONS IN
AMERICAN HISTORY
Number Four

Greenwood Publishing Corporation
Westport, Connecticut

Library of Congress Catalog Card Number: 78–95502

SBN: 8371–2345–3

Greenwood Publishing Corporation
51 Riverside Avenue, Westport, Conn. 06880
Greenwood Publishers Ltd.
42 Hanway Street, London, W.1., England

Printed in the United States of America

FOR MY PARENTS

Contents

Tables

Introduction

THE discussion of the New Deal would be sadly disrupted if respected historians were suddenly to suggest that in their considered opinions there had really never been a depression in the 1930s, and that the events of that decade would have to be interpreted within a different framework and with altogether different questions in mind.

Mercifully we have been spared that kind of New Deal revisionism so far, yet something similar has happened to the historiography of the 1920s. For years, the established view had held that farmers did not share in the widespread prosperity of the 1920s, that in fact they suffered through a decade of depression which foreshadowed the national economic crisis of the 1930s. This was the analysis of the farmers themselves, and historians were not disposed to dispute it.

When the challenge finally came in the 1950s, it was registered as one aspect of a far-reaching reevaluation of the role of agrarianism in American history. Traditionally seen as the embodiment of all things good in American life, the farmer was now toppled from his lofty perch, and in some instances was even recast as the villain of the piece. The decade of the 1920s was one of those instances.

The pivotal essay in this redefinition of the 1920s was an attempt by Richard Hofstadter to explain the growth of McCarthyism in the 1950s.[1] Hofstadter argued that American politics is characterized by struggles over status (prestige) and class (economic) matters. Both, he said, are always present in some balance, but status politics tends to prevail during periods of prosperity, while class issues dominate the politics of hard times. Furthermore, he continued, status conflict, because it is rooted in frustration and aimed at prejudice, is irrational and unreal.

It is a fascinating hypothesis which gives hope of illuminating some of the darker corners of American social and political history. Applied to the 1920s, it suggests that rural dwellers, temporarily freed from the burdens of economic hardship, threw their weight into such pseudo-issues as prohibitionism in an almost hysterical attempt to shore up their prestige in the face of increasing urbanization. Thus Hofstadter became the first historian to assign a truly major role to the general cultural conflict of the 1920s, and to set it within an analytical framework.

A few years later William Leuchtenburg introduced this hypothesis into a full-scale study of the 1920s. Leuchtenburg stated that the economic grievances of farmers in those years were really best understood as a reaction to a sharp drop from the "astronomical levels" of wartime farm prices, and to the disproportionate burst of prosperity in the cities after 1921.

---

[1] Richard Hofstadter, "The Pseudo-Conservative Revolt," ed. Daniel Bell in *The Radical Right* (Garden City, N.Y., 1963).

He concluded that "the poverty of farmers in the 1920s has been exaggerated" and that "most of them were actually better off than in the pre-war days so far as return on their crops was concerned." [2]

By opening up new fields of inquiry the status historians have made an immense contribution to American historiography. Indeed they have virtually reshaped our thinking about the basic problems of the American past. Prior to the 1950s, historians seemed somehow embarrassed that such absurdities as prohibitionism and fundamentalism should have crowded their economic assumptions about the 1920s. Either they treated these issues as sideshow freaks in a circus whose main attractions were political clowns, moral acrobats, and economic jugglers, or they ignored them altogether. It is doubtful that cultural conflict will be so lightly dismissed in the future.

Yet for all that has been written in recent years about cultural conflict, there has been relatively little hard research done on it. It has been more than a decade, for instance, since Hofstadter developed his hypothesis about status conflict, and Leuchtenburg related it to the 1920s, but we still do not know how much stock to put in it because nobody has seen fit to check it out empirically. This book was conceived in part to find out whether that political model provides a reasonable description of the 1920s.

Before proceeding, however—in order to fend off irate historians who might feel that their areas of special competence have been curiously neglected—it would be prudent to discuss briefly what the book is not about. Although it discusses rural economic problems, it is not *about* the farm economy; it includes a fairly extensive description of rural images and values, but it is not *about* the "rural mind"; it examines legislative

---

[2] William Leuchtenburg, *The Perils of Prosperity*, pp. 100–101.

voting in some detail, but it is not really *about* such political footballs as taxation and road construction. The farm economy, the rural mind, government regulation—each of these merits book-length treatment in its own right, and indeed some have received it. Here, however, they serve another purpose.[3]

Instead this book is about a wide and often confusing array of rural responses to an urbanizing nation. Specifically it describes how farmers and townsmen in the Midwest perceived and evaluated a changing environment, and how they tried to shape that environment to their own ends by legislative action. There are really three elements to this conceptual scheme. First, there is the matter of *objective conditions,* which might include anything from the number of tractors on the farms to the number of immigrants in the cities. Secondly, there is the question of the *subjective impressions* that rural people had of these objective conditions. Finally, there is the problem of the *political behavior* that grew out of these impressions. The interrelationship of these factors is the framework within which I have worked on the problem.

Illinois and Iowa are ideally suited to such a study. Together they make up the heart of the corn belt. Including some of the richest farm lands in the world, and flecked with hundreds of towns and villages that served the farmer's immediate needs, they also contained a number of smaller cities with miniaturized industry, labor strife, suburbs, and even ethnic ghettos. What set the two states apart as nothing else did was Chicago, a sprawling giant of transportation and heavy in-

---

[3] I have deliberately avoided footnotes and bibliographical citations to works on these and other issues discussed in the book, except where they bear directly on the matter at hand. Thus in Chapter 1 I do not cite the numerous monographs on the farm economy in the 1920s because they did not provide me with factual data specifically for Illinois and Iowa or with a theoretical or methodological framework.

dustry that curved toward the bottom of Lake Michigan and spilled over into adjacent Indiana. Ill-hidden behind its fragile veneer of lakefront beauty lay a city which appeared to farmers as somehow foreign, radical, snobbish, dirty, ugly, oppressively congested, artificially complicated, and snidely cosmopolitan. Culturally, economically, and ideologically, Chicago was the nemesis of everything that ruralites knew and venerated.

Because statehouses were commonly the arenas in which rural interests were pressed, I have made extensive use of quantitative legislative analysis as the method best suited to reveal the issues, to gauge their dimensions, to see how they related to one another, and to detect shifts in the nature of the conflict and the fortunes of the combatants. *The reader who wishes to make sense out of the tables that summarize the evidence, and to understand the assumptions on which I constructed them, is urged to read the methodological appendix.*

I have been unusually fortunate in the people who have read all or parts of this book, and have offered their comments on it. I am deeply grateful to William Aydelotte for sparking my interest in history to begin with, and for steering it gently toward the mysteries of quantification. Samuel Hays first drew that interest toward American history. This book began as a dissertation under his direction, and he has been prodigal with his time and thought about it in the several years since. Christopher Lasch painstakingly combed through an early version of the manuscript for stylistic snarls and conceptual confusion. Allen Bogue assisted greatly with his knowledge of farm economics and of quantitative techniques in political research. Loren Baritz, Lowell Dyson, Samuel McSeveney, Stow Persons, Jack Roth, Joel Silbey, Allan Spitzer, and Charles Wrong all shared their time and insights with me. At an important juncture, Irwin Flack generously assisted with the research. A University Fellowship from Roosevelt University allowed me to finish the research and writing, while a grant from Simon Fraser University assisted in the preparation of the manuscript. Library personnel everywhere were most helpful. I am obligated to those at the University of Iowa, the State Historical Society of Iowa, the State Archives of Iowa, the State Historical Society of Illinois, the University of Illinois, the Illinois Agricultural Association, the Newberry Library, the Mid-West Inter-Library Loan Center, the University of Chicago Law School, and Roosevelt University.

At some cost to her own professional commitments, my wife, Teresa, patiently listened to the entire manuscript with the trained ear of a linguist, helped to clarify my thinking and writing, and somehow communicated her cheerfulness and energy to me at those times when I was in danger of losing both.

1

The Nature of
Rural Problems

I

IN THE two decades before the 1920s, midwestern farmers were
the happy beneficiaries of a generally expanding farm prosperity. As this trend accelerated after 1914 because of the demands
generated by a war economy and the immediate needs of a
starving Europe after the war, prices soared to what would
have been levels of pure fantasy in earlier years. When farmers
turned to the postwar world it was with a buoyant optimism
sustained by the longest and steepest economic upswing since
the Civil War. They might have grumbled about the excessive
wage demands of labor in 1919, but they did not get seriously
steamed up about the working class while prices remained
high. They had always known that there were large profits to
be harvested from the rich soil under the proper circumstances,
and now at last the proper circumstances prevailed. Ardent
students of the Bible though many of them were, they had
somehow forgotten the parable of Joseph and the grain, and
acted instead as if the years would wax fat forever.

Optimism dimmed in 1920 when farm prices began to slide,

and disappeared completely in 1921 when the bottom dropped out of the rural economy. After cresting at almost $1 billion in 1919, farm income in Iowa plummeted to $336 million two years later, and wavered between $400 and $600 million for the remainder of the decade.[1] This disaster reflected the conditions of individual farmers. The average gross income on Iowa farms was $2,000 in 1910, and then rose steadily to over $3,000 in 1917. It tailed off to $2,600 in 1919, and then sank sharply to $1,500 in 1921. By 1924 it had climbed back to nearly $2,300, but then prices broke again and incomes dipped below $2,000 for the rest of the decade.[2]

Obviously farmers could not absorb a 30 to 50 percent cut in income without at least a twinge of discomfort. Still, gross income by itself is not a very reliable indicator of economic conditions. There are other factors that can act to cushion the shock. If the farmer owns his land and machinery free of debt, for example, he may at least be fairly certain that he will ride out the crisis without losing his farm. Or if falling prices are accompanied by an equivalent drop in costs then real income remains much the same. And in the unlikely event that land values remain high when prices drop, then at least the farmer's capital investment is not affected. Unfortunately for many farmers in the 1920s, none of these cushions was there to absorb the shock.

For the business-minded farmers of Iowa and Illinois, no problem was more alarming than the severe decline in capital investment after 1920. Between 1910 and 1920, when times were good, the value of farm lands and building more than doubled in Iowa, and increased by nearly 75 percent in Illinois. During the same years the value of implements and machinery trebled in both states. By 1925, however, $2.5 billion had been pared away from Iowa farm values, a loss of over one-third, and in the next five years another $750 million was lost. The relative decline in Illinois was almost as bad in the first half of the decade, and worse during the next.[3] In both states the value of implements and machinery also skidded between 1920 and 1925, before increasing slightly during the rest of the decade as farmers in the more substantial cash-grain areas began to replace outmoded equipment with motorized tractors.[4] Furthermore, the shock of capital loss hit with roughly equal impact in all parts of the corn belt. Farms in the best cash-grain regions had been worth up to $60,000 in 1920, but a decade later they were worth only half as much. At the other extreme, in such marginal areas as Decatur County, Iowa, farms valued at nearly $24,000 in 1920 had fallen below $11,000 ten years later.[5]

It might be argued that the decline in farm values was a healthy symptom of the end of wartime inflation, and that a sense of reality had finally been restored to land prices. Yet this argument sounds uncomfortably like the official proclamations from the White House in 1930 and 1931, when the nation was being reassured that what had sounded like a loud bang on Wall Street was only the whimper of a lunatic fringe of investors being shaken out of the market. The argument also ignores the human dimensions of the situation. It is unlikely, after all, that farmers were much comforted by the thought that things were finally returning to "normal" now. The problem was especially acute for the thousands of farmers who, urged on by rising prices for crops, had invested in land and machinery at the very peak of wartime inflation. These people did not simply lose speculative suet; they lost bundles of solid cash.

The manner in which this contraction of capital bore on the perennial problem of farm mortgages made their situation even more painful. Farmers are incurable optimists when times

are good. The prospect of high profits clouds their memories
and they go about their business as if prosperity were the natural and permanent condition of mankind. They are plungers
at such times. They reason that if they can clear $1,000 on 200
acres, then they can clear proportionately more on 300 acres.
And so they borrow to buy land and they borrow some more to
buy the extra machinery they will need to farm it; and of
course they do their borrowing and buying at inflated price
levels. The steep mortgages which they incur do not worry
them as long as crop prices hold up. The trouble is that prices
usually don't hold up, and when they break, farmers inevitably
entertain some ugly second thoughts about the implications of
their debts.

That is exactly what happened in the corn belt between 1910
and 1930. At first there was a stunning increase in the amount
of mortgaged indebtedness, but it caused no concern because it
was matched by a sharp rise in crop prices and farm values. As
a result, the ratio of indebtedness to value held steady and so
did rural nerves. When prices dropped, however, values chased
them downward but mortgages remained high. Thus, farmers
who had owed about one-fourth the value of their capital in
1920, owed nearly half of it in 1930. There were counties in
northwestern Iowa where nearly three out of four farmers
were debtors. In the marginal counties perhaps only half the
farms were mortgaged, but the mortgages were often larger
than elsewhere.[6] A sizable majority of midwestern farmers were
saddled in this way with mortgage payments pegged to high
prices and land values at a time when prices and values were
in fact falling. Their real costs thus rose sharply. Economic
complacency does not grow from such conditions.

The squeeze was not a new one for farmers, nor was there
much novelty in the sour response it drew from them. If there

was an added intensity to their protest it was provided by the steeply rising taxes of the 1920s. It is difficult to get precise and extensive information on farm taxes for those years,[7] but it is evident that expanding state and local expenditures were falling heavily upon farmers, since they owned most of the property and property was the major source of taxation. To meet the many new financial pressures, the Illinois legislature raised property taxes in 1919 and again in 1927, while it fought off several rural attempts to impose an income tax in the state. In Iowa, the legislature opened the way to higher property taxes in 1929 by raising the limit to which a county could go into debt, and it consistently beat down efforts to levy a state income tax which would have distributed the burden more evenly.[8]

The implications of heavier expenditures were best explained by the owner of an eighty-acre farm in southern Iowa, who wrote of his plight to the *Iowa Homestead,* a farm journal with a loyal following in the marginal areas of the state where farm discontent ran high. During the two years of the war, when prices were shooting up, this farmer's taxes had held steady at about $120. By 1920, however, when prices were beginning to fall rapidly, his taxes had almost doubled. In 1923, when conditions were improving, his taxes had climbed to over $260, and the next year, when there was another break in prices, he paid $400 in taxes. Through good times and bad his taxes had swept irresistibly upward. In six years they had more than tripled while, at the same time, the value of his property was melting and prices, overall, were declining. The chief reason, as he explained it, was that the number of farmers locally was declining but school taxes were not. With fewer farmers left to pay the same amount, the burden fell more heavily than ever upon those who remained. This farmer was one of only four who were paying the entire school tax for Hocking, Iowa.[9] By the 1920s it was becoming rather costly to sustain the ideal of the family farm in southern Iowa.

In those districts where consolidated schools were replacing the old one-room country schoolhouses, the tax levy was even heavier. *Wallaces' Farmer,* a respected and widely read farm journal in the Midwest, saw the implications of this problem in terms of an agrarian dilemma:

> The childless farm landowner perceives that he pays a tax of per-haps $4 an acre on farm land in a consolidated school district and only $2 or possibly $1.50 an acre on similar land which is not sup-porting such a school. Even men who have children and who are enthusiastic about the type of education furnished by the con-solidated school oftentimes feel that they are forced to oppose plans for a consolidated school because they can not afford the increased tax.[10]

At four dollars an acre even the small farmer was contributing heavily, and this was early in the decade with further increases still ahead. The solution to the problem, as Wallace saw it, was to restore farm prices to the levels of a fondly remembered yesterday, so that farmers could pay higher taxes for better schools without sacrificing to do it.

The situation was a difficult one for ruralites. The costs of government were being multiplied at the local level by new kinds of schools with more teachers receiving better pay, and at the state level by increased services, larger bureaucracies, and higher salaries. Farmers were the primary source of government income, but the number of farmers was dwindling. As a result, the per-capita tax load for those who remained was even higher than it would have been with a stable farm population.

Falling income, a punishing loss of capital investment, the

pressure of high, fixed mortgage payments, rising taxes and swelling farm costs all combine to suggest that the 1920s were not the best of years for corn-belt farmers. But just how bad were they? Was there really a farm depression or was there merely a decline from a few abnormally good years? For that matter, at what point does a "decline" become a "depression"?

It is easy enough to describe economic conditions in clinically dispassionate terms by referring to various statistical compilations. With care and thoroughness it can be a comfortingly objective exercise for the historian. However, when it comes to interpreting his data—when it comes to evaluating a period as one of prosperity or depression—the historian's decisions must be relative and altogether subjective. The concept of depression almost by definition demands a comparison between two sets of conditions. There is a depression *from* one condition to another. Only the historian can select the conditions to compare, and only the historian in the end can evaluate the human impact of the conditions he chooses to describe. His data may be perfectly objective; his choices cannot be.

He might choose, for instance, to minimize the farm crisis of the 1920s by filtering his appraisal through the bitter conditions of the 1930s. By 1932, most farmers would have been eager to return to what they had called a depression ten years earlier. True enough, but this is a patently unhistorical argument. In 1922, farmers had not yet felt the 1930s, and so could not have felt depressed from them.

The impact of economic change must be understood not by looking forward from the 1920s, but by looking backward from them. And gazing backward one sees fully two decades of expanding farm prosperity with only one or two brief interruptions. The war did exaggerate the trend, but it did not start it. The older farmers had to stretch their memories through more

than twenty years of good times to recall the squeeze of the
1890s. The younger ones—those who did not begin to farm
until after the turn of the century—had never really experienced hard times. In other words, most corn-belt farmers had
learned from long experience that a decent living could be
made from the soil, and they had keyed their expectations to
that experience. The collapse of 1920–1921 was sudden and
drastic, and its effects lingered. Farmers did not sink below
the subsistence level, but then neither did most of the depressed
urban middle class a decade later. The point is not that many
farmers bought cars in the 1920s, and therefore could not have
been depressed, but that almost all of them suffered heavy
losses and felt that reasonable expectations had been betrayed.
In the end, it is how people respond to economic change that
effectively determines whether there is a depression. Evaluating the worsening conditions and the sharp responses to
them, it is difficult to conclude that the corn belt was experi-
encing anything less than a serious depression in the 1920s.

The troubles of midwestern farmers were further com-
pounded by the realization that their problems were growing
in the midst of plenty—indeed, in some perverse and ironic
way, that they were growing precisely because of plenty. What
kind of justice was there, after all, in a system which penalized
success? Surely it did not square with the old American values
which they had learned as toddlers. This bitter paradox was
even reflected in occasional fragments of verse that were sung
in the countryside. In southern Iowa one balladeer lamented:

> Oh, the corn is ripe in Iowa
>   And the oats are in the bin,
> And it's time to dig the taters,
>   Tho the crop is mighty thin;

The bloom is on the clover
  And the farmer ought to sing
For this year's bumper harvest
  Which doesn't mean a thing!

Oh, the corn is ripe in Iowa
  And the freight rates still are high
The taxes too, are mounting,
  While the farmers moan and sigh
As they haul their grain to market
  For whatever it will bring—
It's g.o.p. prosperity
  But it doesn't mean a thing.[11]

It is probable that these stanzas embarrassed Calliope more
than Harding, and it may be that most Iowa farmers felt little
sympathy for the Democratic politics of this paper, but there
were doubtless few among them who did not feel the same
frustration over some of the problems which the poet lamented
in those bleak days of the price collapse of 1921. During the
war, every effort had been made to encourage farmers to increase production, but increased production proved to be a
difficult habit to break and a costly one to continue when
market conditions changed.

Unable to cope with the depression effectively in other ways
at the national level, farmers sought relief through legislation.
The extension of farm credits, the encouragement given to
cooperatives, and above all the passage twice of a program of
federally supported farm prices (vetoed both times by a profoundly aloof President) do not reflect the free-will offerings
of a kindly Congress as much as they do the depression politics
of troubled farmers now operating more shrewdly than shrilly

as a pressure group in both parties. When their efforts were
stunted by a hostile chief executive some of them were stirred
to warn darkly that "it takes a lot of slaps and cuffs to rouse
the farmers and unite them in any organized effort, but just a
little more will be enough." [12] With a nationwide depression
approaching rapidly, this editor was a better prophet than he
might have imagined.

Thus, in Washington, farmers tried to counteract the depression with legislation designed to affect prices and certain costs.
Because they were beset by common problems at this level, they
were able to pull together in Congress and to achieve some
noteworthy legislative victories. At the local level, however,
their stakes and interests varied greatly, and in state politics,
where these interests were played out, they fell to fighting
among themselves.

The range of economic differences among farmers in the
corn belt was enormous. They ran from the heavily capitalized
and mechanized farmers in the fertile cash-grain areas to those,
especially in the southern sections of both states, for whom
questions of boom and bust in the market economy were almost
irrelevant. For these marginal farmers—"dirt farmers" they
were known locally—times were always hard and changes were
marked largely in degrees of relative impoverishment. They
were barely able to scratch a living from the soil even in the
best of times. One such area in Iowa was Appanoose County,
where farmers worked an average of only 140 acres with about
$600 worth of machinery in 1925. At the same time, farms in
Plymouth County, in the lush northwestern corner of the state,
were more than one-third larger, and were operated with nearly
$1,500 in machinery.[13] It is hardly surprising that they pro-
duced almost three times as much income as the poorest counties.[14] In Illinois, the contrast was even more exaggerated. The

farms in a cluster of counties in the southern tip of the state averaged less than 100 acres and only about $325 worth of machinery. In the central part of the state, farmers owned almost twice as much land and worked it with machinery valued five times higher.[15]

These dirt farmers were trying to survive on small farms with poor soil and inadequate machinery. Compared with their highly mechanized neighbors to the north they were inefficient producers, and in an era when the potential to over-produce held prices down, efficiency was the key to survival. Thousands of dirt farmers lived in a state of almost constant panic. The many who did not make it constituted a major source of emigration from the rural areas to the cities. Those who managed to hang on made up a class of chronically de-pressed, a source of perpetual ill-will from which the verbally militant Farmers' Union drew many of its members during the 1920s, and virtually a separate economic interest group in the political tong wars that took place every two years in Des Moines and Springfield. In fact, the in-fighting that ranged farmers against farmers often enabled urbanites to compensate for the political disability imposed upon them by malappor-tionment, and worked with devastating effect to pinch in the borders of rural influence. It was a natural outcome of the fact that there were different classes of farmers working for different ends by different means.

Only by 1928 and 1929 did the pressures slacken for many of them. Finally their complaints and threats diminished as they began to contemplate the pleasant prospect of joining in the national treasure hunt. Once again, the optimism of 1919 glowed in the corn belt, and it was reflected in the frequent assertions that farm real estate held immense promise for future rewards. No longer cowed, the plungers were reappearing. One

Iowa editor illustrated the trend by claiming that "no one will dispute that the governor is right in urging Iowa farm mortgages as the safest investment on earth." [16] As it turned out, he was a decade or more premature, and there were already a few speculators who might have disputed the governor. It had been just one month since the crash on Wall Street; it would be many months more before rural editors would again commend their readers to farm mortgages as "the safest investment on earth."

II

Economic problems in the rural areas were serious enough, but they were not the only problems. Reaching far beyond them were changes of a more durable nature that were transforming the nation from a basically rural to an increasingly urban society. In its most tangible form this transformation was felt in terms of a long-continuing change in the nature and distribution of the population.

The rural population of Iowa declined by almost 170,000 between the beginning of the century and 1930. While much of this loss occurred in the first decade, the process persisted with a cumulative impact that was most distressing. During these same years, the urban population shot up from less than 600,000 to nearly 1 million, increasing by more than 10 percent in the 1920s alone. Furthermore, this growth took place primarily in the larger urban centers. The population of cities over 25,000 rose by one-third during the decade, while the number of inhabitants in towns between 5,000 and 25,000 declined. [17]

In Illinois, the process was much more advanced. At the

turn of the century, the population was split almost evenly between rural and urban areas. By 1920, the balance had shifted to a two-to-one majority living in the towns and cities, and ten years later nearly three out of four people lived in urban areas.[18]

The major difference in Illinois was the existence of an immense metropolitan area whose ungainly growth served only to distort the situation. In Iowa the towns ranged from small county seats through local hubs of commerce to the middling industrial centers strung out along the rivers which bordered the state on the east and west. In the aggregate their weight was felt increasingly, but no one of them could reasonably stand as the symbol for a world gone wrong as Chicago did in Illinois. Chicago's size and power placed it by itself, a thousand times more ominous than the lesser cities. Between 1910 and 1920, its population grew by almost 25 percent, and by that much again in the next decade. By 1930, Chicago had thirty times the population of the next largest city in Illinois, and nearly a million and a half more people than the total rural population of the state.[19]

This urban growth was fed by two streams of population. One of them originated in the rural areas, and it presented agrarian apologists with a problem. It was their contention not only that rural life was superior, but that any clear-headed individual, given the chance, would recognize the superiority at once.[20] And yet there were thousands of farmers, or children of farmers, who chose the bright lights of the cities to the economic uncertainties of the soil. The repeated warnings of country editors did nothing to stem the flow.

More significant than the renegade farmers who left for the cities were the immigrants flooding into them from southern and eastern Europe. Since the 1880s, these "new immigrants" had been arriving in swelling numbers, bringing with them customs, traditions, values, and religions that were often sharply at odds with New World norms. By 1920, the accrued weight of these awesome folk migrations was pressing unbearably on the countryside, charging ruralites with a current of fear for the very survival of "the American way of life."

It was not that the new immigrants were pouring into the country districts—the rural citadels of Americanism were spared the embarrassment—but that they were nesting in the cities at precisely the time when cities were threatening to destroy the old rural society. The urban threat thus grew as much from the kinds of people who lived in cities as from the economic pressures that attended metropolitan growth, and ruralites were perfectly clear about who these people were.[21] It was not simply that the proportion of "foreign stock" to "native stock" was greater in the cities.[22] To be sure, nearly two out of three urbanites in Illinois were of foreign stock, while seven out of ten rural dwellers were natives. Yet the most heavily alien counties in Iowa were strictly rural, and still they caused no excessive concern among natives because they had been settled from northern Europe.[23]

No, the distinction made was not whether one had come from Europe, but where in Europe one had come from. In these terms the rural counties were, without exception, free from the taint of impure origins. Only in areas like the mining counties of southern Illinois might one encounter a few hundred Poles or Lithuanians, and a thousand or two Italians. And in these few semirural industrial counties the new immigrants were a minority among the foreign born and only a minuscule element in the total population.

It was in the cities where the new immigrants were to be found, and among the cities it was especially Chicago which seemed to exemplify to the rural eye the whole sad situation. There were 800,000 immigrants in Chicago in 1920, and more than half of them had come from southern and eastern Europe. In the southern tip of the state, on the Kentucky border, lay Pulaski County, named after the Polish count who had been martyred in the Revolution. In 1920, there were two Poles living in Pulaski County. In the same year, there were more Poles living in Chicago than there were people in any other city in the state. In Poland itself, only Warsaw had a larger Polish population. The Russians in Chicago, mostly Jews, were almost as numerous as the total population of Des Moines. One out of four counties in Illinois and Iowa had fewer than 500 immigrants, and almost all of them had come from the British Isles, Scandinavia, and Germany. Chicago had more Syrians, Joliet more Yugoslavs, Herrin more Italians, and Cedar Rapids more Bohemians.[24] One had only to gauge the distance from his farm to any one of these cities to realize how imminent the peril was.

The fervent response of country folks to this threat was fed by the religious hostilities which have recurred like malarial spasms since they were first brought here in the seventeenth century. In obvious ways the Catholics and Jews who made up the bulk of the new immigration were distinct minorities in what for three centuries had been a Protestant society. Each group was much smaller than the total of Protestants, and both were dissenters from a prevailing religious tradition. In the eyes of rustic Protestants, however, the situation looked quite different. They agreed that this was a Protestant nation, and were deeply concerned that it should remain one, but their knowledge of current trends gave them cause to fear the future.

By the 1920s the Roman Catholic Church was the largest single religious body in the United States. It was four times

the size of its nearest competitor in Illinois, and even in Iowa
was 40 percent larger than the next denomination. There were
more than 1 million Catholics in Illinois, and almost 90 percent of them lived in cities.[25] No less shocking to ruralites, the
recent migrations from eastern Europe had vaulted Jews over
Methodists as the second largest religious group in Illinois,
and Jews were even more urbanized than Catholics.[26] Indeed
there were more Jews in Chicago alone than there were Methodists, Presbyterians, and Disciples of Christ in all of Iowa.
Not only Chicago, but such cities as Joliet, Peoria, Dubuque,
and Davenport ranged between 40 and 75 percent Catholic
and Jewish.[27] With few exceptions, on the other hand, rural
areas were completely dominated by Protestants.

Because the public creed of the nation preached religious
toleration, hostility toward these minorities often remained
covert, but it was not passive. On the contrary, these feelings
often involved a passionate commitment, and it does not seem
unnatural that the explosive potential of the commitment
should have been directed against the cities in the Midwest,
and especially against Chicago where well over a million of
these outsiders lived.

In some ways more insidious than any of these threats to
rural hegemony was a rapidly changing outlook among the
middle and upper classes of the large cities. The evidence here
is largely literary, but if it is imprecise next to the flinty-cold
figures of the census, it is no less important. Of course, there is
no way of knowing how many people were reading such writers
as Mencken and Masters and Fitzgerald, or who they were or
where they lived, but that is of no consequence here. What is
important is that these authors represented a trend that was
making it fashionable either to mount a literary assault on

farm and village, or to praise the virtues of city life. The message of the new literature was perceived—sometimes vaguely, sometimes quite directly—and resented in the countryside.

Easily the most stinging of the new critics of rural America was H. L. Mencken. Who but he could have written of the "humble husbandman" as a "tedious fraud and ignoramous, a cheap rogue and hypocrite . . ." in short, as a "prehensile moron"? [28] Mencken's aim in writing about "The Husbandman"—apart from giving his genius for contumely its daily workout—was to expose the farmers, and their panegyrists in Congress, for the hypocrites he thought them to be. The farmer, said Mencken,

> . . . takes on, in political speeches and newspaper editorials, a sort of mystical character. He is no longer a mundane laborer, scratching for the dollar, full of staphylococci, smelling heavily of sweat and dung; he is a high priest in a rustic temple. . . . The farmer, thus depicted, grows heroic, lyrical, pathetic, affecting.

For Mencken, though, the farmer was neither mystical, nor heroic nor lyrical. "There has never been a time, in good seasons or bad," he wrote, "when his hands were not itching for more; there has never been a time when he was not ready to support any charlatan, however grotesque, who promised to get it for him." Of course, nearly everybody in Mencken's universe was grasping and hypocritical, but there was something special about farmers that made him single them out as the most depraved of a race which he usually defined only in gradations of depravity. For it was the farmers who had invented prohibition, and they had done it, according to Mencken, as an exercise in pure malice. "What lies under [prohibition], and under all the other crazy enactments of its category," explained Mencken, "is no more and no less than the yokel's congenital and incurable hatred of the city man— his simian rage against everyone who, as he sees it, is having a better time than he is." Once again, Mencken belabored rural hypocrisy, pointing to farmer-inspired loopholes in the Volstead Act that did not prohibit such abominations as hard cider, "but simply the use of alcohol in its more charming and romantic forms."

Equally repugnant to Mencken was the farmer's double standard of sexual morality. It was they who had been responsible for the Mann Act, he claimed, because they had wanted to stop what they thought were "the byzantine debaucheries of urban Antinomians," and they had passed state laws "forbidding the use of automobiles 'for immoral purposes,' " while conveniently overlooking "barns, cow-stables, hay-ricks and other such familiar rustic ateliers of sin." The moral fervor of farmers, he concluded, "never prohibits acts that are common on the farms; it only prohibits acts that are common in the cities."

Farmers had probably been fair game for city people since the founding of the Republic, but in the past most of the derogation had been patronizing rather than vicious. The caricatures of farmers as hicks, bumpkins, and hayseeds had been drawn with the same kind of almost good-natured ridicule that is usually reserved for the village or neighborhood idiot. And over the years, farmers and their choruses had given much more and better to the cities than they had received. With Mencken, however, the rules changed. The farmer was no longer seen as a relatively harmless simpleton. He was a gouging, grasping, conniving, loutish hypocrite who was as responsible as anybody for the fevers which racked the national body politic. It is scarcely surprising that Mencken was treated with a certain lack of graciousness from time to time in the village press.

Alongside Mencken, Edgar Lee Masters's rejection of the bucolic life was almost tame, but then Mencken was not an easy act to follow, especially for someone performing essentially the same act. However, while Mencken might be damned in the rural press and dismissed as an urban loudmouth who did not know what he was talking about, Masters could not be so easily ignored. When he tore apart the country village he spoke as a product of it. Masters's shot at village life in *Spoon River Anthology* had not gone unnoticed in the corn belt, but it was quickly forgotten—or repressed—until he visited Des Moines in 1925. In an interview there he reopened old wounds by asserting that the way to national self-respect could only be cleared if the church were eliminated completely from American society. "The country must fight her way back to liberty," he said, "and throw off the incubus of prohibition laws, censorship, William Jennings Bryanism, ignorance and scriptural dogmatism." [29] The Reverend James Kellems, a Des Moines evangelist, replied by attacking Masters's adopted home town of Chicago, and by suggesting that if Masters did not like it here he could solve his problems by removing himself to Russia where he would find all the modernism he wanted.[30] Similar invitations were issued elsewhere in the Iowa press.

F. Scott Fitzgerald did not enjoy the same renown in the country districts as Mencken and Masters, probably because he was content to write about other things, but the frame of mind that he represented—his absorption in the dazzle of urban life—was sensed in the rural areas. In the past, the American literary tradition had not been kind to the metropolis, but now all at once the national literature was saturated with city life, often fascinated with the very things in it which the farmer despised and feared. Fitzgerald himself might have felt deeply ambivalent about the life he lived and the society he described, might even have had Nick Carraway preparing to return to the Midwest at the end of *The Great Gatsby,* but in both his life and his writings he was unable to resist the attraction of the brightest of lights. He indulged his nostalgia from a safe distance, and while he had Nick packing to return West, he himself was packing for Europe, a few light-years distant from the wheat fields of his native Minnesota. "So we beat on," he concluded, "boats against the current, borne back ceaselessly into the past." Fitzgerald's boat, meanwhile, had no trouble cutting through the current, mocking his own past as it sailed ever eastward through the decade.

The ruralite was finding that in song and story the ethos of millions of Americans was changing in a novel and dangerous fashion. He had neither sympathy nor patience with the new literature. "Down east," said one village editor, "certain would-be highbrows . . . pretend that every few weeks a great novel is produced by some American writer." The fact is, he continued, that today's best writing does not begin to compare with the fiction in the "dime and half dime novels" of our parents' generation. With unbounded confidence in his aesthetic sensibilities he pronounced that "there are epochs in art and literature. Today's is not one of the great epochs in American fiction." [31]

There was a challenge to the ruralites rising from among the restless urban middle classes, and it was being shaped, contrary to rural judgments, by a brilliant young generation of artists. Ruralites could ignore the challenge only at the risk of losing their traditional position as custodians of the American ethos, and of losing their self-esteem as well. They had no intention of surrendering either. In the past, they had been able to rely upon poets, novelists, and essayists for reassurance, but that was no longer so surely the case. Now they would have to proceed alone.

There was a dual assault upon rural America in the 1920s. One wave threatened to swamp the traditional way of rural life; the other eroded a hard-won farm prosperity. Both were real and both were critical, and they left ruralites bewildered and angry. One thing was clear, however: both sets of problems had their source in the city.

NOTES

1. Howard Bowen, *Iowa Income: 1909–1934.*
2. Ibid.
3. United States, Bureau of the Census, *Fifteenth Census of the United States, 1930* (hereafter cited as *Census, 1930*).
4. Ibid.
5. Ibid.
6. Ibid.
7. Certain tax data were made available in the 1930 census, but were not enumerated in 1920. As a result it is not possible to measure changes in the tax loads of farmers except by visiting every county court house in the Midwest.
8. See Chapter 5 for a discussion of these and other tax problems that were racking the legislatures at the time.
9. *Iowa Homestead,* February 26, 1925.
10. *Wallace's Farmer,* December 15, 1922.
11. *Fremont County* (Iowa) *Herald,* September 15, 1921.
12. *Carrollton* (Illinois) *Patriot,* May 31, 1928.
13. *Census, 1930.*
14. Ibid.
15. Ibid.
16. *Monticello* (Iowa) *Express,* November 28, 1929.
17. *Census, 1930.*
18. Ibid.
19. Ibid.
20. *Ames* (Iowa) *Daily Tribune,* August 29, 1923; *Monticello* (Iowa) *Express,* April 4, 1929; *Carmi* (Illinois) *Tribune-Times,* November 1, 1923; *Galena* (Illinois) *Gazette,* February 26, 1920.

21. See Chapter 2 for a discussion of some of the implications of rural nativism at this time.

22. "Foreign stock," as opposed to foreign *born*, refers to immigrants and to native Americans with at least one foreign-born parent. "Native stock" describes native-born people whose parents were both native-born Americans. These are definitions used in the census.

23. *Census, 1920.* Only four counties in Iowa had as many as 15 percent foreign born at the time. Of these, Audubon County was predominantly Danish, Winnebago County was strongly Norwegian, Sioux County was overwhelmingly Dutch, and Lyon County was essentially Dutch and German.

24. Ibid.

25. United States, Bureau of the Census, *Census of Religious Bodies, 1926.*

26. Ibid. It is doubtful that there has ever been a more valid stereotype than that of the Jew as urbanite. Of 340,000 Jews in Illinois only 58 lived in rural areas, and not a single one of Iowa's nearly 13,000 Jews lived outside a city or town.

27. Ibid.

28. H. L. Mencken, *Prejudices: A Selection*, chosen by James T. Farrell. All of the quotations here are taken from Mencken's essay, "The Husbandman," pp. 157–169.

29. *Des Moines Register*, March 20, 1925. This interview took place well before the Scopes affair in Tennessee.

30. Ibid.

31. *Elkader* (Iowa) *Register*, September 22, 1921. From one year before this editorial to one year after it, some interesting literary works were published, including *This Side of Paradise* and *The Beautiful and the Damned* by Fitzgerald, *Main Street* and *Babbitt* by Lewis, *Three Soldiers* by Dos Passos, *The Waste Land* by Eliot, and *Emperor Jones, Anna Christie,* and *The Hairy Ape* by O'Neill.

2

The Rural Image
of the City

I

DOMINATING the farmer's image of the city were its people. Rich and poor alike, immigrant and native, laborer, radical, and plutocrat, they crowded together in the foreground, a series of stereotypes whose common purpose in life was to define and enhance his misery.

In past eras of economic crisis, farmers had often directed their wrath at eastern wealth. They had attacked the Wall Street financier whose gold mentality had thwarted their inflationist aspirations. Or they had ranted at the railroad magnates whose freight rates had bled them dry. In either case, the farmer had expressed very specific economic grievances against the urban rich as the unwanted masters of his destiny.

Once again in the 1920s the farmers were in trouble. Once again, drawing from their historic reservoir of ill-will, they sniped at the urban rich. Only now there was a curious difference, because it was not the capitalist's economic power that the farmer attacked as much as his way of life. Increasingly, he

removed the capitalist from his economic context and ab-
stracted him to a kind of generalized symbol of indecency.

Of course, there was still much residual hostility toward
economic exploitation in the Midwest, and the chief spokesman for it was the Farmers' Union, which ordinarily represented the most embattled farmers. Even before the volatile
Milo Reno became its president early in the decade, the Iowa
Farmers' Union was firing a stream of invective at capitalist
exploitation, at the "exorbitant interest, rents and taxes" levied
against the farmers by bankers and businessmen.[1] Again and
again throughout these years the *Union Farmer* was filled with
pungent rhetoric attacking businessmen, and especially bankers.

Yet this attitude was no longer really prevalent in the corn
belt. It was less the capitalist's exploitation of the farmers that
was criticized than the way he made his living and the way he
lived his life. Speaking the disgust of many ruralites, an editor
in southern Illinois noted that

> There are between the City Hall in New York and the Battery
> Wall—a distance that can be walked in ten minutes—thousands of
> high binders in the world of speculation who have never done an
> honest day's work in their lives, but who make often in a day and
> frequently in a week as much if not more than the average farmer
> makes in a year.[2]

Although there were perhaps some overtones of jealousy for
wealth in this statement, what really nettled the editor was less
the sheer existence of wealth than the way in which it was acquired. The ruralite was outraged at a world in which chica-
nery was rewarded so generously. Even more deeply embedded
was an implied judgment of what really constituted work. The

financier did not work for his money, he speculated, he gambled, and was therefore engaged in a fundamentally dishonest occupation. Work in any meaningful sense was done only by the farmer, who was presumably the more honest and dignified for it.

Disparaging references to "capitalists" were common in the rural press, and the stubborn refusal of farm prices to mirror the growing prosperity of the nation only heightened the farmer's hostility. One editor, lamenting the poor state of the agrarian economy, added angrily that "it don't help matters at all to have some fat, sleek, prosperous chap from the industrial centers tell us that we are getting along all right now." [3]

It was not only the advice of that fat, sleek, prosperous chap that infuriated farmers, however; it was his whole approach to life. As farmers saw it, the capitalist was unable to create a meaningful existence in the city, and so he and his family dulled their senses in a kind of Roman voluptuousness that was utterly depraved. The triviality of their way of life was depicted in a cartoon which showed the copy boy of a country paper—a kind of Tom-Sawyer-with-a-green-eye-shade—saying to the editor:

> The big city papers kin poke fun at us fer tellin' 'bout Paul Jones' new chicken coop—but, by Hek! We never fall fer no guff 'bout Mrs. Algernon Morganbilt's pomperanian [*sic*] pup "Piffle," havin' the pip and a lotta other items like that, witch them city papers print, do we, boss? [4]

The terse "Nope" from the boss shows that the generations concurred in their scorn for the idle rich. As if to underscore the point, the same paper noted a few days later that a New York judge had denied a divorce decree to a man who had pleaded that his wife's smoking was evidence of her bad character. The editor commented that Iowa women weren't "jaded by the mad craze for sensation until cigarets [*sic*] are necessary to soothe jangled nerves." [5]

If Mr. Morganbilt was lazy and dishonest, if he shunned the satisfaction of work for the profits of speculation, his wife was spoiled, pleasure-mad, and corrupt. Worse still, the future held little hope for improvement because the children were as bad as the parents. One editor discovered that urban juveniles "must have a movie mellerdramer a day, or perish of ennui . . ." and he concluded that "such youths will be of no value on the farm, nor anywhere else, until they have learned the art of living rationally, simply and therefore, happily." [6]

Further hostility toward urban wealth was expressed in connection with Prohibition. Shortly after the Eighteenth Amendment had been ratified, an Iowa editor triumphantly pointed to the "dazed" New Yorkers who "never took stock in the sentiment of the country." He continued, "the overfed rich who wash their pate de fois with champaigne [*sic*], never believed that prohibition would ever get beyond Maine." [7] Here too, the theme of urban decadence runs near the surface, but it was laced this time with a dash of the bitters of vengeance.

Whether the ruralite judged the urban rich at work or at play, he found them guilty of corruption and depravity, condemned to live in a revolting madhouse where there was little hope for a cure. On the whole, however, the attacks against wealth, whether on economic or moral grounds, were sporadic and relatively infrequent, considering the way in which farmers had responded to depression circumstances in the past.

The upper classes were portrayed essentially as a moral disgrace, but not usually as a direct threat to the farmer. Such a threat existed, all right, but it was to be found infesting Chicago's West Side or the Lower East Side of Manhattan rather than Wall Street. None of the city's people was subjected to such a steady stream of verbal abuse from the ruralite as the immigrant. If the Wall Street financier was unwholesome, the immigrant was positively un-American. Fulminations against him welled up soon after the war was over and continued throughout the decade.

A paper in northeastern Iowa was only one of the many that alerted its readers to the dangers inherent in the soaring numbers of immigrants. Alluding to the recent arrival of a shipload of immigrants from seventeen nations, the editor noted ruefully that "none was from the British Isles or the Scandinavian countries or Holland. . . ." These immigrants shared nothing in common with "original stock" Americans, and as if to accentuate and perpetuate their differences the new arrivals fled instantly to their respective urban ghettos, which were already packed beyond "decent" human conditions. Dubiously, he noted:

It has been maintained by the advocates of unrestricted immigration that some of this human overflow . . . will reach the agricultural sections. And what if it does? The American farmer is not likely to be able to speak Yiddish or Croatian. . . .

Moreover, there is a reasonable doubt whether the American farmer wants this new type of immigrant to turn the land (because the farmer would be forced to compete with men who would work for very low wages).[8]

This editor had launched his assault two weeks earlier by informing his readers that "nine-tenths of the Bolsheviki and anarchists in the United States can hardly speak English." In view of this, he wondered whether "American citizens who know better [would] allow this canker to grow in their midst until it overwhelms them." [9]

Here was the description of the immigrant which the country press was to broadcast over and over during the 1920s. There was, first of all, a deep awareness of the distinctions between the "original stock" and the newer immigrants. One specifically lamented the prewar influx "of the most undesirable type— those from southern Europe, the most of whom never fitted into our ways . . . [unlike] our best immigrants . . . from England, Holland, Scandinavia, Germany, Scotland, and Ireland." [10]

In addition to the exotic customs and appearance of the new immigrants, they seemed different from the old in the way they resisted assimilation by rushing to their own people as soon as they got off the boat. In short, they were clannish, and the ruralite found this distasteful for two reasons. For one thing, it seemed to imply a rejection of the American way of life, by which he meant his own way of life. Since rural life was already being challenged as never before, this additional rebuke was not likely to warm the farmer's heart. Secondly, the foreigner's apparent exclusiveness only packed more closely the slums that lent such a vile tone to urban life. This did not mean that the farmer was prepared to welcome those immigrants who might want to escape from the city's slums. Not only was he unwilling to cope with the customs and languages of these aliens, he was reluctant to compete with men who would work for next to nothing. The immigrant, it seemed, was damned for wanting to live in the slums, and damned again if he wanted to leave them.

Those who still retained a scrap of compassion for the new immigrants were further cautioned that these people were willfully destructive of the very fabric of democracy. The red scare of 1919–1920 still weighed heavily on the nation, and for

beleaguered ruralites the alchemy of fear might easily trans-
mute the statement that 90 percent of all radicals were foreigners into a fear that 90 percent of all foreigners were radicals.
Once they were acquainted with this problem, it was unlikely
that true Americans would permit such a "canker" to destroy
the nation. Those who failed to grasp this were flirting with
trouble when they called for a return to unrestricted immigration. Restriction had to continue, and it had to continue specifically to restrict the new immigrants.

Restriction, however, was only a partial solution to the problem, for while it would prevent undesirable aliens from entering the nation in the future, it could do nothing about those
who were already here. Citing statistics released by the Department of Labor, one Iowa newspaper pointed out that of the
17,500,000 aliens in the nation "nearly 12,000,000 . . . still re-
tain their foreign allegiance. . . ." [11] The fact of the matter, according to this editor, was that America's famed melting pot
had not succeeded very well in melting the millions of immigrants in the pot. The solution, he continued, was to press for
the "Americanization" of these immigrants, though he did not
explain what he meant or how this was to be accomplished.

A part of the campaign to alert rural America to the dangers of aliens on our shores was the propagation of specific
ethnic stereoptypes. The laws of libel and slander being what
they were, editors had to tread with some caution on these
matters, but the barriers were not insurmountable for the dar-
ing and imaginative among them. One of the more openhanded
of the country papers in this respect was the *Monticello Express*. A subject of urgent concern to the *Express* was the threat
posed to American society by the Jew. In its campaign to inform Iowans of the extent of this problem, the *Express* borrowed freely—as did several other papers—from Henry Ford's

Dearborn Independent, which was justly famous as a veritable mine of information on the Jewish question. On one occasion, the *Express* drew from the *Independent* to warn its readers about the effects of Jewish influence in the movie industry. The argument asserted that it was Jews who were responsible for the growing commercialization of American life, and held that if they were now to dominate the production of motion pictures completely, nothing could prevent them from using this agent of mass propaganda to subvert the basic values of American life, and to transform the nation into something alien and repulsive.[12]

Even among those who were not ready to swallow Ford's line whole there were some who felt that so much smoke had to indicate at least a little fire. One northwest Iowa editor, a bit dubious about the extremes of Ford's accusations, wondered nevertheless whether urban Jewish pressures to ban street sales of the *Independent* did not after all "suggest [the] basis of [an] unpalatable truth" in what the automobile tycoon was saying.[13]

It remained for the *Express,* however, to explore the most evil implications of the peril. Hammering away again at the theme of Jewish commercialization, it noted:

> Those [New York Jews] of Russian birth have superceded the German Jews in the clothing trade, and it is well known that leading bankers and financiers of New York are of the Hebrew race. They are out for the dollars, and they usually capture them, by hook or by crook, or by the honest method which sends money into service by the month or the year at stipulated rates.[14]

The editor emphasized the reluctance of well-to-do New York Jews to aid fund-raising drives seeking to relieve Russian Jews from famine, and quoted a Jewish philanthropist as saying that "while their cousins in Russia are being driven to cannibalism, the Jews in New York are driven to expensive restaurants where they eat like gluttons."

Obviously, in its original context, this statement was meant to shame New York's Jewish population into a greater display of generosity. Here however, appended to an editorial which had already stressed the dishonesty and greed of money-oriented Jews, it was intended to embellish the charge of dishonesty with one of cruelty, and to bloat greed into gluttony.

The anti-Semitism of the rural press was not ordinarily an expression of economic discontent, though it was commonly portrayed in an economic stereotype. Exceptions to this rule were printed regularly in the *Iowa Union Farmer*. Actually, the instances where this sentiment was smoked out into the open were few. However a few of the jokes that were used as fillers at the bottom of a page embodied pejorative stereotypes. One, for example, entitled "A Jew-el of a Story," told in dialect of a "Hebrew trader" named Abie who, when duped by a Scotsman into buying a dead racehorse, turned the deceit to his profit by raffling off the horse to unsuspecting speculators at two dollars per chance. Asked how he could satisfy the winner with a dead horse, he replied, "Him, I'm giving back his two dollars." [15]

A much better measure of this journal's point of view was published regularly in its economic editorials. In one which asked, "Who speaks for the farmer?", the editor answered sardonically, "Every long-nosed, pinched-faced, bleary-eyed, red-nosed, squeaky-voiced or loud-mouthed, gold-brick stock salesmen [sic] speaks for the farmer." After expanding the list with a few more of the farmer's "helpers," the editorial concluded bitterly that "not [one of them] . . . will come out in the open and help the farmer build his own market, or muzzle the dogs snapping at his heels." [16]

Even before Milo Reno became president of the Iowa Farmers' Union, he carried variations of this message across the state on his speaking engagements. Letters of thanks for this exciting speaker were printed often in the *Union Farmer*. In one of these, the writer praised Reno's illuminating example of the farmer who sells ten pounds of raw wool for two dollars and buys it back as a suit for forty or fifty dollars. "Question," said the writer, quoting Reno, "Where is the Jew?" Reno's answer at the meeting was that "they are every where [*sic*] dealing, speculating, profiteering in our products." [17]

After Reno rose to the presidency, he wrote a regular column in which he could sound the alarm to a much larger public. He could not afford to be specific any more, as he had been in his speaking engagements, but there is no reason to believe that he was any less effective. By 1923, his paper was quoting often from the *Dearborn Independent,* and he was cheerfully offering Henry Ford to his constituents as the next President of the United States. Ford's public anti-Semitism had become somewhat subdued since his appearance in court, but his outlook was already well known, and the *Independent,* while more discreet than before, was not really subtle, merely borrowing from the hoary folklore of anti-Semitic stereotypes instead of naming the villain outright. Reno borrowed from the same stock of images. In a signed editorial entitled "Posterity Should Not be Mortgaged to the Usurers," Reno reminded his audience:

> Henry Ford's paper is handing out the dope on finance straight from the shoulder. He is saying through the paper *the very things I have talked over and over again* to the membership. I assert that it is a crime to mortgage posterity to the usurers of the earth. . . . Yet every effort is being made by those who fatten from usury to destroy [our] rights to life, liberty and the pursuit of happiness.[18]

Later that year, Ford gave Reno the shock of a lifetime by coming out in favor of Calvin Coolidge for the Presidency in 1924. Thereafter, Ford joined Reno's long list of economic enemies, but the discrediting of the hero did not discredit the hero's ideas. Reno's attacks on usurious international finance continued unabated throughout the 1920s. The frequent repetition and conjunction of these images leaves little doubt that the *Union Farmer* was not just tangentially anti-Semitic, but that it used the image of the Jewish usurer and international banker to explain the very basis for the farmer's economic problems.[19]

The political radicalism of some Jews in the East provided the final ingredient of agrarian anti-Semitism. It established the grounds for the ruralite to threaten that "Communists, Bolshevists, Anarchists and any other ists who may not be satisfied with our laws and customs had better 'loog a leedle oud, yet' . . ." and to warn "foreigners" that there were legal means by which "real Americans" could take action against them.[20] The use of dialect here served effectively as a literary device to portray the Jew as a radical. Yet in pointing this out, the editor completed that curious paradox of American anti-Semitism, the double negative of the Jew as a greedy and exploitive capitalist and a menacing radical.

The emergent image of the Jew, if something less than adulatory, and perhaps not too accurate in describing the lives and commitments of the hundreds of thousands who were crammed into the nation's ghettos, was at least consistent with the larger conception of the immigrant as an undesirable who was opposed to American standards of honesty and compassion, a person who was unfamiliar with the morality of common decency.

Questions of consistency or accuracy are, of course, irrelevant in such stereotypes. What was important was that the ruralite saw no inconsistencies and was aware of no inaccuracies. Thus, there was nothing to prevent him from expressing his concern publicly at a time when the idea of selective restriction was ripe for congressional action. And just to make sure that the point was not lost through subtlety, the *Galena Gazette,* on the eve of a vote on a restriction bill, said bluntly that "this country is not in need of the offall [*sic*] of foreign countries and we have had quite enough experience with that class of undesirables." [21]

With the structure of immigration restriction legislation effectively completed by 1924, the public expressions of nativism ebbed somewhat. They never disappeared entirely, however, and indeed as the decade waned they began to recur with some urgency once again. The catalyst to this revival was the repeated association of aliens with crime, a process that almost inevitably called forth nightmare visions of the murderous Italian or Sicilian. Thus, it was not surprising that the distant thunder produced by the electrocution of Sacco and Vanzetti should have rumbled faintly in the Middle West, where one paper noted that "their kind have been permitted to 'run wild' for so long a time that they have come to believe that there is no power above them. . . ." [22]

That "their kind" had been disproportionately active in homicidal affairs by no means came as a revelation to the farmer. In fact, he had been kept abreast of some of the more sensational occurrences all through the 1920s. Commenting early in the decade on the impending execution of five convicted murderers, an Illinois editor alerted his readers to the "striking significance in the names of these murderers. . . ." [23] Unless it was that there were two Sams in the group, the striking significance seems to have been in the obvious Italian origins of the last names. And it should be noted that the readers were expected to pick this up without another clue.

Some years and many murders later, the *Monticello Express,* ever on guard for the peccadilloes of immigrants, observed that both the victim and his slayers in a recent murder in Chicago's Loop had been Sicilians. How, wondered the editor, could there still be some who favored a return to open immigration? "This country," he concluded, "is too good to become the nesting place for gangmen and racketeers from Sicily." [24]

Another important aspect of this nativism was the underlying racism that was commonly used to explain it. Racism was significant in this context for two reasons. First of all, it implied that the differences between old and new immigrants were insurmountable because they were rooted in genetic factors. Secondly, because racism paraded in the guise of biology, it was able to claim all of the prestige and unassailability of science. Thus couched in the phrases of a pseudo-scientific mystique, the arguments of the nativists raised some disquieting questions about the ultimate role of the immigrant in American society. It hurled a particular challenge at the assumptions of melting-pot theoreticians who had been arguing in favor of assimilating immigrants by "Americanizing" them. How, after all, could any group which was genetically un-American ever be Americanized?

At the least complicated level, this rural racism was expressed in a fear that the immigrant was simply unassimilable. Such doubts were articulated throughout the corn belt each time immigration restriction became a matter for serious congressional consideration. Nowhere was this elemental rural racism more succinctly stated than in a letter to the *Iowa*

Union Farmer from A.C. Davis, the national secretary-treasurer of the organization. After pointing out that only the "captains of industry" wanted unrestricted immigration, Davis got to the crux of the matter by suggesting that "in the face of the fact that the class of immigrants now coming do not assimilate, there is strong reason for closing the gate." [25] Except that it was more tersely stated than most, this assertion of the racist position was typical of many that were being carried in the country press at the time.

For the more discriminating reader, there was no lack of sophisticated statements of the same commitment. Occasionally, they were made all the more effective by being framed in images that made direct contact with the farmer's experience. Such an image was developed by perhaps the most respected of all the farm journals in the Midwest, *Wallaces' Farmer*. When its editor, Henry C. Wallace, packed off for Washington in 1921 to become Harding's Secretary of Agriculture, the blue pencil was passed on to the hands of Wallace's capable son, Henry A., who was then at the beginning of his meteoric career. An advocate of the most progressive methods of agricultural production, and himself no mere novice in plant genetics, the young Wallace was thoroughly familiar with the advantages of crop hybridization, which he saw as a handy metaphor to dramatize for the farmer the dangers of unchecked immigration. In an editorial published only a few months after he had assumed responsibilty for the *Farmer's* opinions, he pointed out that a continuation of unrestricted immigration would actually work to the farmer's economic advantage, since 97 percent of the immigrants remained in the cities, and opened that many more mouths for the farmers to feed. If the issue were decided purely in terms of economic self-interest, the farmer would unquestionably fight any attempt to limit immigration. But Wallace demonstrated that there was a more basic issue involved here:

> ... the farmer who is experienced in the breeding of grains and live stock has come to have a more genuine appreciation of hereditary characteristics than any other class of our nation. Even tho they lose money by it, farmers can see the peril of allowing admission of large numbers of people of low grade intelligence from southern and eastern Europe. . . . If the farmer was the selfish individual which some people think that he is he would be clamoring vigorously for unrestricted immigration.[26]

The strain of racist convictions appeared in other Wallace editorials on the city and its people during the 1920s. In most of them there was a tone of reasoned restraint that was characteristic of Wallace, but if he never reached the level of shrill emotionalism attained by other rural journals, he was nonetheless effective as a tutor for the rural mind.

The crowning achievement of midwestern racism, however, was the product of a mind professionally trained to think through such problems. The man was Edward Wiggam, cited approvingly by a small-town Iowa paper as a "noted biologist-lecturer." Leaving little to the imagination except the means for proper action, Wiggam probed the deepest meanings of the question, and emerged brooding at the prospects for the future of his country. "Our beautiful women soon will cease to exist except in pictures and statuary," he warned. And then he spelled out the doom of the nation in the incontrovertible terms of statistical trends:

> On an average one child is born to every three of the graduates of our leading women's colleges. But one low-class, broad-backed, flat-chested, stout-legged, high-necked, stupid, ugly immigrant woman will in the same time produce three.

By this process the average American woman is rapidly becoming ugly. With a decline in beauty, there always comes a decline in intelligence. Every decline in intelligence brings a decline in morals. The crime wave is no mystery to biologists.[27]

Here at least was a biologist with a synoptic vision. In an astonishing tour de force that fused aesthetics, genetics, and logic, he was able clearly to demonstrate the cause of one of the nation's most sorrowful problems. Meanwhile the American farm father, terrified by this nightmare of ugliness, fecundity, stupidity, and crime, might well quake with anxiety at the prospects for his daughter's future, and with mortification at the thought of being the doting grandfather to a houseful of little Neanderthals.

The economic counterpart of the cultural blight brought by the immigrant was organized labor. When a rapid postwar inflation threatened to erode the wartime economic gains of the farmer, he found a ready explanation in the wave of strikes that swept the nation in 1919. One paper found the connection between labor and inflation deplorable, and warned that no relief was in sight.[28] Another, aroused by the great power of railroad unions, saw little hope for improvement as long as senators and congressmen were intimidated by labor's political power. Things might be very different, this editor suggested, if the farmer himself were to strike for the privileges already enjoyed by labor.[29] Something would obviously have to be done, and one editor proposed the solution that others were considering when he suggested that the need to stop strikes was as urgent as the need to abolish war.[30]

Even the Farmers' Union, which was the one farm organization that cried out during the 1920s for an alliance of the "progressive" forces of agriculture and labor against the "reactionary" powers of high finance, found that it was expedient to put its rhetoric into cold storage when faced with the inflationary implications of labor's actions after the war. After paying lip-service to the noble aims of labor in the past, the Union complained that "too much success and too much power has [*sic*] crazed them and we now find them exerting influences which are fatal to the welfare of society, including the workers themselves." [31]

Such tender concern for the welfare of union labor, however, was never allowed to blur the vision of Henry A. Wallace. In 1921, when Samuel Gompers expressed some interest in an alliance between farmers and workers, Wallace refused to be taken in. "The fact is," he said, "that the farmers are suffering more now from the leaders of labor than from the leaders of industry or finance." [32]

Shortly before that, Wallace had explained the problem in greater detail, and had proposed some solutions to it. He noted, first of all, that "more than any one thing, it is the city laboring man" who is responsible for the high cost that farmers were forced to pay for what they bought. Coming as it did during a drastic farm depression, this explanation had very serious implications. Wallace's assumptions led him to assert that businessmen did not care really how farmers and laborers divided their share of the national income, as long as they did not interfere with profits. He contended that there was a limited national product to divide and that capital ultimately determined who was to get how much of it. Generously allocating 40 percent for itself, capital tossed out the remainder to farmers and laborers, and was perfectly content to watch labor grab off 90 percent, leaving farmers to share what little remained. Well, if that was the way it was, if organized power rather than justice played the key role in apportioning the

national income, then the only solution was for organized agriculture to back capital in cutting wages, so that the farmer's
share would increase. And if necessary, Wallace concluded,
"the farmer is quite justified in reducing production . . . to
bring Capital and Labor to their senses." [33]

Explaining the farmer's difficulties in terms of the unreasonable demands of organized labor, in fact, became almost a habit
with Wallace for the entire decade, and was an attitude that
prevailed throughout rural Iowa and Illinois. It is particularly
worth noting here that labor was saddled with the burden of
guilt at precisely the same time that business was being freed
of it by most farmers.

What made the laborer's actions even more reprehensible to
farmers was his inexcusable propensity to loaf. The farmer,
caught up in a constant round of hard work, could not tolerate
this, and the country press was quick to say so. It was unfair
for workers to "sleep and loaf 18 hours per day for five days
in the week and 24 hours per day the remainder of the week,"
while farmers were forced to put in sixty, seventy, and more
hours weekly just to feed them cheaply.[34]

Thus, again it was emphasized that urban people did not
really work. The capitalist gambled and the laborer loafed.
Only the farmer, toiling in the earth from dawn to dusk, in fair
weather and foul, knew the meaning of honest work.

It may be that the farmer entertained some strange ideas
about work in the city, but these notions formed an important
part of the inferences he drew from the world as he perceived
it. As a result, labor was made to assume its share of responsibility in the farmer's troubles, and thus joined the legions of
his foes in the city. From the rich, there came the challenge of
an insidious immorality. From the immigrants, there came the
threat of an alien and altogether unacceptable way of life.

From the laborer came the threat of higher costs to the farmer in a decade of falling prices. Together they constituted a formidable array of opponents who were threatening to destroy both the cultural and economic bases of rural life.

II

Each of these urban types represented a specific grievance to the ruralite. Collectively, they helped impart to the city a certain tone which was unpleasant and extremely dangerous. Indeed, the city seemed to be almost ineluctably evil, and yet it became a kind of mission for ruralites to try to purify it.

To the rural mind, nothing symbolized urban corruption more than the liquor problem. On this issue there was absolutely no public dissent. Even before the Volstead Act had been passed to implement the Eighteenth Amendment, the monthly publication of the Iowa Republican party attacked Woodrow Wilson for calling for the return of liquor. "Thus lightly does our nation's president pass over the greatest issue since Lincoln faced the slavery question," said this partisan journal. "The great labor vote of the East is the flesh pot for which the president has bartered his conscience." [35]

Unimpelled by the need to make a party issue out of Prohibition, other papers reflected the bipartisan rural nature of the dry crusade. The first fruits of victory were sweet, and confidence in the law to achieve a moral revolution was unbounded. This was, after all, no mere statute, it was the Constitution; and the distinction was not lost in the rural areas. With the force of the fundamental law of the land behind Prohibition, it was clear, as one editor saw it, that "a better U. S. A. is in prospect. After July first the spectacle of drunken men on the streets of our cities, towns and villages will be a thing of the past." [36]

Before long, however, it became clear that alcohol would not evaporate as quickly as many had hoped, and that the very law which had been intended to promote the cure was being used to evade it. One of the loopholes in the Volstead Act was a stipulation that allowed liquor to be sold for medicinal purposes on prescription from a doctor. As soon as the implications of this provision became clear, a strange new virus sent an epidemic of parched throats raging through the cities. The only treatment, it seemed, was not only alcoholic, but disgustingly legal. "New drug stores," observed the *Galena Gazette,* "have sprung up in the large cities where stocks are confined to a few medicines and a huge supply of intoxicants." [37] This particular violation of the spirit of Prohibition was related to another urban evil, since it was the rich who could most easily afford the high costs of purchasing liquor through doctors. Perhaps an alternative solution would be to regulate the sale of liquor so that the less affluent would at least have an equal chance to purchase it, one paper suggested. If not that, then "put the stuff out of business altogether." [38]

By the early 1920s the optimism of the first year of Prohibition had become clouded with the realization that urban resistance would be stiff. This only strengthened rural determination, and before long the battle was on in earnest. One observer saw the issue not only as a wet-dry controversy, but also as a related struggle between urban and country press. Rural newspapers had spoken with one voice on behalf of "temperance and law enforcement," he suggested, while the urban newspapers for unfathomable reasons had aligned themselves with "the destructive liquor interests" in an attempt to block effective implementation of the law. And then the argument swelled into a veritable call to arms:

Now comes the country editor and his thousands of clear-thinking and unprejudiced brethren . . . ready to defend and uphold the law. . . . They have no selfish motive in thus enlisting on the side of right. . . .

It was the strength of the moral forces in the agricultural states that made possible the early enactment of the law which the enemies of society are now seeking to nullify. This same courageous electorate will see to it that no backward step is taken.[39]

Here was the rhetoric of the crusade, with all its overtones both of piety and combat. Under attack from "the enemies of society" the "clear-thinking and unprejudiced brethren" among the "moral forces" in the agricultural states had no alternative really but to "enlist" in order to defend "the side of right" and "fight the battle" against the minions of evil in the cities.

The call to battle was even issued in the imagery of an earlier American crusade, the antislavery movement of the nineteenth century.[40] When prohibition was elevated to the same moral plane as abolition, the point was not lost that slavery had only been eliminated finally by force.

The fond rural dream of a dry America was turning rapidly into a chimera, but faith in the righteousness of the cause never flagged. Faith alone, however, was not enough; nor were words. It was all well and good to pour out a rhetorical barrage, but the fact was that the cities stood coldly impervious to the heated oratory. With utter disdain they continued to flout the Constitution, and as if to rub salt into the wound they did it with the complicity of the very machinery of the law—mayors, aldermen, judges, and policemen.

As the Prohibition conflict intensified, it became apparent that the problem was closer to home than New York and Chicago, that it was even infesting the smaller cities of the Midwest. What was one to think when a judge in Quincy, Illinois, was forced to dismiss nine out of twenty-four prospective jurors in a Prohibition trial because of their open hostility to the Volstead Act? [41] At the same time, Iowa papers were growing alarmed over wet sentiment in their own cities. "Cedar Rapids is getting quite modern," said one editor sarcastically, "with a 'bootlegger king' who claims to rule the city with a pass for the undisturbed traffic of his teamsters.'" [42] Two years later, when the Iowa legislature was considering stricter enforcement laws, a country editor pointed to the state capital as the place where a clean-up ought to begin. He doubted a recent accusation that Des Moines was crawling with a thousand bootleggers. At that rate, with one for every seventy-five drinkers, there would not be enough business to go around. But he had no illusions about the effectiveness of enforcement, and was plainly disgusted with a recent, widely heralded investigation which had turned up exactly one bootlegger in the city.[43]

A major reason for the persistence among ruralites of stout opposition to liquor was their certainty that the chief violator of the law was the immigrant. Assertions linking aliens to booze ran freely, and served to reinforce both the nativism and the prohibitionism of the countryside. After a tour through the East, a one-time Iowa state senator reported that while the "better element of the population" there supported Prohibition, strong opposition came from the predominant "foreign element," most of whom could not even speak English. "The best Americans," he concluded, "are inclined to stand by the law. . . ." [44] Another rural spokesman found that the greatest opposition came from New York, Illinois, and California, all of which contained cities with heavy immigrant populations. However, "in Pennsylvania, where the largest city—Philadelphia—is more American in the character of it's population," most people opposed any retreat from the current laws.[45]

In addition to the liquor problem in the cities, and often tied closely to it, were the problems of crime and politics, which were by no means the exclusive property of the huge metropolitan areas. Clearly, graft was where you found it, and where you found it was in all cities. One Iowa commentator noted sourly that Des Moines was a "storm center of graft" in Iowa, just as bad as Springfield, the capital of the state across the river.[46]

In the end, however, there was no doubt that the really big loot was to be found in the really big cities, and none served better to illustrate this lesson in political immorality than Chicago. Commenting on a city official who had been indicted for violation of the prohibition law, the *Monticello Express* found it only to be expected inasmuch as "an education in the Chicago school of politics has in several instances in the past made men heedless of the law in the pursuit of wealth." [47] The interrelation of crime and politics still disturbed this editor late in the decade, by which time Chicago was acquiring a measure of renown far beyond the Midwest for this kind of thing. "Poor old Chicago!" he exclaimed sympathetically. "The city is becoming a byword for crime, and seems to be in the grip of alien gunmen, and political mountebanks, one almost as bad as the other." [48]

In 1928, when Henry Wallace asked, "Is there something about congested life in great cities that stimulates crimes of violence?" he was expressing more than idle curiosity. He pointed out that during the past quarter of a century the population of the thirty-one largest cities had doubled, while the annual rate of murders in those same cities had quadrupled.[49] This bit of intelligence confirmed Wallace in his fear of cities, and encouraged him to continue his decade-long struggle against them.

In rural Iowa, the crime and politics of Chicago served as an object lesson in the demographic distribution of immorality, and was mentioned fairly often. In Illinois, it involved the control of the state's destiny, and was discussed incessantly. Here was one reason, for example, why much of the rural press in Illinois opposed the initiative and referendum when those hallmarks of agrarian discontent came before the voters of the state in 1919. In a series of pre-election editorials, the *Carrollton Patriot* warned darkly that a favorable voter response on these proposals would be disastrous to the state, "especially to the downstate rural section. . . ." [50]

Similar fears were expressed a few years later over the question of legislative reapportionment. Rural critics pointed out that Chicago's gangsters exercised too much influence in the city to allow it to dominate the state's lawmaking apparatus.[51] "Cook County, and especially that portion of it known as Chicago," said one editor, "is blessed with a bunch of politicians and schemers who have for a long time endeavored to direct the affairs of the state. . . ." [52] Obviously farmers could never tolerate redistricting.

As if they did not already have enough to worry about in the cities, the farmers were also forced to take note now of an alarming increase of crime in the country districts. Originally at a loss to explain this, the country press soon found the answer. As the cities applied pressure, their "hardened criminals" were being forced out, and with their urban source of income temporarily cut off, they had no choice but to ply their trade in the country.[53] In reality, there was little evidence to support such a charge. On occasion, of course, a city criminal was apprehended for some crime in a small town. More often, though, the offender came from the surrounding area, or else the crime went unsolved altogether. Legal evidence, however, was not needed to prove what the ruralite already knew. He knew that it was only natural for crimes to be committed in cities because criminals naturally abounded there. He knew also that the ordinary crimes committed in the rural towns could be explained in terms of a few well-known local characters who had gone wrong. It followed that any rise in the rural crime rate had to be explained not in terms of more ruralites going wrong, but in terms of more urban criminals going rural. It was the only explanation that would fit his assumptions. Short of abandoning these assumptions, there was no other reasonable way to understand it, and ruralites had no intention of abandoning their assumptions about this phenomenon.

There was no doubt in the country districts that the mother lode of crime in the Midwest was Chicago, and that a contributing factor to its spread there was the flabby effort of policemen and politicians to clean it up. With gangsterism growing bolder and more lurid in Chicago, the rural press could hardly be blamed for turning cynical by mid-decade. When "Big Bill" Thompson was reinstalled as mayor after a one-term absence during which a reform mayor did not reform very much, nobody in or out of Chicago could take seriously his pledge to drive out the gangsters. "Should he redeem his promise," said the *Bardolph News* wryly, "Chicago will become a mighty lonely place." [54] It is perhaps to Thompson's credit at least that no alarming increase of loneliness was reported in his city during the ensuing months.

All of these vices, and the people who practiced them, combined to produce a shorthand of interrelated symbols in the rural areas. The mention of any one of them was likely to evoke hostile feelings toward the others. *Immigrants were dirty and radical and vice-prone opponents of the American way whose drinking supported the criminal and murderous bootleggers who corrupted city officials who fawned before laborers and sold their souls for the votes of dirty and radical and vice-prone immigrants.* And thus the circle was closed around the city, the one symbol which completely summed up all the others.

In part because he was better educated and far more widely read than most of his colleagues among country editors, in part because his mind ran toward grand designs, and in part simply because his voice reached more farmers in the Midwest each week than any other, Henry Wallace was the outstanding spokesman for those people who raised the ultimate questions about the place of the city in the United States.

Actually Wallace was more preoccupied early in the decade with specific instances of urban evils than he was with the city as an abstraction of evil. He railed against labor constantly, held racist attitudes toward the new immigrants, abhorred the profit orientation of businessmen, and feared the way in which cities bred crime. By mid-decade, however, his discontents had drawn together into a more integrated view of the nation's basic problem. That problem was nothing less than a clash between conflicting kinds of civilizations. The United States, which had developed as a rural nation, was now moving toward a severe crisis produced by the overexpansive urbanization which characterized the twentieth century.[55]

One expression of the problem, Wallace held, appeared in the realm of values, where the mindlessness and artificiality of city ways were beginning to worm their way into the country. Urban amusements, which were vicarious to the point of automatism, were now attracting more and more rural people. Too few people were actually participating in their own recreation any more; they were simply sitting by passively and letting it happen to them. In the long run, such a development could only undermine the "individuality and vigor" that had once been characteristic of American life.[56] In this way—meta-phorically—cities developed the instruments which might "kill" American civilization.

When Wallace referred to cities as the "death chambers of civilization," however, he used the term not metaphorically but quite literally.[57] At times alluding to artificial aspects of urban life—to the automobiles, electric signs, jangling noises, and crushing crowds that played havoc with man's nervous system—and at times referring to the "fog of coal smoke and the exhaust from gas engines" which tarnished man's lungs, Wallace went to considerable lengths, literally and statistically, to demonstrate that cities "sapped the vitality," which was Wallace's delicate way of alluding to man's procreative powers.[58] Wallace was deadly serious about this, and even went so far as to argue that cities would perish without the continuous stream of people flowing into them from the farms and from Europe. The trouble with this situation was that native Americans quickly succumbed to the ennervating forces of urban life, while the immigrants, somehow immune to these forces, continued to reproduce at an astonishing and perilous rate.[59]

In the end, Wallace trapped himself in a dilemma concerning America's future, if urbanization were to continue unchecked. Either "foreign blood" would win out and we would become a nation of aliens (the racist mind, by definition, does not distinguish among generations); or cities really would prove to be death chambers and America would meet the fate "of the old civilizations that have been buried for centuries under the sands of Asia. . . ." [60] In either case, prospects for the future were not terribly bright.

Wallace felt very strongly for the older America which seemed to be slipping away from him. Although he never completely surrendered to his pessimistic tendencies, he constantly

portrayed the situation in its most frightening aspect by reducing it to a struggle to the death between two inimical
civilizations, a struggle in which all the momentum, for the
time being at least, lay with the process of urbanization. It
should not come as a surprise then that rural Americans waged
a battle in the 1920s on behalf of civilization, for that is exactly
the way that many of them saw it.

And it should not be surprising either that the accumulated
wrath of the rural Midwest was vented in 1928 against Al
Smith, a man who exuded the new America in the very words
he spoke and in the way he spoke them, a man who represented
every evil that ruralites despised: liquor, political corruption,
crime, labor, immigrants, and Catholicism.

In the forefront was the liquor question again, largely because Smith had chosen to put it there. Republican papers in
the villages gleefully hammered away at this issue in 1928.
Even the Democratic papers were forced to equivocate on the
matter. In the spring of 1928, one of them predicted that a
major Prohibition party would be the result of both parties
nominating wets, but after the nomination, it tamed down and
supported Smith without much enthusiasm, pointing lamely to
the hypocrisy of Republican attempts at enforcement during
the decade.[61] Another Democratic paper in rural Illinois boldly
announced that the two major issues in this campaign were
modification of the Volstead Act and farm relief, and then
quietly abandoned both of them to concentrate on the need
for religious tolerance.[62] The Republican rural press, free from
the burden of political commitments, returned time and again
to Smith's stand on prohibition.

But they had more than liquor to work with in this campaign. They had Tammany Hall, a phrase, an epithet, an image
whose implications were so familiar that space-consuming des-

criptions were unnecessary in the press. One Illinois editor cautioned that a Democratic vote was a vote "to open the gates of graft to Tammany and its cohorts . . ." while a Republican vote would register a belief in the "home and the safeguarding of the same against the aggression of the liquor and the vice lords who are bending their combined efforts to elect Governor Smith. . . ." [63]

Elsewhere Smith's bold attempt to cut into the normally Republican, but now very angry farm vote was ridiculed in terms of his long-time affiliation with "Tammany farmers," and his frequent rejection by New York's rural areas.[64] No amount of Democratic ballyhoo, apparently, could convincingly transform the Tammany tiger into a domesticated animal.

One of Smith's more severe liabilities in the rural areas was his plea to reopen the question of immigration. Once again, nativism reached a great pitch of excitement, with one paper predicting that Smith would "open the gates to the horde of European immigrants . . ." if he were elected.[65] Few papers were as direct in exposing the issue, and indeed in getting at the very marrow of the campaign as the *Knoxville Journal,* which asserted:

> The great cities with their crowded foreign populations are largely for Al Smith. Indeed many of the shrewdest and keenest newspaper correspondents declare that the issue in this election is the city against the country, the foreign-born people against the native Americans.[66]

The fear of foreigners was nearly as widespread as the liquor issue during that autumn. It was pointed out that 80 percent of New York's "white population" were either first or second-generation immigrants, that this "metropolis of aliens" was

dominated by the Tammany machine, and that the combina-
tion of machine leaders and immigrant followers had developed "a New York viewpoint, a New York trend of mind and
thought which is alien per se and alien to the beliefs of the rest
of the country." [67] Al Smith had been bred in that environment, and Al Smith was seeking to become the President of the
United States. The line from the immigrant through Tammany
to Smith ran straight as an arrow.

Everywhere in the rural press during the campaign the same
issues were repeatedly emphasized. The arch-symbol of the
city, New York; the arch-symbol of crime and corruption, Tammany; the arch-symbol of human weakness, alcohol; and the
arch-symbol of human degradation, the immigrant—all of
these were strung tightly together in the rural campaign
against Smith, and they were not mere cryptograms for Smith's
Catholicism. Each had its own intrinsic charge, and in each case
the charge was intensely negative.

What was remarkable in this nativist-tinged campaign was
that the press never raised the specter of Romanism as a spur to
the electorate. On the contrary, where the issue surfaced at all
it was to repudiate the anti-Catholicism that was being whisp-
ered about. One Hoover paper claimed that "it would
strengthen and establish our claim to religious liberty to some
time elect a good Catholic to that office, not because of his
religion, but regardless of it, and because of his pre-eminent
fitness for the office." [68] Another, which had pulsed with
nativism throughout the decade, asserted the irrelevance of the
religious issue by pointing out that it would be just as wrong to
vote for Smith because he was Catholic as it would be to vote
against him because he wasn't.[69]

If one is to look for expressions of anti-Catholicism in rural
America during the campaign, he should look not at what the

press was arguing for, but at what it was arguing against, because just as surely as one after another of these papers exhorted its readers that religion must not be allowed to become an issue, so it becomes more and more certain that it already had.

There is little doubt that Smith's Catholicism hurt him in many parts of the rural Midwest, but as several recent studies have demonstrated, this was an issue which cut both ways on a national level.[70] There is every reason to believe that if the Democrats could have dug up a Tammany Methodist to run, he would have fared little better than Smith in the corn belt. This was not merely a Catholic who was running; it was a man who stood for the running sore and dimming hopes of Prohibition, for crime, graft, and foreigners. All of the farmer's fears were bundled together in him, and he was running for the highest office in the land.

When the voters of Greene County, in western Illinois, returned a majority for a Republican presidential candidate for the first time in their history, while remaining faithful to the Democrats for local offices, they were expressing their pent-up resentment in what was to them a national referendum on the city.

NOTES

1. *Iowa Union Farmer,* July 2, 1919, reprinted from the *Colorado Union Farmer.* The frequency with which attacks were reprinted from other state branches suggests that this was a national, rather than merely an Iowa, point of view.
2. *Carmi* (Illinois) *Tribune-Times,* June 8, 1922.
3. *Knoxville* (Iowa) *Journal,* May 15, 1924.
4. *Ames* (Iowa) *Daily Tribune,* January 2, 1920.
5. Ibid., January 7, 1920.
6. *Rossville* (Illinois) *Press,* July 17, 1919.

7. *Monticello* (Iowa) *Express,* July 24, 1919.

8. *Elkader* (Iowa) *Register,* March 31, 1921.

9. Ibid., March 17, 1921.

10. *Monticello* (Iowa) *Express,* August 23, 1923.

11. *Fremont County* (Iowa) *Herald,* December 2, 1920. The substance of the rest of the editorial suggests that by "foreign allegiance" the editor meant illiteracy in the English language.

12. *Monticello* (Iowa) *Express,* April 21, 1921. Ford was brought to trial for slander early in the decade, and although he was acquitted, country papers were less eager to borrow his editorials thereafter, and rural nativism became rather less explicit.

13. *Sac* (Iowa) *Sun,* March 31, 1921.

14. *Monticello* (Iowa) *Express,* March 2, 1922.

15. *Iowa Union Farmer,* March 14, 1928.

16. Ibid., July 2, 1919, reprinted from the *Colorado Union Farmer.*

17. Ibid., May 4, 1921.

18. Ibid., March 7, 1923. Italics added.

19. In his book *The Tolerant Populists: Kansas Populism and Nativism* (Chicago: University of Chicago Press, 1963), Walter Nugent argues that although Kansas Populists condemned Jewish bankers, they were not really anti-Semitic. Their hostility, in other words, was really directed against bankers, and not against Jews. Nugent's reasoning here escapes me entirely. The Populists did not dip blindfolded into a thesaurus because they felt that "banker" would be a nice noun to modify with the first adjective that came along. Obviously, Jewish bankers were singled out because the Populists shared a negative stereotype of Jews that was pervasive in Western society, and which consequently was almost bound to evoke hostile feelings. Precisely what this anti-Semitism *meant* to Populism, if anything, is another question altogether.

20. *Galena* (Illinois) *Gazette,* February 26, 1920.

21. Ibid., May 12, 1921.

22. *Rock Rapids* (Iowa) *Reporter,* August 25, 1927.

23. *Bardolph* (Illinois) *News,* February 17, 1921.

24. *Monticello* (Iowa) *Express,* September 13, 1928.

25. *Iowa Union Farmer,* May 18, 1921.

26. *Wallaces' Farmer,* June 10, 1921. In view of the sources of Wallace's support in his Presidential bid in 1948, his stand on restriction in 1921 is ironic indeed!

27. *Ames* (Iowa) *Daily Tribune,* October 26, 1923.

28. *Galena* (Illinois) *Gazette,* June 5, 1919.

29. *Bardolph* (Illinois) *News,* August 7 and September 11, 1919.

30. *Carrollton* (Illinois) *Patriot,* September 7, 1922.

31. *Iowa Union Farmer,* December 17, 1919.

32. *Wallaces' Farmer,* June 24, 1921.

33. Ibid., April 22, 1921.

34. *Bardolph* (Illinois) *News,* November 20, 1919.

35. *Iowa Forum,* June, 1919, reprinted from the *Marengo* (Iowa) *Republican.* The word "East" was a common euphemism for New York and for the city generally.

36. *Galena* (Illinois) *Gazette,* January 23, 1919.

37. Ibid., May 6, 1920.

38. *Oblong* (Illinois) *Oracle,* December 18, 1925. A dry Democratic paper, the *Oracle* was one of the few to warn its readers from the beginning that moral revolutions do not occur overnight.

39. *Carmi* (Illinois) *Tribune-Times,* October 24, 1923.

40. *O'Brien County* (Iowa) *Bell,* June 14, 1923.

41. *Bardolph* (Illinois) *News,* July 2, 1925.

42. *Monticello* (Iowa) *Express,* November 3, 1927.

43. *Knoxville* (Iowa) *Journal,* March 7, 1929.

44. *Ames* (Iowa) *Daily Tribune,* July 31, 1923.

45. *Monticello* (Iowa) *Express,* August 17, 1922.

46. Ibid., January 4, 1923.

47. Ibid., April 26, 1923.

48. Ibid., March 29, 1928.

49. *Wallaces' Farmer,* July 6, 1928.

50. *Carrollton* (Illinois) *Patriot,* October 30, 1919. Basically, the proposition before the voters assumed the form of a referendum on the referendum, but in fact it was toothless because the referendum had no standing in law. Only legislative action or a constitutional amendment could legitimize these proposals for direct democracy. Since a constitutional convention was imminent, however, a favorable vote on the proposal could be interpreted as a popular mandate to the delegates, and would be a powerful weapon in the hands of its proponents at the convention itself.

51. Ibid., February 12, 1925.

52. *Galena* (Illinois) *Gazette,* June 25, 1925.

53. *Ames* (Iowa) *Daily Tribune,* January 3, 1921; *Bardolph* (Illinois) *News,* June 9, 1921.

54. Ibid., April 14, 1927.

55. See Don S. Kirschner, "Henry A. Wallace as Farm Editor," *American Quarterly,* June, 1965, for a detailed discussion of Wallace's views at this time.

56. *Wallaces' Farmer,* June 8, 1923.

57. Ibid., November 2, 1923.

58. Ibid., *passim.* See, for instance, November 2, 1923, June 6, 1924, September 18, 1925, July 9, 1926, November 5, 1926, and September 7, 1928.

59. Ibid., May 9, 1924.

60. Ibid., April 14, 1922.

61. *Bardolph* (Illinois) *News,* May 24, 1928, and August–November, 1928, *passim.*

62. *Oblong* (Illinois) *Oracle,* August 24, 1928, and September–November, 1928, *passim.*

63. *Galena* (Illinois) *Gazette,* November 1, 1928.

64. *Knoxville* (Iowa) *Journal,* July 26, 1928.

65. Ibid., August 30, 1928.

66. Ibid., August 2, 1928.

67. *Monticello* (Iowa) *Express,* July 5, 1928.

68. *Carrollton* (Illinois) *Patriot,* August 2, 1928.

69. *Knoxville* (Iowa) *Journal,* September 6, 1928. There seems to have been an awareness, more or less vaguely expressed in a number of rural papers, that Smith's religion would win votes for him as well as lose them, as in fact it did.

70. See especially David Burner, *The Politics of Provincialism;* Samuel Lubell, *The Future of American Politics* (New York, 1952); and Richard Hofstadter, "Could a Protestant Have Beaten Hoover in 1928?" *The Reporter* (March 17, 1960).

3

Rural Life: The Image
and Some Realities

IN STARK contrast to the city, in the rural mind, stood the ruralite and his way of life, a living testament to the values that had
made the United States a great nation, a beacon of virtue that
cut through the darkness of a world gone wrong.

A chronic indulgence of the rural press during these years
was to sing hymns of praise to the virtues of country life and
the farmer. As chorus after chorus welled forth, several basic
themes emerged. The favorite among these emphasized the
basic simplicity of the country districts, a simplicity made all
the more attractive when it was contrasted with the illusory attractions of the city. Warning the restless younger generation
on the farm against the mirage of city life, one editor noted
that "in every city we find men of mature years, heads of
families, who would give anything to get back to the sanity and
purity of country life—but they can not." [1] There was almost
universal agreement that it was better to "be a 'Busher' or a
'Rube' and live in peace and security in a country town than be
a sport and live in a large city." [2] The profound changes in

American life implicit in these comparisons were celebrated with different emphasis by Tin Pan Alley. A generation earlier, Americans had sung nostalgically of the "Banks of the Wabash." Now, however, all too many of them were singing "How You Gonna Keep 'Em Down on the Farm." One editor commented that the youths to whom this song was directed would "be of no value on the farm, nor anywhere else, until they have learned the art of living rationally, simply and therefore, happily," [3] an art which they were as unlikely to cultivate in New York or Chicago apparently as in "Paree."

Similar expressions of contentment with this pastoral paradise appeared constantly during the 1920s in the rural press, and regularly they led directly from sanity and purity, peace and security, reason and simplicity, to happiness, and this in spite of the fact that the farmer had been sounding much less happy when he directed his attention to other matters.

Among the fundamental elements of this happy simplicity were the sights, sounds, and smells of the countryside, or of the small country town nestling like a gem in the natural beauty of its rural setting. There is an abiding peace, noted one editor, in the "little country town where the only lights come from the windows that glitter down the lane," and where the silence is punctuated only by "the lowing of the cattle in the fields and the sighing of the winds through the trees. . . ." This really was "God's country." [4]

Coupled with a love for this soothing rusticity was pity for the unfortunate denizens of the urban jungle who were not aware that a kind of earthly salvation lay at hand in the sensuous joys offered in the country. Among the most unfortunate, because they were powerless to change their lot, were the children of the city's slums, condemned to a life of punishment in the fenceless internment of their tenement prisons.

The Illinois Agricultural Association commonly spoke of such things in its annual drive to organize rural support for a program to bring children from Chicago's slums for a two-week "outing" on Illinois farms. An IAA article widely reprinted in the Illinois press called attention to the way in which slum children were "hemmed in by dingy walls," ignored by the impersonal crush of the city. Worse still, they were not even aware of the "heritage of which they [had] been robbed. . . ." They had never encountered "the smell of meadow grass after a summer shower" or any of the other bounties "that even the poorest country child accepts as his natural right." [5]

Earlier in the decade, when the program to bring these children into contact with nature was just getting under way, the Association had begged farmers to cooperate in "one of the greatest works of mercy Illinois has ever known. . . ." To the more wary among the prospective hosts, it offered the reassurance that each child would be "carefully examined for dirt and disease by a physician the day he leaves for his outing and will come to the farm neat and clean." These outings, the article continued, are more than mere vacations; "they are life itself. In addition to saving lives," they would make "real Americans" out of the children by showing them some truly "wholesome American homes." [6]

Actually, this invitation to share in a mission of mercy was rooted in some of the same fears that haunted Henry Wallace. Man is basically a natural animal, a creature of nature who must live with nature in order to flourish. From these assumptions, the line running from logic to value judgment was inevitable: since what was rural was natural, and what was natural was good, then what was rural was good. By the same line of reasoning, since what was urban was unnatural, and what was unnatural was evil, then what was urban was evil.

Even city men had to be aware of this, if only deep in the recesses of their memory. How else explain the crowds gazing "respectfully, earnestly and even longingly" at the exhibit of a farm-living room in a New York store. The editor concluded:

> You can transplant people from the natural and plank them down for a lifetime into the unnatural, but you can't stamp instinct out of them. That's why New York, blasé and gaudy, crowds to this simple farm house window and feasts its eyes on independence and sane living.[7]

Here they were, all the key words strung together—"natural," "simple," "independence," "sane"—and they were all rooted in the inviolable wishes that grow from instinctual direction.

This love of the simple and the natural carried over to women as well, and was what made the country belle so much more attractive than the city girl. It was a sad fact, though, many editors noted, that too many of them nowadays were being misled into thinking that cosmetics enhanced their beauty. As soon as they realized "that their painted cheeks and rouged complexions create unfavorable impressions they [would] get back to the more beautiful simplicity of nature, and that badge of good health, a clear skin." [8] One editor even came to the defense of shorter skirts in these terms, and he did so in the face of a certain amount of rural indignation over this particular kind of upward mobility. "It is the state of mind and not the length of a dress that breeds indelicacy and vulgarity," he insisted, and then proceeded to reason that freedom of movement led to greater health, and that consequently women's skirts should be even shorter.[9] As the arbiters of haute couture continued to raise hemlines for reasons not especially related to health, however, a small outcry went up in the rural areas. One editor was dubious about the long-run healthfulness of short skirts. As he saw it, for every accident in the boarding of street-cars that was prevented by women wearing short skirts, one was probably caused by some poor man stumbling and falling while he gaped at the sight.[10] A more gripping concern was felt by those who were convinced that such exhibitionism contributed to the rise in delinquency.[11] Obviously a compromise would have to be struck somewhere between health and morality, and the compromise would have to be negotiated well below the knees. In the final analysis, nature was best appreciated as landscape, it appeared.

Paramount in the rural structure of values was the conviction that the beautiful countryside provided the context within which the most profound advantages of rural life were to be found, the immeasurable joy of kinship and the warm human relationships that were found in one's family and neighbors. To the country dweller, neighborliness implied a sincere personal concern for the well-being of friends. Although the dazzle of city lights must ultimately dim, "the firm steady glow of the loving hearts in the old home town can never be extinguished." [12]

The neighborliness of rural life was its own reward, of course, but its blessings could bring tangible bonuses on occasion also:

> In an ordinary city neighborhood if a man breaks a leg and is laid up, his neighbors, if they happen to hear about it, will say, "Too bad," and go on about their work. In the country somebody comes over to milk the cows and feed the pigs and a deputation may be over in a day or two to see that the corn gets plowed.[13]

References to sociability, friendship, and warm affection were the ruralite's way of spelling out his commitment to intensely personal values. As often as not, these human feelings for other humans were simply abbreviated in a symbolism that placed heavy emphasis on the home, the fireplace, and the family. Any one of these might be used to suggest the whole nexus of personal values to which the farmer was committed. The common references to these virtues were summed up in one warning to all who cared to listen:

> The true American family can only be found in the rural districts. So said an official of the Federal Department of Agriculture. . . . "The common occupation of the farmer's family [he said] . . . tends to weld more firmly the family idea. The rural home and family become, therefore, a type in the nation. The city family has long ceased to be the type of American family. The rural home is holding the line for the family idea in the nation. This is the reason rural life is significant. If the rural structure crumbles, the nation crumbles." [14]

This reverence for home and family expressed a heartfelt commitment to a way of life believed to exist nowhere else, and, as with so many other facets of rural life, it broadened the basis for a harsh judgment of the city. What the urbanite referred to as a family was really no more than a cluster of people huddled together by habit and for convenience. Only in the country were these people suffused with the warmth and human concern that breathed life into them as a family. And now the family—this cornerstone of the nation—was in jeopardy of being shattered by the ruthless advance of the city.

Two of the prime virtues of rural life, then, were simplicity and warm human feelings. To these, the farmer added the old American virtues of freedom, individualism, and patriotism. As with the others, the natural habitat of these qualities was held to be rural America. It was here that they had been born and nurtured, and it was only here that they could be preserved.

"The independent life on the farm," observed one editor, "is far more preferable than a hand-to-mouth existence in the bright light district of the city." This is what explained the vision he had of farm boys, now disenchanted with the city life they had sought after the war, returning to their homes.[15] The country home was spoken of as a "bulwark of independence." Occasional doubts about the impact of the farmer's independence on the level of farm prices were never related to the purely symbolic value of independence. There was nothing in the corpus of rural values to suggest that farm areas weren't the "heart of the real America," circulating freedom throughout the land.

The farmer had become painfully aware, however, that the traditional values and institutions which he revered were being confronted by a serious challenge from a hostile culture. Adding to his discontent was the possibilty of permanently depressed farm prices, a prospect made all the more vexing by his knowledge that while he suffered, the urbanite prospered. As a result, he could not be content merely to defend his way of life in ideological terms. The seriousness of the whole situation called for action, and to devise and justify a course of action the rural mind bent considerable efforts after the war.

Farmers had long since learned that action stood little chance of succeeding unless it were organized, and yet they had not been able to devise a systematic course of action that both succeeded and endured. Still, after the war they persevered, suggesting a number of possibilities, trying some of them, and agreeing more and more on one of them.

It seems almost anomalous that one of the solutions proposed in the rural areas was, of all things, the strike. Yet after all, why not? Perhaps it was traditionally a weapon of labor, but who was America's true laborer, anyhow? Who was it that really

earned the right to strike with the sweat of his brow? Certainly
not the unionized worker. The nation would do well to remember that when "some communist pro-labor orator starts spout-
ing in favor of protecting the downtrodden working man, it
might be wise to first ascertain just who is the working man . . .
if not the farmer." In fact, warned this editor, considering "the
treatment the farmers have been receiving, it should not be at
all surprising, were they to finally stage a modern up-to-date
strike." [16] Repeatedly in those years of despair the rural press
resorted to the threat of a strike as the means by which the
farmers might seek redress for their many justifiable grievances.
Nowhere was this device more consistently urged than in the
Farmers' Union. Yet it is difficult to escape the conclusion that
there was more bluster than substance in this kind of talk.
Those who spoke of a strike seemed to have no idea of what it
would involve for the farmer. In addition, strike talk was almost bound to run aground on the ruralite's contradictory
demand to curtail the right of organized urban labor to strike.
As a result, even the Farmers' Union did not really give serious
consideration to the possibility of this mode of action in the
1920s. As a yardstick to measure rural frustration such talk was
revealing, but as a proposal for action it was little more than a
hollow threat.

When the time came for action, it was not to the urban
workingman that most farmers turned for their inspiration, but
to the urban businessman. Certainly this development represented one of the striking changes of attitude among farmers
by the 1920s, and perhaps begins to explain the shift in the
nature of the farmer's attacks on businessmen. In the past, the
businessman had been pilloried for economic exploitation; by
the 1920s, his major offense, it seemed, was moral decadence.
What was new here was not a redirection in the nature of farm-
ing. Actually the farmer had long since become a petty capital-

ist, fully committed in a commercial economy to loans, mort-gages, and investments, immediately subject to fluctuations in a market economy, and hopeful of profits that were dependent upon such related factors as prices and costs, production and in-ventories. In addition, he had long since adopted certain of the organizational techniques of businessmen to promote his own economic interests. The change that took place during the 1920s was less one of techniques than of growing consciousness. To be sure, the farmer was a businessman, but he had been slow to accept the identification in his own mind. Now at last he was confronting this reality and breaking through the earlier limitations of his own vision. And in the process of reshaping his self-image he was making it easier to throw himself fully into the business methods necessary to protect his investments and increase his profits.[17]

Signs of this redefinition were evident all through the farm areas of Iowa and Illinois. While the aroma of the Teapot Dome scandal was still fresh in the land, one editor pointed to the "oil crowd's" efficiency of organization as a model for farm-ers to emulate. When that day arrived, he suggested, the farm-er's quest for prosperity would end. "Of course some of the white collared fellows may go hungry," he continued with a feeling for social justice that was also worthy of the oil crowd, "but John Henry Farmer will get his." [18] Other comments were less vindictive, but they consistently reflected an awareness that the farmer's strength lay in "business-like united action" rather than his "historic individualism." [19]

The inspirational leader of this redefinition was the Ameri-can Farm Bureau Federation, first formed as a federation of ex-isting state organizations in 1920. The Farm Bureau, among its many businesslike activities, organized a cooperative advertising service in 1921, which was to operate without cost to farmers in connection with cooperative marketing associations to stimu-

late demand by advertising. Applauding this development, the
Illinois Agricultural Association, which was affiliated with the
Federation, noted that it should "prove to the consuming public that the farmer is capable of taking hold of and solving his
own problems in a businesslike way." [20]

The following year, Illinois farmers were told of an address
made by the president of the National Federation to the National Association of Manufacturers. He cited an identity of
interests between the two groups in that both had to show a
profit or go bankrupt. Then he told the industrialists:

> Just as the consumer of food has a right to protest against agri-
> cultural waste, so has the consumer of industrial goods the same
> right to protest against industrial waste and mismanagement. It
> is a matter which concerns us all, and I trust I will not be con-
> sidered out of my proper sphere of functioning if I call your
> attention to the joint necessity of efficiency of production.[21]

With the arrival of a day when the farmer could commiser-
ate with the industrialist over common problems, a day, in fact,
when he ventured to advise the manufacturer on the need for
more efficient production methods, the farmer had indeed
come of age as a businessman. Not long thereafter the IAA noti-
fied its members that it had hired a consulting accountant, a
man who was also employed by some large corporations in
Chicago. Lest this cause undue concern, the organization assured its members of the need for modern accounting techniques in the farm economy. Too many farm cooperatives in
the past had gone under because they had failed to understand
the "fundamentals of business and finance." Although it had
been an expensive lesson for farmers to learn, it was now time
for them to begin to avail themselves of the long-time experience of the business world to solve their own problems.[22]

Farm organizations in the corn belt were becoming more and

more involved in time-tested business techniques and processes to solve what were essentially business problems. Thus the proliferation of cooperatives served at the same time to eliminate the costs of middle men and to gain a measure of control over marketing. Advertising was used to stimulate consumer demand, a process which hopefully would eat into the problem of overproduction. Modern cost-accounting methods were introduced to rationalize the varied business endeavors of farmers. Prodded by such organizations as the IAA, the farmers were even founding their own insurance corporations. If organization to eliminate waste and restrict competition had been the watchwords of the trustification of business enterprise in the late nineteenth century, then midwestern farmers by the 1920s were experimenting with a quasi-trustification adapted to the peculiar needs of their own variety of business enterprise.

A more standard field of action considered by farmers during those years was partisan politics. In 1924, when the cup of agrarian discontent had filled to overflowing, many farmers turned to the possibility once again of third-party action. Confronted with what they felt to be a choice between Tweedledum and Tweedledee, whom the major parties were running brazenly as the political spokesmen for eastern industrial and financial interests, many midwestern farmers gathered again in a Progressive party, and marched forth behind the spirited leadership of Robert LaFollette to political annihilation. Whatever the reasons for the failure of LaFollette's party in the corn belt, it seemed obvious that there was little hope for growth in it, and the party disintegrated even more rapidly than had been the case with most other third-party efforts.

In the long run, a more successful course of political action during the postwar years was to apply pressures on farm congressmen of both major parties for relief through legislation. The grass-roots support for this pressure was organized and directed by the Farm Bureau through its various information agencies.[23] In this way, the Bureau was able to supply a wide range of information, covering everything from the proper techniques of manuring to the proper limits of constitutional reform. The Bureau thus served not only to keep the farmer abreast of new agricultural methods, but to educate him as well in the roots of his problems and in the measures needed to overcome them.

Characteristic of the Bureau's efforts at propaganda was its willingness to utilize the most modern devices to convey its messages. One of its significant contributions was in the production of moving pictures, which served at the same time to entertain and educate farmers by fictionalizing many of their problems and dramatizing the solutions. Judging from the Bureau's own immodest reviews of these movies, the haphazard products of the early 1920s were being replaced by increasingly slick articles by mid-decade, and by the time of the crash had achieved a level of artistic accomplishment fully worthy of Hollywood's efforts at the same time, if perhaps on a somewhat smaller scale. One of these films, *The Romance of Sleepy Valley*, had been "widely viewed" in 1928, according to the Bureau. It told the story of "a backward rural community, 'Sleepy Valley,' which eventually woke up and found prosperity through the unselfish labors of a County Agent and the earnest efforts of the County Farm Bureau leaders." [24] Like so many of the Bureau's films, *The Romance of Sleepy Valley* was intended to purvey farm propaganda in the sugar-coated pill of motion-picture drama, and to hammer home the point ultimately that the farmer's economic salvation was to be found in the methods of the Farm Bureau.

Not all of these films were such arid attempts to alert farmers to the blessings of the county-agent system. There was, for instance, the story of *A Rural Cinderella,* which was decidedly not set in a backwater rural community. On the contrary, it told of the degree to which country people were escaping from such communities:

> Into the action enter a football game, a girl, a party dress and a college fraternity dance. Glimpses of the game in the packed stadium of the State College of Agriculture, with the battling teams, blaring bands and hysterical rooters will thrill any audience, but back of it all runs the story of the Farm Bureau Home and Community work and the labors of a Home Demonstration agent on a sewing project.[25]

Interestingly enough, the Bureau sought to capture its audience with football games and fraternity dances at the State College of Agriculture, although of course once the plot frills are stripped away from the movie its only apparent difference from *The Romance of Sleepy Valley* is that a sewing agent had been substituted for a county agent.

Still another rural problem—and it was one that was often aired in the country press—was the steady defection of farm children to the city. To help ruralites cope with it, the Bureau produced the film *Transformation* in 1928. In order to lure its readers to the movie, the *Bureau Farmer* outlined the dimensions of the drama:

> "Is there anything about this old house to make me want to spend my evenings here?" the independent little Miss Sue scornfully asks her tearful parents in a family council.
>
> If you have ever been there you will know how that cuts in. And your hearts will leap with delight when you see the wonderful transformation wrought from the impulse of little jazz-mad Sue's cruel question.[26]

Since the description ends abruptly at that point we cannot be absolutely certain how little Sue solved her problem, but the leap of delight in our hearts leaves us suspecting strongly that she overcame her jazz mania and returned to the farm, no doubt to find happiness at the hearth.

Throughout these descriptions runs a message of a different kind of transformation, however, a message which suggests that there were immense underlying changes taking place in rural life, changes which could narcotize Sue with jazz, or cast a farm girl into the social hysteria of modern college life, and, perhaps above all, of changes in the nature and extent of communications in the rural areas, for it is no mere coincidence that the farmer's organizational medium was using motion pictures— not documentaries, but full-fledged movie stories—to illuminate the problems of farmers and to suggest how they, with the aid of the Bureau, would be able to solve them. Not only was the farmer coming to realize the meaning of his business commitment, not only was he becoming more and more committed to the use of technological innovations in his economic life, he was also snapping up the wondrous mechanical advances in communications, and was rapidly growing to depend upon them in his daily life.

Few editors could resist commenting upon the salutary changes that these new devices were effecting in the rural areas. Dante Pierce, editor-publisher of the *Iowa Homestead,* suggested that the movies might prove to be a means of slowing the rush of population from farms to cities. "In one sense," he argued, "the moving pictures take the place of travel, bringing the entire world in review. . . ." Perhaps even more important were those movies that provided a vicarious way to share in the "romance" and "excitement" of the city, thus "removing the desire to experience them in person." [27] Predictably, Henry Wallace condemned the average motion picture because it was a form of passive entertainment; but he had great hopes for the educational potential of the medium. *The Covered Wagon,* he

noted, was a film that "puts into dramatic form the most important factor in American history, the influence of the frontier." If more people went to worthwhile movies, and fewer attended such brainless trivia as *Did She Slip—or Was She
Pushed?* ("A Drama of Sex and Society"), Hollywood's movie-
makers, according to Wallace, might realize that there could be
profit in quality as well as in trash.[28]

Perhaps Wallace remained skeptical about the entertainment
potential of motion pictures, but even he fell victim to the fas-
cination of radio. As early as 1922, he spoke hopefully of the
radio as a godsend to farmers, although he did not think that it
would become a reality for most of them until some time in the
remote future. Within two years, however, Wallace himself had
become an addict of the wireless, and by the end of 1925 he was
offering prizes through his journal for letters relating the most
interesting radio experiences.[29] It was left for the *Iowa Homestead,* however, to bring the winner of that award to the attention of Iowa farmers. The *Homestead* related the tale of a
housewife who had been startled in the quiet of her kitchen as
"the strains of 'Ave Maria' filtered from a pan of beans simmer-
ing on the electric range. . . ." Puzzled, to say the least, since she
did not even own a radio, the poor woman "stirred the beans
vigorously. In answer a whole chorus burst into a hunting
song. . . ." [30] The technical explanation that followed was not
important really, nor was the fact that the woman lived in a
California city. To midwestern farmers, who under the proper
conditions were able to pull in both coasts, Canada, Cuba, and
even Europe on their crystal sets,[31] this was simply another
example of the everyday miracles they were coming to expect
as a matter of course in the new world of mechanical gadgetry.
Naturally, radio blessed them as an economic boon which
brought regular weather and market reports, but they were
twice-blessed because it was also a "never-failing and ever-

changing source of entertainment" which at last broke through the curse of rural isolation.[32]

Even the rhetoric of midwestern churchmen was being radically altered by these changes in rural America. In a speech before a meeting of Methodist dignitaries, William H. Perdew framed his message in what must surely be one of the most breathtaking metaphors in all of English prose:

> The "good fight of faith" is not a scrimmage, but a real battle and only the high courage and unfaltering purpose of the preacher whose spiritual radio receiver is keyed to the wave measure of God's broadcasting has saved the church from being gassed to suffocation by the murky damp of indifference, blind avarice and unbelief.[33]

This call to battle not only invoked images of technology from the recent war, but also of the growing craze for college football, and above all of the new radio technology.

The following year another church leader, Thomas Osborne, addressed a similar gathering. In his discussion of the recent decline in contributions for benevolent purposes, he chose a different kind of mechanism as the inspiration for his metaphor. He explained that

> traveling at a high rate of speed in the early days [of the campaign], upon a pavement of mixed enthusiasm and daring, it is not wholly surprising if our speed should slow up as certain novel . . . parts of our financial mechanism wore down or that we should slow up still more when we reached the end of the five year pavement and struck newly made dirt roads. . . . That we should have been compelled to put on chains and to resort to the shift of gears should not have been wholly unexpected. . . . In any event, having once driven the speeding auto, we shall not again return to the ox-cart method of benevolent financing. . . .[34]

These men who spoke of scrimmages and wave lengths, of pavement and dirt roads, of tire chains and shifting gears—

these men were not pandering to mass audiences, or merely trying to make a point graphically in the Sunday sermon. These were leaders of the church speaking to other leaders of the church, most of them ministers, caught up in a devastating series of images that would have been as impossible in 1904 as they were inevitable in 1924.

Nor was the farmer delinquent in adopting another characteristic of the New Era, the pursuit of governmental assistance in promoting his economic interests. Not only was his course of action premised upon the existence of a positive government, but he was not the least bit timid about making the fact known. "The province of government," said one editor, "is to create prosperity, the greatest good for the greatest number. . . ." On these grounds, he demanded "equitable legislation" for the farmer.[35] Such spokesmen for the farmer as Henry Wallace, Dante Pierce, Milo Reno, and the entire Farm Bureau might often have disagreed over the specific legislation needed, but not one of them would have taken issue with the broader implications of that statement.

Here was no Jeffersonian dream of limited local government. On the contrary, in the process of examining anew the fundamentals of his predicament, the farmer had reaffirmed his old commitment to the idea of a dynamic and creative government. Two generations of farmers had grappled with these problems since the Civil War. They had solved them not at all by action through state governments or by third-party ventures at the national level. Now, during the 1920s, the farmer finally perfected the techniques he has used ever since: bipartisan political action through the two-party system facilitated by pressure groups with a broad base of grass-roots support, and social action, often by the same groups, to soften the harshness of country life.

During the 1920s, the rural mind was a maze of conflicting

images and impulses. It achieved its greatest degree of unity in its view of urban people and their way of life. The consistency in this rural view of the city was important because it provided the farmer with an explanation for many of his problems, and justified the actions he took to solve them. Further justification for these actions grew out of the mellowed vision he had of his own way of life. Life in the country stood for personal warmth, independence, and simplicity, whereas life in the city represented physical proximity without feeling, human action without independence, and human living without sanity altogether.

Yet in many of the techniques that farmers were exploring to solve their problems there was a danger lurking just beneath the surface, for these were techniques which had been pioneered and developed in the very cities which stood as the farmer's arch enemies. If ruralites continued to incorporate them into their mode of life, they were running the risk of undermining the whole battery of images that described their world. From cost accounting and advertising to motion pictures, farmers were snapping up the procedures and products of a new and more materialistic way of life. But what might happen if they were made to face the fact that the images and values that they cherished were contradicted by the lives they were living?

NOTES

1. *Carmi* (Illinois) *Tribune-Times,* November 1, 1923.
2. *Galena* (Illinois) *Gazette,* April 28, 1921.
3. *Rossville* (Illinois) *Press,* July 17, 1919.
4. *Carmi* (Illinois) *Tribune-Times,* quoting the *Goshen* (New York) *Democrat,* July 20, 1922.
5. *Illinois Agricultural Association Record,* June 20, 1925 (hereafter cited as *IAA Record.*

6. Ibid., July 7, 1921.

7. *Oblong* (Illinois) *Oracle*, May 27, 1921.

8. *Monticello* (Iowa) *Express*, August 7, 1924.

9. *Ames* (Iowa) *Daily Tribune*, February 12, 1921.

10. *Bardolph* (Illinois) *News*, May 26, 1921.

11. *Galena* (Illinois) *Gazette*, December 2, 1926.

12. Ibid., February 26, 1920.

13. *Monticello* (Iowa) *Express*, August 25, 1927, quoting *Wallace's Farmer*.

14. *Henry* (Illinois) *News-Republican*, January 5. 1925.

15. *Galena* (Illinois) *Gazette*, April 9, 1925.

16. Ibid., June 24, 1926. See also the *Bardolph* (Illinois) *News*, September 11, 1919; the *Rossville* (Illinois) *Press*, May 15, 1919; and the *Ames* (Iowa) *Daily Tribune*, October 28, 1920.

17. The research for this chapter was completed, and many of the conclusions reached, several years ago before I read the pioneering article by Paul H. Johnstone, "Old Ideals Versus New Ideas in Farm Life," *Farmers in a Changing World, Yearbook of Agriculture, 1940*. Still, it contributed much to my thinking about these problems (hereafter cited as *Yearbook of Agriculture*).

18. *Knoxville* (Iowa) *Journal*, February 14, 1924.

19. *Galena* (Illinois) *Gazette*, January 8, 1925.

20. *IAA Record*, September 22, 1921.

21. Ibid., May 11, 1922.

22. Ibid., December 5, 1923.

23. In addition to its own journals and newsletters, the Farm Bureau quickly gained access to the country papers, many of which ran regular columns of Farm Bureau news.

24. *Bureau* (Illinois) *Farmer*, November, 1928.

25. Ibid.

26. Ibid.

27. *Iowa Homestead*, March 31, 1921.

28. *Wallace's Farmer*, June 26, 1925.

29. Ibid., February 1, 1924, and October 9, 1925.

30. *Iowa Homestead*, January 3, 1929.

31. *Osceola* (Iowa) *Tribune*, July 30, 1925.

32. *Bureau* (Illinois) *Farmer*, July, 1927.

33. *Iowa Conference of the Methodist Episcopal Church, Minutes of 1923*.

34. Ibid., 1924.

35. *Rossville* (Illinois) *Press*, June 8, 1922.

4

The Fight to Preserve Purity

RURALITES suffered from a dreadful vision of cities spreading out to smother them, yet they knew that their fate was bound to those cities. Indeed they were even coming to realize that this could be made to work to their advantage, if somehow they could harness the city to their own purposes. Painfully, however, they learned what a difficult task they had cut out for themselves. The educational process took place as much as anywhere else in the state legislatures.

Perhaps the most spectacular aspects of legislative conflict flared over the cultural differences that existed between ruralites and urbanites. These collisions involved the kinds of differences that grow from attitudes, customs, traditions, and values. In other words, they involved opposite ways of looking at life rather than opposite ways of making a living.

Among the issues that grew from cultural estrangement one rose tall enough to dwarf all the others, for this was the era of Prohibition, the era when some men undertook to reform all mankind. Of course, the advocates of temperance knew that it would take a few years to educate the entire world, but for a start they were willing to settle modestly on setting the necessary example at home. That example, they felt, could most meaningfully be given by distilling the moral tone of the city.

The fight to drain the alcohol from the nation's cooling system had been long and arduous, yet in the end amazingly successful. Beginning in the 1890s, the Anti-Saloon League, enlisting the active support of the evangelical Protestant churches and operating on a bipartisan political basis, proceeded to dry up the nation patch by patch at the grass-roots level. By the time the war broke out in Europe, nearly half of the American people lived under at least nominal prohibition. American entry into the war provided the final impetus for the dry crusaders. For the first time they were able to argue in terms of the patriotic need to conserve the grains ordinarily used in brewing and distilling, and at the same time to direct the anti-German hysteria against the brewers, many of whom were German-Americans. In December, 1917, Congress sent the Prohibition amendment to the states, and in little more than a year the heavily rural legislatures ratified it.

From the outset, the nation's large cities had fought the coming of Prohibition, but step by step they had been forced to give ground. Early in 1919, the issue was on the edge of resolution as legislatures met and put ratification as the first order of business. As the General Assembly of Illinois debated this fateful issue, the *Chicago Tribune* warned that "nations when they act wisely do not put social correctives into their organic law." [1] That this sentiment reflected the concern of many Chicagoans was demonstrated in the local elections of April, 1919, in which the ballot included a local-option proposition to dry out Chicago. The more than 500,000 voters who responded answered with a resounding "No!" Perhaps it did not surprise the prohibitionists that four out of five men in Chicago voted wet, but they must have been shocked to discover that women, who had been the very heart of the temperance movement, voted by more than 60 percent to prevent Chicago from going dry. In all, nearly three out of every four votes on the proposition were dripping wet.[2]

Still, the important question in 1919 was not local option, it was national option, and that question was not to be answered in the precincts of Chicago; it was to be thrashed out in the legislature, which was rather more friendly to the amendment. In a strikingly polarized vote on ratification the near unanimous support of the rural districts overcame stout resistance in Cook County, with only a handful from each group defecting to the enemy. And so Illinois joined the national parade which that month marched onward to the great experiment.[3]

Later that year, in order to implement the amendment, Congress passed the Volstead Act over President Wilson's veto. Those who wished had until the beginning of 1920 to accumulate a store of memories—and as large a stock of liquor as they could find and afford at rapidly inflating prices—to fortify themselves for the nights of nostalgia that loomed ahead. Yet it was not as simple as that. There were still many important questions to be raised, and the entire fate of Prohibition depended upon how they would be answered. Who, for instance, was going to enforce the dry laws? Behind that question lay a maze of conflicting authorities among federal, state, and local agencies that could conceivably work more to inhibit enforcement than to promote it. The implications of the problem became clearer in the years that followed when Congress proved quite reluctant to make the large-scale appropriations necessary to police the nation's thirst. As a result, much of the responsibility for enforcement was thrown back upon state and local agencies. However, there were justifiable doubts about the reliability of local authorities in the very cities which had so desperately opposed Prohibition from the beginning. It would be too much, of course, to expect docile acquiescence from the huge blocs of first- and second-generation immigrants in a city like Chicago. Legal restraints were obviously called for. But

TABLE 1
Illinois
Ratification of
Prohibition
1919

| | Rural | | | | | Cook | |
	1	*2*	*3*	*Total*	*Urban*	*County*	*Total*
Dem.							
F	9	6	3	18	2	0	20
A	2	5	2	9	4	28	41
O	0	0	1	1	1	0	2
Rep.							
F	12	15	12	39	10	12	61
A	1	1	0	2	10	16	28
O	0	0	0	0	0	1	1
Total							
F	21	21	15	57	12	12	81
A	3	6	2	11	14	44	69
O	0	0	1	1	1	1	3

what was the likelihood of the law being faithfully enforced by a police force made up predominantly of Irish-Americans who were more in sympathy with the potential "criminals" than with the law? What were the chances for success in a city where it became a standing joke that the quickest way to find a speak-

easy was to "ask the nearest cop"? Thus even without considering the possibility of wholesale bribery among law enforcement officials (which was always a possibility in the Windy
City), the prospects for Prohibition in Chicago were dim at best.

In spite of the early optimism of the prohibitionists, questions such as these arose and were responsible for the introduction of several measures into the legislature designed in one
way or another to discourage urbanites from slaking their thirst
illegally. The recurrence of such measures provides an insight
into the intensity of the struggle during the 1920s, and into the
nature of important changes that began to take place after the
first few years.

Even before the prohibition issue had been resolved on a
national level in 1919, it was being pressed relentlessly forward
in the Illinois legislature. Still operating on the principle of
drying up the state piecemeal, the drys introduced into the
house a bill to prohibit the sale of liquor outside the limits of
cities, towns, and villages. Prior to this time, sales had been
restricted to relatively small quantities, and had been responsible for a proliferation of "gallon houses" in the country districts. This bill aimed to destroy the evil, and to discourage
those who might try to sneak past the law, by levying fines of
$200. The intent was to close still further the vise of temperance
around the cities, and the vote on the measure consequently
produced a well-defined urban-rural split. It received overwhelming support from the downstate rural areas, and passed
the house comfortably despite sharp resistance from Cook
County.

That was only a start. In the same session of the legislature
a bill was received which anticipated national Prohibition by
banning the manufacture, use, or possession of liquor in dry
territory except for medicinal, sacramental, chemical, or manu-
facturing purposes. In fact, this measure was even more drastic

than the federal law that was taking shape. The Prohibition amendment did not outlaw the possession or use of alcohol, but only its manufacture, sale, and transportation. As far as the federal government was concerned, it was perfectly legal to go on a private five-year binge beginning in 1920, as long as the

TABLE 2

House Bill 239

Illinois, 1919

Restrict Sale of Liquor "Gallon House" Bill

| | Rural | | | | | Cook | |
	1	*2*	*3*	*Total*	*Urban*	*County*	*Total*
Dem.							
F	9	5	4	18	2	1	21
A	2	5	2	9	5	23	37
O	0	1	0	1	0	4	5
Rep.							
F	12	15	12	39	12	12	63
A	1	1	0	2	7	13	22
O	0	0	0	0	1	4	5
Total							
F	21	20	16	57	14	13	84
A	3	6	2	11	12	36	59
O	0	1	0	1	1	8	10

liquor had been purchased before Prohibition. Now Illinois was proposing to push the prohibitionist argument to its logical conclusion by defining the very act of drinking as a crime. Even the mere possession of a bottle was to be considered presumptive evidence of the intent to commit a crime.

Understatement is never one of the virtues of statehouse

oratory, but on this occasion some of the speakers were swept beyond mere exaggeration to a state of near-ecstasy rarely experienced even in Springfield. There was the delegate from

TABLE 3
Senate Bill 130
Illinois, 1919
Re: Prohibition

| | Rural | | | | | Cook | |
	1	*2*	*3*	*Total*	*Urban*	*County*	*Total*
Dem.							
F	9	5	4	18	2	1	21
A	2	5	2	9	5	25	39
O	0	1	0	1	0	2	3
Rep.							
F	12	14	12	38	12	11	61
A	1	2	0	3	8	15	26
O	0	0	0	0	0	3	3
Total							
F	21	19	16	56	14	12	82
A	3	7	2	12	13	40	65
O	0	1	0	1	0	5	6

southern Illinois, for one, who climaxed a lengthy lecture by roaring to the hall:

> I say to you now, that no less than the navy, the army, the home, the State, the Nation, the church, the school, honest business, motherhood and girlhood are all behind this bill, and want it passed at this time.
>
> I ask you today, to ask yourself, "Choose ye, this day, who you

will serve," and in the words of the late lamented Roosevelt, answer the question by saying, "We will stand at Armagedon [*sic*] and we will battle for the Lord." [4]

To this impressive list, later speakers added Jesus Christ, George Washington, and Abraham Lincoln, among others, and, thus linked with patriotism, morality, and divinity, the ruralites administered another crushing defeat to the wets.

A final prohibition measure that year was concerned not with defining the issue, but with administering it, and consequently carried an even greater threat to Chicago. It proposed the creation of a state commission to enforce the liquor laws uniformly in Illinois. In so doing, however, it ran afoul of complications. As far as Chicago was concerned, it meant a sacrifice of local authority at a time when she was arguing for more autonomy in her economic and political affairs. A concession on this issue could vitiate the strength of Chicago's demands for "home rule," even apart from the immediate prospect of more stringent enforcement of dry laws than Chicago police were likely to provide. At the same time, for the rural areas a state commission pointed to heavier expenditures at a time when the farmer's tax load was beginning to create a measure of discomfort in the rural areas. As a result, Cook County opposition was even stronger than usual, whereas rural support, still very heavy, thinned just enough to throttle the proposal.

There were minor variations in the votes on these bills, but what stood out was the great cohesiveness within the contesting factions, and the dramatic polarization between them. The opposition in Cook County and the support in the country districts both enlisted about four out of every five legislators. The votes on these bills clearly illustrated the line of battle. The results, together with the federal legislation, provided the framework within which legal action could finally be taken against the cities.

Such an unprecedented flurry of activity on the liquor question at the national and state levels sent a streak of excitement shooting through the rural areas in 1919. Hopes ran high

TABLE 4

House Bill 620

Illinois, 1919

Re: Prohibition

| | Rural | | | | | Cook | |
	1	*2*	*3*	*Total*	*Urban*	*County*	*Total*
Dem.							
F	8	5	2	15	2	0	17
A	2	6	3	11	5	24	40
O	1	0	1	2	0	4	6
Rep.							
F	11	13	12	36	12	8	56
A	2	3	0	5	7	16	28
O	0	0	0	0	1	5	6
Total							
F	19	18	14	51	14	8	73
A	4	9	3	16	12	40	68
O	1	0	1	2	1	9	12

among the drys that year. However, by the time the Illinois legislature convened in 1921 the first signs of disillusionment were already appearing. It was beginning to look as if the moral revolution might not occur overnight after all. Indeed, one globetrotter for the dry cause, a man well known in the villages as "Pussyfoot" Johnson, was already warning his followers that the nation might never be completely dry.[5] Taking heed of Pussyfoot's alarming prophecy, one editor pinpointed the trouble spots when he suggested wryly that

> Chicago is going out of the liquor business for good and it is said that it is so dry in Manhatten [*sic*] that were it not for the large body of water adjacent to that burg the people who are so unfortunate as to live there would die of thirst and yet Pussyfoot says that this country will not go dry.[6]

By the end of 1921, other signs of disenchantment and frustration were appearing. An awareness that morality was not likely to spread like some kind of beneficent contagion was admitted now even in such heroic quatrains as *The New West:*

> "Curse you!" he snarled,
> And reached for his hip:
> Ten men trampled over him
> Fighting for a sip! [7]

Of course, *The New West* was not wholly a message of despair. On the bright side was the knowledge that the stuff was, after all, increasingly difficult to find. But somehow this ray of hope was dimmed by the human stampede set off at the mere hint of a hip flask. The conversion of the cities was apparently still off somewhere in the future. To hasten the arrival of that day, the drys again prepared some stern measures to tighten the law. They were upset that the drinking of pre-prohibition liquor at private affairs was still legal.[8] Of course, if they could prove that such liquor had been purchased since 1920, they could take steps to prosecute, but there was little chance that they would be able to procure the necessary evidence. Although the Constitution appeared to suggest that drinking was wrong,

Congress, in passing the Volstead Act, had been too timid in its interpretation of the Eighteenth Amendment. To correct this deficiency the Illinois General Assembly sought once more to outlaw the possession or use of alcohol. The passing of two years and the election of a new legislature had little bearing on

TABLE 5

Senate Bill 450
Illinois, 1921
State Prohibition Law

| | Rural | | | | | Cook | |
	1	*2*	*3*	*Total*	*Urban*	*County*	*Total*
Dem.							
F	6	7	2	15	2	0	17
A	1	2	2	5	5	25	35
O	1	0	2	3	0	0	3
Rep.							
F	13	13	14	40	13	10	63
A	2	1	1	4	6	19	29
O	0	0	0	0	1	3	4
Total							
F	19	20	16	55	15	10	80
A	3	3	3	9	11	44	64
O	1	0	2	3	1	3	7

the house vote. The chasm was wider than ever as intensive rural support served to guide the bill successfully through the house over militant Cook County opposition, and this time through the senate as well. Henceforth, it would be a criminal act for a man to carry a bottle of liquor to the house of a friend.

As the cities continued to flout Prohibition contemptuously

during those early years, it became evident that one of the major obstacles to enforcement was the nagging shortage of funds allocated for the purpose by the parsimonious rural-dominated legislature. Designed to mend this deficiency, a bill was introduced into the 1923 general assembly that approached the problem from several directions simultaneously. The over-all aim of the bill was to encourage stricter enforcement with-out additional outlays of cash. It provided that the attorney general would receive all fines from convictions in cases where the evidence was secured by his office. These new revenues were to be used solely for further prohibition enforcement. If some other agency uncovered the evidence, the fines were to be turned over to the county which secured the conviction. Half of this windfall was to be plowed back into county enforce-ment, and the remainder was to be turned over to the county's schools.

If all the possibilities of this bill were realized the benefits for the rural districts would be almost immeasurable. First of all, the bill would be a great stimulus to state and local authorities for whom funds would now grow in direct proportion to efforts made at enforcement. The more diligent their efforts, the greater their rewards; the greater the rewards, the more dili-gently they could pursue violators in the future. And the bill added the piquant irony that not the taxpayer, but the boot-legger himself would finance the great manhunt. The intent of the bill carried far beyond the creation of new funds for en-forcement, however. Once passed, it would not only force violators to finance their own extinction, but would also en-courage them to become patrons of education, contributing generously to the molding of tomorrow's citizens. With the trends in public education creating vast new pressures for local funds, the harassed farmers might hope in this way to satisfy these demands without adding further to their tax load. The measure even had its own built-in propaganda device, for if Chicago politicians chose to fight it they would be placed in the unfavorable public position of blocking educational improvements which could be made without dunning the taxpayer.

TABLE 6

House Bill 561
Illinois, 1923
Prohibition

| | Rural | | | | | Cook | |
	1	*2*	*3*	*Total*	*Urban*	*County*	*Total*
Dem.							
F	9	6	4	19	4	1	24
A	3	5	2	10	4	27	41
O	1	0	0	1	0	0	1
Rep.							
F	10	12	13	35	10	10	55
A	1	0	2	3	8	19	30
O	0	1	0	1	1	0	2
Total							
F	19	18	17	54	14	11	79
A	4	5	4	13	12	46	71
O	1	1	0	2	1	0	3

Chicago politicians, however, did continue to vote unswervingly as they always had on prohibition measures, and with the same lack of success. Once again the farmers drew together tightly, and managed to see the bill through the house by a very narrow margin.

The continuing need for new enforcement machinery, how-

ever, only heightened the awareness in rural areas that something had gone radically wrong. The cities were evading the law
with virtual impunity simply by ignoring it. Worse still, they
seemed to be positively enjoying their criminal behavior, and
even broadcast it through the nation in novels, short stories,
and popular songs. True, the voters of Chicago had ousted
Mayor Thompson in 1923, and had replaced him with a reform
candidate, Mayor Dever. But Dever's reform campaign had
been pitched more against the alleged corruption of Bill
Thompson's regime, and the glaring rise in crime, than against
the mass violations of the Volstead Act, which nobody in
Chicago seemed to consider crime. Reform or not, once in
office the new mayor had little visible impact upon either the
quantity or quality of intoxicating beverages consumed in his
town. Discretion, to be sure, dictated that Al Capone and his
colleagues depart from the once-congenial ambiance of Chicago's notorious First Ward for the safer political climate of
suburban Cicero. The Exodus was a mere formality, however,
as demonstrated by the mounting tidal wave of beer and liquor
washing over the city, and the corpses which were discovered
with embarrassing regularity here and there, on the streets, in
the alleys, and in nearby forest preserves. Chicago, in fact, was
gaining a reputation in what was coming to be called the fight
for "personal liberty" with almost heroic dimensions achieved
by no other city. The reform mayor was able to do nothing to
dim the valor of these latter-day captains of industry as they
struggled to bring order to a chaotic new area of entrepreneu-
rial endeavor in the time-honored fashion of American businessmen—by eliminating competition.

This massive urban resistance to Prohibition only spurred
ruralites to greater efforts in order to guarantee compliance
with the laws. When the 1925 general assembly convened, bills

were sponsored in both houses to set up a state Prohibition commission made up of four administrators and twenty-five investigators. In a decade when rural legislators commonly rose up in wrath against suggestions that would even slightly expand the costs of government, they advanced a bill here that, if

TABLE 7

House Bill 264

Illinois, 1925

Prohibition Commission

| | Rural | | | | | Cook | |
	1	*2*	*3*	*Total*	*Urban*	*County*	*Total*
Dem.							
F	7	6	2	15	1	0	16
A	2	2	2	6	4	24	34
O	2	1	1	4	2	2	8
Rep.							
F	11	13	13	37	15	8	60
A	1	0	2	3	5	20	28
O	1	1	1	3	0	3	6
Total							
F	18	19	15	52	16	8	76
A	3	2	4	9	9	44	62
O	3	2	2	7	2	5	14

passed, would add more than $20,000 annually to the state payroll. Such a proposal might easily have generated a conflict of interests among downstaters, since they were committed both to make Prohibition work and to hold down state expenditures. The misgivings that ruralites usually harbored about public spending did not prevent them from voting for the house-sponsored bill, as usual overriding urban opposition, and they voted overpoweringly also for the senate version of the bill.

But it was not the intensification of rural dedication that made this legislative session a memorable one. More significant was the fact that in 1925 Chicago launched a counteroffensive of its own in Springfield. It was the first major step in a process which was to culminate eight years later in the repeal of the Prohibition amendment. Emboldened by their success in withstanding several years of the experiment, yet obviously impatient with some of the inconveniences that it entailed, Chicago legislators cast about for a means to give expression to what they believed was a growing public sentiment against Prohibition. They were fully aware that the rural legislature was unlikely to assist them in this matter, yet they were forced to work within the system. Seeking a way out of the dilemma, they sponsored a bill to hasten repeal of the Illinois prohibition acts of 1919 and 1921 through the device of a statewide referendum. If they could ram this bill through the legislature somehow, and bring the issue before the voters at large in the state, where one Chicago vote really equaled one rural vote (and sometimes more, the farmers charged), they stood a good chance of achieving their ends. Of course, ultimately the legislature would have to confirm a favorable vote in the referendum, which was improbable, but even here defeat could be turned to some advantage, since Chicagoans had been urging from the beginning that Prohibition had been foisted on the nation by a minority. If the legislators ignored the request for a referendum, or if they flouted the anticipated results if it were held, the wets would be able to turn their propaganda organs loose on the rural minority for violating the sacred norms of democracy. What else was there to say about an entrenched minority that willfully denied the pressing desire of the majority? Of course in the end, no matter what happened in the referendum and in the legislature, the wets would have to come to grips with the disturbing reality that Prohibition was a constitutional mandate, and not merely a local nuisance. But they might at least be able to destroy the stricter state legislation, and at the same time strike a blow in the national struggle for personal

TABLE 8

House Bill 24
Prohibition Referendum
Illinois, 1925

| | Rural | | | | | Cook | |
	1	*2*	*3*	*Total*	*Urban*	*County*	*Total*
Dem.							
F	3	3	2	8	4	26	38
A	5	6	3	14	1	0	15
O	3	0	0	3	2	0	5
Rep.							
F	1	1	3	5	6	19	30
A	12	13	13	38	14	9	61
O	0	0	0	0	0	3	3
Total							
F	4	4	5	13	10	45	68
A	17	19	16	52	15	9	76
O	3	0	0	3	2	3	8

liberty. Thus just as the campaign for Prohibition had begun at the local and state levels, the campaign to abolish it was beginning to gather momentum at the grass roots as well.

By 1925, it was becoming clear that the dry campaign was bogging down. It had not yet stalled completely, but the initiative was changing hands. For the first time since 1919, Chicago went on the offensive and forced the rural areas to ward off an unexpected countercharge. The urbanites did not succeed this time because they were not able to alter the basic alignment of forces. With little ceremony the bill was laid to rest by the rural delegates.

TABLE 9

Vote to Modify Prohibition (November 2, 1926)

Area	Yes	Percentage	No	Percentage
All Rural	32,895	44.1	41,643	55.9
1–25 Percent Urban	50,658	48.5	53,854	51.5
25–50 Percent Urban	114,328	47.2	128,147	52.8
Rural Total	197,881	46.9	223,644	53.1
Urban	151,630	54.2	128,470	45.8
Cook County	487,163	70.6	202,474	29.4
		60		40

Although the cities failed with this repeal attempt in 1925, they did succeed in getting a different measure on the ballot. This one had even more far-reaching implications because it tackled the question at the national level. Stripped to its essentials it aimed to hobble the Volstead Act by allowing the states to define what was an "alcoholic beverage." [9] The immediate goal of such legislation would be to legalize light wines and beers, but there is little doubt that it was meant to be only the first step in the ultimate repeal of the Eighteenth Amendment.

The results of the voting on this proposition in the 1926 election must have sent a quiver of anxiety through the dry legions. The 70 percent majority for it in Chicago was unpleasant but it was not news. The upsetting revelation in this referendum was the degree to which bone-dry sentiment had been moistened in the rural areas, where 47 percent of the vote agreed that a modification of the Volstead Act was desirable. On a statewide basis the resolution carried 60 percent of the voters and gave credence to wet charges that Prohibition did not reflect

TABLE 10

House Bill 3
Illinois, 1927
Prohibition Referendum

| | Rural | | | | | Cook | |
	1	2	3	Total	Urban	County	Total
Dem.							
F	4	2	3	9	8	24	41
A	4	6	2	12	1	4	17
O	3	0	0	3	0	0	3
Rep.							
F	1	0	1	2	12	24	38
A	12	10	10	32	15	4	51
O	0	0	1	1	0	1	2
Total							
F	5	2	4	11	20	48	79
A	16	16	12	44	16	8	68
O	3	0	1	4	0	1	5

majority opinion in Illinois. In fact, by mid-decade it only barely reflected majority feeling in the countryside.

This triumphant expression of antiprohibitionism at the polls renewed the determination of urban forces to destroy the state's dry laws. Again in 1927 they demanded that the legislature approve a statewide referendum on the laws of 1919 and

1921, and this time those who might have laughed off such a maneuver by underrepresented Chicago in 1925 were brought face to face with some of the ruder facts of political life in the state. As always, the split between Chicago and downstate on this bill was sharp, but this time the outcome was different. Cook County legislators were even more firmly behind the reso-

TABLE 11

House Bill 13

Illinois, 1929

Prohibition Referendum

	Rural				Urban	Cook County	Total
	1	*2*	*3*	*Total*			
Dem.							
F	5	2	5	12	10	25	47
A	5	6	1	12	1	0	13
O	0	0	0	0	0	2	2
Rep.							
F	0	0	1	1	8	21	30
A	13	10	11	34	14	4	52
O	1	0	0	1	2	4	7
Total							
F	5	2	6	13	18	46	77
A	18	16	12	46	15	4	65
O	1	0	0	1	2	6	9

lution than they had been in 1925. At the same time, there was a slight increase in support of it from the smaller cities, and a perceptible moderation of rural opposition. The result was instructive. While the cities remained generally opposed to Prohibition, and the rural areas remained generally opposed to drinking, a thin shift in favor of the bill among all the legislative forces meant the difference between defeat and victory for the wets. The bill foundered in the rougher rural waters of the senate and was put out of commission there until the next session when once again it squeezed by in the house. In spite of their ponderous numbers in the house, ruralites were finding out that they had to pay an enormous price for anything less than near unanimity on the liquor question.

By 1929, Prohibition was still very much the law of the land and of Illinois, but after a full decade there was little evidence that the nation had experienced a pervasive moral transformation, unless it was in the direction of greater public immorality. Americans were drinking perhaps as much hard liquor as they had before the war, only now they were paying more money for poorer whiskey, and in the process they were financing a sensational rise in organized crime.

Across the river in Iowa the issue produced fewer fireworks, but only because the contest had been settled before the war when Iowa voted dry, and because there was no locus of concentrated opposition to Prohibition in Iowa such as there was in Chicago. Even then, the matter proved to be not completely repressible. The rural press kept up a constant sniping criticism of Iowa's cities for tolerating continued violations of the law, and finally in 1929, a bill was introduced into the house to stiffen the penalty for a second violation of the state's liquor laws to three years in prison. If bootleggers persisted in peddling their poison, the solution appeared to be to give them ample time and solitude in which to reflect upon the implications of the career they had chosen. The predictably heavy rural support in the house was enough to ease the measure through over futile urban resistance.

In the final analysis, of course, one might believe whatever one wanted to believe about how well Prohibition was working out in Iowa. As late as 1927, the Committee on Temperance of the Methodist Church was proclaiming that it was delighted by "the splendid achievement of the Eighteenth Amendment in bringing sobriety and prosperity to our nation. . . ." In spite of the liquor interests who were spending "billions of dollars" to end Prohibition, this Committee was "able to observe that the consumption of alcoholic liquors [was] constantly decreasing, and that the sources of supply [were] speedily disappearing." [10]

TABLE 12

Senate File 163
Iowa, 1929
Prohibition Enforcement

| | Rural | | | | | |
	1	*2*	*3*	*Total*	*Urban*	*Total*
F	14	27	13	54	10	64
A	6	6	14	26	16	42
O	2	0	0	2	0	2

Other eyes cast in other directions, however, were observing that the consumption of alcoholic liquors had merely become more discreet. As the 1927 session of the Iowa legislature was drawing to a close, one reporter noted nostalgically that in the old days "the parting of friends meant one foot on the rail, elbows on the mahogany" and a cheerful discussion of legislative accomplishments. Nowadays, little knots of men stood furtively around the halls until finally one of them might whisper, " 'Let's go into Executive Session.' 'Any objections?' 'The chair hears none.' 'Who's got one?' " [11] To this seasoned observer, the sources of supply were not disappearing at all, even in the hallowed corridors of the statehouse itself.

Prohibition was the great rallying point for cultural discontent during the 1920s, but it was not the only one. Among the other issues that served to galvanize rural values into action were the attempts to legalize boxing in both Illinois and Iowa.

Boxing had been encouraged as a recreational outlet in the armed forces during the recent war. Tens of thousands of young men had been brought into contact with it for the first time, some as participants, far more as observers. This was no doubt one reason why the newly formed American Legion was an important source of pressure to legalize professional boxing after the war. Over the years, however, the strongest pressures for legalized boxing came from the cities in these two states. The reasons have never been fully explained, but it seems probable that a variety of factors contributed to this mounting pressure. For one thing, there were the vast new reservoirs of leisure time upon which many urban middle- and even working-class Americans were avidly drawing by the 1920s. The sensational boom in such spectator sports as baseball and college football reflected this condition, and boxing enjoyed its own measure of profit from it. The fact that there were hundreds of thousands of people willing to spend money watching athletes earn it created other pressures from the cities. All kinds of businessmen, including hotel and restaurant owners and merchants, stood to make sizable profits from boxing matches that might attract thousands of tourists to a city for a few days. In addition to the men of commerce, the urban newspapers had their own stakes in boxing. As these journals began to sense the groundswell of enthusiasm for sports they responded by gradually expanding the amount of space devoted to sports coverage. When they discovered that sports news sold papers they grew still bolder, so that the relatively innocuous sports *page* that was characteristic of many urban newspapers in 1919 grew into the much more ambitious sports *section* of 1929, with banner headlines of its own, staffs of experts on different sports, regular columnists and, by the way, some of the best journalistic writing of the decade. Once these papers had acquired a vested interest in athletics, they needed no special prodding to serve as the propaganda outlets for all the other groups interested in promoting boxing.

Even many of the ethnic minorities in the cities were developing an interest in prizefighting, for it was in this sport more than any other that the sons of immigrants might find an avenue of escape from the poverty which had so many of them trapped. It was no coincidence that Irish names had dominated boxing for years and were now being joined by the more difficult names of the newcomers. Many among these ethnic groups probably did not know the difference between a haymaker and a hayloft, but they could all feel a sense of pride in the accomplishments of kinsmen who rose to pinnacles of wealth and fame as fighters. It gave them a vicarious sense of achievement in a world where they were virtually shut out from success in any of the more socially respectable occupations.

It was a curious jumble of all of these interests that formed an image of boxing in the rural mind that included crude commercialization, cheap sensationalism, unearned money, immigrants, and, in addition, the gamblers and criminals who were alleged to have had heavy investments in boxing. Nor did it appear likely that the profits from fighting could dissuade the farmer from his principles, if only because the profits would almost certainly remain in the cities.

The various pressures for boxing made themselves felt as soon as the war was over. In Iowa, a bill appeared in the 1919 legislature to legalize boxing under the supervision of a state athletic board. At the same time another was submitted to the Illinois Senate to create an athletic commission of three men who would serve without pay, and a secretary who would receive an annual stipend of $3,600. This Illinois commission would function to license and control matches in those areas where they were not prohibited by local law. Obviously anticipating rural hostility, the sponsors of the bill hedged it with provisions whose purpose was to disarm the critics. First of all, they put boxing on a local option basis. In this way the voters of a particular area could avoid the blight merely by voting it out of their home territory without at the same time interfering with the desires of others elsewhere to witness exhibitions in the noble art of self-defense. A more mundane inducement

TABLE 13
House File 191
Iowa, 1919
Legalize Boxing

	Rural					
	1	*2*	*3*	*Total*	*Urban*	*Total*
F	6	12	7	25	16	41
A	9	27	17	53	6	59
O	1	4	2	7	1	8
Total	16	43	26	85	23	108

was held out in a clause which provided that 5 percent of the gross receipts from all matches would be turned over to the state treasurer. Thus if the farmers protested that they opposed the creation of still another state job, they could be answered that the treasurer's share of boxing receipts would be far in excess of the $3,600 he would pay out, and that the rural areas would share in the anticipated surplus. As a hedge against the moral fulminations that were almost sure to come thundering out of rural pulpits, the sponsors further adorned the bill with provisions that banned Sunday matches, made the use of liquor illegal (the Eighteenth Amendment had not yet been ratified), prohibited gambling on the matches, and penalized "fixed" fights. Gymnasiums, universities, playgrounds, and YMCA's, where the sport was practiced for the sheer animal joy of it, were to be exempted from control by the commission.

TABLE 14
Senate Bill 245
Illinois, 1919
Legalize Boxing

| | Rural | | | | | Cook | |
	I	2	3	Total	Urban	County	Total
Dem.							
F	4	3	4	11	5	26	42
A	3	4	0	7	2	1	10
O	4	4	2	10	0	1	11
Rep.							
F	4	3	2	9	12	19	40
A	8	7	8	23	6	2	31
O	1	6	2	9	2	8	19
Total							
F	8	6	6	20	17	45	82
A	11	11	8	30	8	3	41
O	5	10	4	19	2	9	30

In fact the bill made concessions to almost every conceivable rural objection except to boxing itself. Yet in this matter such factors as prohibition and gambling were only peripheral issues which could always be disposed of in separate bills, as indeed they were. Boxing was the matter at hand here, and it was over that issue that the rural areas drew together. In Iowa, the measure was swamped in spite of solid support in the cities. In Illinois, however, rural solidarity was not as strong as it was on prohibition, and the powerful support received from Cook County was enough to put the bill through the house. It was not until it ran aground in the senate that it was stymied in 1919. Round one had been lost by the cities, but while they had

TABLE 15
House Bill 688
Illinois, 1921
Legalize Boxing

	Rural				Urban	Cook County	Total
	1	*2*	*3*	*Total*			
Dem.							
F	2	2	6	10	4	24	38
A	4	6	0	10	2	0	12
O	2	1	0	3	1	1	5
Rep.							
F	6	3	3	12	14	22	48
A	5	10	11	26	2	3	31
O	4	1	1	6	4	7	17
Total							
F	8	5	9	22	18	46	86
A	9	16	11	36	4	3	43
O	6	2	1	9	5	8	22

been outmaneuvered they had not been mauled, and were to come back strongly later in the fight.

When the legislatures convened two years later, boxing again became an issue in both. While there were no major changes in the Iowa measure, the bill in Illinois was somewhat bolder than its predecessor in 1919. Instead of calling for a staff of three unpaid public servants, the new measure proposed an athletic commission to be headed by three men salaried at $5,000 annually, and a secretary who was to be paid $4,000. The provisions designed to minimize rural opposition were retained. Again the bill cruised through the house over considerable rural opposition, and again it died in the senate. In Iowa, meanwhile, the fortunes of the urban areas improved as rural opposition diminished and the bill cleared the house. In the senate, however, it met the same fate as its counterpart in Illinois.

TABLE 16
House File 387
Iowa, 1921
Boxing

	Rural				Urban	Total
	1	*2*	*3*	*Total*		
F	10	23	8	41	18	59
A	12	12	16	40	4	44
O	1	0	3	4	1	5

By this time, the rural forces were growing alarmed. Only the senates had prevented these bills from becoming law, and there was no telling how long the senators would be able to hold out. Taking official notice, for the first time, of the dire prospects of legalized boxing, Illinois Methodists now passed a resolution urging the "hearty support of legislation that would check the fearful scourge of prize fighting and gambling which . . . is afflicting the country." [12]

The connection between athletic events and gambling was no accident, and it is not surprising, in view of this, that the Illinois legislature entertained a bill in 1921 to outlaw gambling on any kind of athletic contest. The bill did not deal specifically with boxing matches, which were not yet even legal, but it was certainly an expression of the same kind of thinking that opposed boxing. Although the usual rural support gave the bill a majority of the votes cast, it did not provide the needed majority of the entire house because of the great number of abstentions, and the bill died quietly.

The rural victories over the devotees of boxing in the spring of 1921 had been harrowingly secured only by the vagaries of legislative apportionment. As it was, an uncomfortable number of rural lawmakers had demonstrated a lack of reliability, and many members of the country press were thoroughly displeased with the trend of events. To add to their discomfort, the impending heavyweight championship bout between Jack Dempsey and the French challenger, Georges Carpentier, was receiving vast coverage in the city press. Interest in the affairs of a man like Dempsey only made things worse because of the charge that he had evaded the draft during the war. The country press had been broadcasting this intelligence for some time now, and it had done little either to gild the champion's reputation or to enhance the prestige of the sport in general. At that, the doubts cast on Dempsey's patriotism were only incidental to the broader barrage of criticism fired by rural newspapers. Most characteristic was the Iowa editor who charged:

> These fights are not promoted through love of clean sport, but as a betting and money-making proposition. . . . Let us boost for clean, manly sports and oppose those widespread tendencies to degrade [men] to the level of beasts.[13]

Boost as they might for clean, manly sports, struggle as they did against the beastly degradation of men, the rural areas were not able to suppress the boxing issue.

Although no serious pressures for legalized boxing were felt again in Iowa for several years, in Illinois the matter continued to bob up for its biennial float through the statehouse during the next session in 1923. The new bill was much the same as its unfortunate predecessors with the one major exception that now the state treasurer's share of the gross receipts was to be 10

TABLE 17
House Bill 584
Illinois, 1923
Boxing

| | Rural | | | | | Cook | |
	1	*2*	*3*	*Total*	*Urban*	*County*	*Total*
Dem.							
F	4	5	4	13	5	26	44
A	7	3	2	12	3	0	15
O	1	2	0	3	0	2	5
Rep.							
F	0	3	5	8	11	17	36
A	8	11	10	29	5	6	40
O	3	0	0	3	2	6	11
Total							
F	4	8	9	21	16	43	80
A	15	14	12	41	8	6	55
O	4	2	0	6	2	8	16

percent instead of the 5 percent offered previously. In an era when the biggest matches were drawing in over $1 million this was a serious offer. The cities had begun to realize that they would never be able to meet the moral objections of the villages to prizefighting as long as those objections were rooted in deeply felt cultural animosities. Instead, they were probing to

see if the principles had a price tag on them. Having twice
failed with a bid of 5 percent, they raised the offer now to 10
percent. Actually, this added inducement was not so much
needed in the house, where similar bills had already been
passed twice, as in the senate, where they had been defeated

TABLE 18
House Bill 338
Illinois, 1925
Legalize Boxing

| | Rural | | | | | Cook | |
	1	*2*	*3*	*Total*	*Urban*	*County*	*Total*
Dem.							
F	7	5	4	16	7	23	46
A	4	4	1	9	0	0	9
O	0	0	0	0	0	3	3
Rep.							
F	5	5	5	15	13	23	51
A	7	7	9	23	7	3	33
O	1	2	2	5	0	5	10
Total							
F	12	10	9	31	20	46	97
A	11	11	10	32	7	3	42
O	1	2	2	5	0	8	13

both times. The time was still not ripe, as it turned out, and the
bill experienced the same fate once more. After having been
approved in the house much as it had been in the past—with
almost unanimous support from Cook County carrying the day
over some rural opposition—it fell in the more heavily rural
senate.

It was not until 1925 that the persistence of the cities was finally rewarded. This time further assurance was given to the farm areas in a clause which provided that fights would only be held within cities, and then only after a majority of voters in a particular city had approved of boxing in a referendum. Now the bill met even less rural opposition in the house than before. More important was the breakdown of resistance in the senate. At last Illinois was to have legalized boxing.

When Gene Tunney outlasted Jack Dempsey for the heavyweight championship the following year in Philadelphia, the stage was set for what was to become the most famous fight of all time—the notorious "long-count" rematch between these two titans. Now that Chicago could legally host such matches, and since it had recently built a stadium large enough to accommodate the tens of thousands who were eager to finance the rematch, it seemed a natural setting for the bout. The reputation Chicago had acquired as a wide-open town made it a very attractive place to boxing fans, a large clique never known especially for their asceticism. Among fight-lovers the match generated intense interest as it approached. In the rural areas, however, the prospect brought considerably less joy. The *Monticello Express,* continuing its crusade against boxing, pointed out that Chicago hotel men had just announced that rooms would have to be paid for in advance. Obviously the innkeepers knew their customers, and they knew also "how the hotel rooms [would] be used, and [felt] justified in charging $10 a day." [14] Precisely how the rooms were to be used was not specified, but the reader was left with no doubt that the "friends of the two pugs" would carry on in ways that would fall rather short of Monticello's moral standards.

When it was all over, many of the rural papers failed even to report the outcome of the fight, although there were isolated bursts of criticism in Iowa.[15] In Illinois, there was a rare silence in the rural press. Perhaps that was because the struggle over boxing was now a closed chapter. On the other hand, it is possible that the editors were simply too busy figuring out how much 10 percent was of over $2 million.

Efforts to legalize the gentlemanly art in Iowa that year failed to generate much pressure in the legislature, in part, no doubt, because of the statewide agitation of the WCTU against it.[16]

TABLE 19
House File 298
Iowa, 1929
Legalize Boxing

	Rural					
	1	*2*	*3*	*Total*	*Urban*	*Total*
F	3	8	10	21	15	36
A	18	24	15	57	11	68
O	1	1	4	4	0	4

Only by 1929 were Iowa's urban areas, probably encouraged by the financial success of boxing in Illinois and elsewhere, able to regroup their forces for another attempt to legalize the sport in their state. Efforts were made to answer criticism by placing boxing under the strict supervision of an athletic commission made up of the athletic directors of the state's three tax-supported colleges, thereby removing the taint of professionalism, the threat of gangsterism, and the horror of adding to state expenditures by the creation of new salaried jobs. It was all to no avail, however. Iowa's cities stood up in favor of the bill by a moderate majority, but this time they were decisively defeated in the house by strong rural opposition.

Even by the end of the decade, then, unremitting rural opposition still kept out of Iowa the rich rewards that Illinois was reaping from the introduction of boxing. The difference between the responses of the two legislatures was much as it had been on the prohibition issue: Chicago was in Illinois and not in Iowa. Iowa's urbanites were truly influential only when they presented a solid front before badly divided rural opinion.

TABLE 20
House Bill 238
Illinois, 1925
Legalize Horse Racing

| | Rural | | | | | Cook | |
	1	*2*	*3*	*Total*	*Urban*	*County*	*Total*
Dem.							
F	5	4	3	12	4	24	40
A	3	5	0	8	0	0	8
O	3	0	2	5	3	2	10
Rep.							
F	2	1	2	5	8	19	32
A	10	8	13	31	9	9	49
O	1	5	1	7	3	3	13
Total							
F	7	5	5	17	12	43	72
A	13	13	13	39	9	9	57
O	4	5	3	12	6	5	23

Rarely did this happen on cultural issues because rural opinion was not seriously divided, and the attempt to legalize prizefighting was no exception.

Of a piece with the drive to legalize boxing in Illinois was the effort to establish horse racing with pari-mutuel wagering on a legal basis. First introduced into the Illinois House in 1925, the bill was defeated because of strong rural reservations. It was reintroduced during the following meeting with numerous provisions, the purpose of which was to lessen opposition from the farmers. The bill would not only legalize the sport of kings, but would regulate it under the Department of Agriculture of the state. Still, pari-mutuel betting was explicitly sanctioned, and that is what was raising all the heat among the ruralites. To counter these feelings, the bill proposed that a portion of the gate receipts be turned over to the Department of Agriculture. Here was an offer that would allow the farmers to pad the funds of a governmental department designed in their own interests without levying additional taxes. In addition, the license fee money for races was to be used for the purchase prizes to be awarded at state and county fairs. And finally, the act was not to apply to harness racing. Trotting races had, of course, long been a highlight at these rural-oriented fairs. Any attempt now to bring them under close regulation or to introduce overt betting at them would unquestionably antagonize the farmers, who preferred apparently to do their wagering in the less conspicuous areas underneath the grandstand. What emerged was a measure to sanction modern horse racing in and around the great population centers. It was to be governed by an essentially rural commission which was enjoined from interfering in any way with rural racing traditions, and finally, it was to provide pecuniary benefits to the rural districts which were to be paid for by urbanites. Such an attractive package was too much for downstaters to resist. The opposition to it was rural, but it was weak, and in spite of the encouragement openly given to gambling by the bill it was passed.

In various forms, these issues—prohibition, boxing, and horse racing—came before the legislatures of Iowa and Illinois on innumerable occasions during the 1920s. They came up during flush times and during bad times. Representatives from the relatively well-to-do cash-grain areas voted on all of them, and farmers from the marginal areas voted on all of them. Prosperity or depression, affluent or poor, however, it made little difference. All of the rural areas, both before the slump and after it, voted in just about the same proportions against them. One of

TABLE 21
House Bill 240
Illinois, 1927
Legalize Horse Racing

| | Rural | | | | | Cook | |
	1	*2*	*3*	*Total*	*Urban*	*County*	*Total*
Dem.							
F	7	2	3	12	8	25	45
A	3	6	2	11	1	0	12
O	1	0	0	1	0	3	4
Rep.							
F	5	4	2	11	11	20	42
A	7	6	0	22	11	8	41
O	1	0	1	2	5	1	8
Total							
F	12	6	5	23	19	45	87
A	10	12	11	33	12	8	53
O	2	0	1	3	5	4	12

the few times that a cultural issue divided farmers along economic lines was in 1929 when the *poorer* farmers in Iowa opposed the boxing bill to a much greater degree than the less depressed farmers, which suggests a correlation between cultural problems and poverty, rather than prosperity.[17] In general, though, economic factors did not appear to shape cultural conflict one way or the other. What was important was that these people were ruralites facing a common problem that had reached crisis proportions for them by the 1920s, and not that they were rich or poor ruralites.

Two other expressions of cultural conflict darted elusively in and out of the scene, yet curiously neither one ever grew strong enough to shape and direct the politics of Illinois and Iowa at this time, as they did in many other states. One of them reflected the resistance of Protestant fundamentalism to the incursions of modernism and secularism; the other was related to the sudden revival of the Ku Klux Klan after the war.

The antagonism dividing fundamentalists and modernists had been growing for many years when the Tennessee legislature finally thrust it to stage center in 1925 by enacting a law banning the teaching of evolution in the state's public schools. The ensuing drama not only focused on an epic struggle between two hostile cultural commitments, it reached also to the very roots of the nation by raising questions about freedom of speech and church-state relations. Its setting—a country village in the South—could not have been more traditionally American, yet at the same time the radio broadcasts of the Scopes trial and the opportunistic hucksterism of local boosters injected a uniquely contemporary tone into the whole affair. Even the major antagonists were the very personification of the issues involved: William Jennings Bryan, evangelist of rural hopes and incurable optimist in the face of unrelenting political disaster, who had recently become a champion of the drive against evolutionism; and Clarence Darrow, patron saint of hopeless causes, urbane, caustically witty, incorrigibly agnostic, and now increasingly pessimistic after a lifetime of remarkable personal victories against forbidding odds. Americans everywhere were absorbed in the unfolding drama because in one way or another they were all involved in its deepest conflicts.[18]

Even before the Scopes trial blazed into the nation's headlines, some of the country editors were airing the controversy over evolutionism, and with surprising consistency they held the fundamentalists up for public ridicule. One of the more pungent critics was the *Monticello Express,* which was also one of the most raucously nativistic and rigidly moralistic papers in Iowa. Early in the decade, when the Kentucky legislature was considering a bill to outlaw the teaching of evolution in the public schools, the *Express* sourly noted that these were the same kinds of people who had tried to suppress Galileo. In that instance, however, concluded the editor, "truth prevailed; authority and tradition were rejected, and the demonstrations of science were adopted." [19] A year later the *Express* criticized the Des Moines police chief for his unsuccessful attempt to bar the teaching of evolution in the public schools of Iowa's capital. Such a man, remarked the editor, would have been more at home during the fifteenth century.[20]

The entire rural press chimed in during the Tennessee uproar of 1925, and while their reasoning varied widely, their conclusions were almost always the same: the state of Tennessee had no right to dictate the subjects taught in its public schools. Launching a direct assault on the fundamentalists, the *Knoxville Journal* asserted that "the idea that [evolution] is antagonistic to the Christian religion is the product of ignorance and bigotry." [21] Clearly the *Journal* had aligned itself with modernism and was hopeful that the trial would serve the useful purpose of generating a rational debate over issues, a process which it assumed could only result in the triumph of its own point of view.

In other instances the press derided the whole thing as a tempest in a teapot with "Bryan in his dotage . . . off on another tangent," or merely expressed indifference to a controversy which would not change anyone's mind when it was all over.[22]

Even partisan politics did not affect the views expressed. One Democratic paper argued that if Bryan's viewpoint triumphed at the trial it would follow that all the sciences and history would have to be "revised and expurgated not to conflict with fundamentalism." [23]

There were even editors who sympathized with Bryan on the religious issues, but could not bring themselves to support his constitutional position. Thus an Illinois weekly said:

> The Tennessee law which forbids the teaching of the theory of evolution should never have been enacted in any community founded upon Democratic principles. Even though we disagree most heartily with the theory which Clarence Darrow says he can prove a truism, we cannot subscribe to the position of [a] law-making body that will legislate against honest and intelligent consideration of any theory. Laws that limit the scope of one's mental range cannot be tolerated. If the Scopes trial results in the repealing of the anti-evolution law it will have served just one purpose.[24]

Here was a fundamentalist editor who opposed the Tennessee law on the grounds that it was an intolerable infringement upon academic freedom and democratic ideals. For him the point at issue was not which side owned a particular truth but the more delicate question of any man's right to pursue and discuss his version of the truth freely, no matter how unsavory or downright wrong his ideas might be. On these grounds he hoped that Scopes's act, if not his ideas, would be vindicated by the trial.

Another Illinois paper took a more equivocal stand. After first suggesting that the matter was not important enough to waste space on, the *Bardolph News* proceeded to waste some by suggesting that perhaps a legislature did have the right to determine what should be taught in the public schools. A week later, however, the *News* quietly reversed its field and said that it would be permissible to teach evolution as a theory, but not as an accepted truth, in the same way that one might teach the various Christian positions on baptism without saying that one was right and the others wrong.[25] Although it was not extravagant in its defense of Scopes, the *News* ultimately supported his right to present alternatives in a classroom, and rejected the more confining views of Bryan and the Tennessee legislature.

Of the few country papers that stood solidly behind the Tennessee law, one said flatly that evolutionary theory "should be prohibited no matter where it is taught." And perhaps to solve the problem for posterity, the editor added that the scientists who propagated such ideas should be "confined in cages like the rest of the tribe of their ancestors, and fed by catching peanuts on the fly." [26]

In all, seventeen rural papers in Iowa and Illinois were sifted on the Bryan-Darrow dispute. Only one of them stood firmly by the right of Tennessee to proscribe the teaching of evolution in its public schools. Eleven of the papers, on the other hand, argued that Scopes did have the right to introduce the subject in his classes, although their reasoning led them in several directions to justify his action. Five other papers were completely silent on the question. Perhaps this was because they did not want to antagonize their readers. Or perhaps it was because they simply did not consider it important enough to discuss. In one or two cases it was due to the fact that the editor-publisher was away on vacation, and during his absence all editorial matter was suspended. In any event, it is clear that public opinion was not strong enough to force the issue in favor of fundamentalism. And these, remember, were the same newspapers which had cried out in unison against the burgeoning evils of an urbanizing America.

There are several possible ways to explain why fundamental-

ism did not surface as a major issue in the Midwest. One is
simply to assume that it had no appreciable following. Yet no
one who has lived in a midwestern small town is likely to make
such an assumption; this was, after all, the Bible Belt as well as
the corn belt. Should one assume then that fundamentalism
was as pervasive and as deeply felt as prohibitionism, but that
somehow it never became a political issue? That argument is
even less convincing. Antievolutionism was perfectly suited to
legislative action, as several states demonstrated at the time. If
rural Illinois and Iowa had been as solidly fundamentalist as
they were prohibitionist, there is every reason to believe that
they would have used their political muscles to force the issue
to a head in the legislatures. That they did not do so suggests
that they could not do so, and if they could not do so it had to
be because they were divided on the question. At this point the
pieces begin to fall into place, especially if we make the further
assumption that fundamentalism was concentrated disproportionately *on the farms themselves,* rather than in the small
towns.[27] Then the failure of rural fundamentalism to pick up
momentum in the Midwest can be explained, at least in part,
in terms of structural changes that were taking place in the
Protestant churches at the time, for the fact is that a blight was
settling over the crossroads churches that was threatening them
with extinction before the decade was over.[28]

The impact of this development was depressing. Whole sessions of church conferences were devoted to the "problem" of
the rural churches. Reports of country churches shuttering
their doors became almost monotonous within a few years after
the war. In 1925, the Methodist and Presbyterian churches in
the village of Oxford, Iowa, had to pool their resources in order
to pay one resident minister for the two of them. In the same
year, a Methodist official in Iowa noted that contiguous rural

churches had been "united" in the Bloomfield district. The rural churches, as a matter of fact, were rapidly being consolidated out of existence because there were scarcely enough people to preach to in them any more.

It was not that farm families had quit going to church, but that they had begun to go to church elsewhere. Perhaps this was because farm children, as one churchman explained, were no longer "satisfied in a little country Sunday school while their chums and playmates [were] gathered in a large school in a nearby city or village. . . ."

In a more basic way, however, the traditional centers of midwestern fundamentalism were fading because the automobile was finally carrying the farmer and his family beyond the crossroads and the nearby village. Time after time at these church conferences references were made to the impact of the automobile on rural piety, and by late in the decade the references were becoming pointed as a full awareness of the problem grew in the minds of concerned clergymen. By 1927, a Baptist field worker lamented that the automobile had been "completely changing the condition of life in the country" for more than two decades already. "The distance between churches," he estimated, "has been reduced at least three-fifths. Once in your car you would just as soon drive ten miles as one." And in the process, he might have added, pacify those children of yours who had been nagging you about their "chums and playmates" in that shiny new Sunday school in the large town ten miles up the road.

As they succumbed by the thousands to the new automobile culture, fundamentalist farmers found themselves facing an unpleasant set of alternatives in the urban churches. They could, if they wished, remain in the more "respectable" denominations, which as often as not is where they had been practicing their fundamentalism over the years. In that case, however, they were apt to find that Methodism at the crossroads was a far different thing from Methodism in the towns and cities, where more and more of the ministers were modernists. For those, on the other hand, who preferred to take their old-time religion straight, there was often no choice but to gravitate toward one of the more esoteric sects. Those among the faithful who were willing to sacrifice social prestige for purity of soul in this way usually found that they had sacrificed broad political influence as well, since the sects were too fragmented to make their weight felt outside of isolated communities. The issue was sealed completely when the fundamentalists tried to force their views within the denominations and were badly defeated. After the showdown at the national convocation of Methodists, an Iowa church official crowed that Methodism had made

> a profound impression upon world wide Christianity . . . when it refused to put its supreme emphasis upon credal statements of belief, whether in the form of fundamentalism or modernism. . . . The substitution of orthodoxy of belief for a Christ-like life borders upon near-tragedy.[29]

When the largest and most influential of the evangelical churches in the Midwest went on record as refusing to go on record, it left the fundamentalists in its ranks without an effective medium through which to channel their sentiments politically about such issues as evolution. Thus, in an age when organization was the key to political leverage, many fundamentalists found themselves forced to choose between fundamentalism without organizational power and organizational power without fundamentalism. Because these alternatives left them helpless to press their views broadly, evolutionism never became more than a local issue in Iowa and Illinois.

In some ways even more elusive than fundamentalism was the soaring revival of the Ku Klux Klan during the postwar years. Reborn in Georgia in 1915, it grew slowly until 1920, when it caught fire and spread rapidly to the Southwest and then through the North from one coast to the other.[30] The Klan's story during those years, however, was not one of unqualified triumphs, even at the peak of its glory.

The reception accorded the Klan in Iowa and Illinois, for the most part, was downright inhospitable. Leading the opposition were many of the country editors who spoke out unhesitatingly against the noble Knights. The *Galena Gazette,* which had supported immigration restriction and had been consistently nativistic and antiurban throughout the decade, attacked the avowed hostility of the Klan toward Negroes, Catholics, and Jews by pointing out that all three groups were capable of producing useful citizens.[31] By no means accustomed to lavishing such praise upon minority groups, the editor was nevertheless willing on this occasion to accept them in order to condemn the extremism of the Klan. Elsewhere in Illinois, the *Bardolph News,* another strongly antiurban paper, clubbed the Klan with heavy-handed irony. It seems that the Richmond (Virginia) klavern of the Klan had recently pressured the city fathers into rejecting the offer of a statue of Christopher Columbus on the grounds that he had been a Catholic. Of the Klan the *News* said, "They should show their disapproval not of Columbus, but of a continent that would allow itself to be discovered by a Catholic. . . . They should pull out and leave the country flat. The whole country would cheer them for that." [32] The year before, precisely when the Democratic party in its convention was preparing to embark upon its venture at self-immolation over the Klan, a rural Democratic paper in Illinois had aired the issue, although it might understandably have been excused for smothering it on political grounds. The *Oblong Oracle* informed its readers that the Klan had been active in Crawford County. With implicit mistrust, the *Oracle* suggested that the Klan operated "stealthily," that its membership was "secret and their methods of doing things are secret." The editor would try to keep his readers informed, however, so that they might be aware of the doings of this mysterious order.[33]

Press reaction in Iowa was, if anything, even more hostile. The *Monticello Express,* an archly nativistic paper, flayed the Klan.[34] And the *O'Brien County Bell* fired off a corrosive blast:

> The federal government is putting up a determined fight against the ku klux [*sic*]. All klansmen are to be driven out of government jobs. This is meet and proper, since government jobs should be open only to Americans, and the klan is one of the most Un-American institutions on record.[35]

Even Milo Reno's Farmers' Union refused to be distracted by the Klan. Approvingly it reprinted a warning from the mayor of Sioux City which charged that the Klan was destructive of American institutions. "KEEP OUT OF THE KLAN," read the warning in capital letters, "AND FORGET IT. IT IS NOTHING BUT A BAIT THROWN OUT BY BIG BUSINESS TO CATCH POOR SUCKERS." [36] There it was—a Wall Street plot to divert the attention of farmers from their real, i.e., economic, grievances.

For the most part, the Methodist and Baptist churches were more prudent than the newspapers and simply avoided the controversy. At that, however, a branch of the Methodist church in Iowa placed itself "on record as condemning the Ku Klux Klan, as being un-wholesome in influence, un-American in method and un-Christian in principle." [37] This was the same organization which at various times in the 1920s had also gone on record against liquor, cigarettes, movies, "salacious and obscene literature and sex magazines," Al Smith, prizefighting, and "commercialized sports and games" on Sunday.

This is not to say that the Klan was nonexistent in the corn-belt states of Illinois and Iowa, or that opposition to it was either universal or militant. Many rural weeklies drew caution from the winds and ignored the Klan for safer subjects, at a time when it took a major effort to ignore the Klan. And from here and there came notices that the Klan was enjoying local successes, some of them rather upsetting. Early in the spring of 1924 an editor in northwestern Iowa served notice that a local klavern was scheduled to be organized in the near future. Even with this forewarning he professed surprise three months later at the extent of the Klan's success in attracting members, considering that it had only recently been organized.[38] Although he hinted mild disapproval in these editorials, he remained silent after that, which is odd in view of the fact that it became a burning issue at the Democratic convention being held at the time, and throughout the country during the following year. In Illinois the Klan held several mammoth rallies in the summer of 1923, and succeeded in turning Williamson County in the south into a gore-drenched battlefield from 1923 to 1926.[39]

With the Klan stirring things up locally it is not surprising that it caught the eye of the legislature. The 1923 session in Iowa, which had four or five Klansmen sitting in the house,[40] entertained a bill to make it a misdemeanor for anyone to appear in a mask, hood, robe, or other disguise. The penalty was not to exceed thirty days in jail. These antimasking bills were already becoming a major political weapon against the Klan in a number of states. At the very least they served a more or less symbolic function by putting a state on record against the Klan and officially discrediting it. And of course any organization that depended upon secrecy for survival could be shattered whenever the state chose to use this weapon for more than symbolic purposes. In Iowa the antimask-and-hood bill stormed through the house without a dissenting vote and with only a handful of abstentions.

TABLE 22

House Bill 208
Illinois, 1921
Religious Libel

| | Rural | | | | | Cook | |
	1	*2*	*3*	*Total*	*Urban*	*County*	*Total*
Dem.							
F	2	4	6	12	5	20	37
A	3	3	0	6	0	0	6
O	3	2	0	5	2	5	12
Rep.							
F	6	5	7	18	12	23	53
A	3	4	2	9	1	1	11
O	6	5	6	17	7	8	32
Total							
F	8	9	13	30	17	43	90
A	6	7	2	15	1	1	17
O	9	7	6	22	9	13	44

In Illinois the Klan, or Klan-related problems, came before the legislature on several occasions. As early as 1921 an attempt was made to discourage libel against religious denominations and sects. The bill stipulated that a violator would be tried in the county where such libel was distributed, irrespective of where it had been published. Actually, it is not clear that the measure was aimed directly against the Klan at this early date, but it was certainly directed against the kind of sentiment that was soon swept up by the Klan. The particular terms in which it was couched were such as to discourage strong opposition, since few legislatures would want to parade before the public in favor of religious libel, and the bill had little trouble in the

TABLE 23
House Bill 8
Illinois, 1929
Klan

| | Rural | | | | | Cook | |
	1	*2*	*3*	*Total*	*Urban*	*County*	*Total*
Dem.							
F	6	6	5	17	10	24	51
A	2	0	0	2	1	0	3
O	2	2	1	5	0	3	8
Rep.							
F	1	1	1	3	11	15	29
A	9	6	9	24	8	5	37
O	4	3	2	9	5	9	23
Total							
F	7	7	6	20	21	39	80
A	11	6	9	26	9	5	40
O	6	5	3	14	5	12	31

house. At that, the resistance it did meet came almost exclusively from the rural areas.

Before long, the Klan itself became an issue. In 1925, a bill was brought in to curb it while the Klan was at the height of its national influence. It provided that any organization with twenty or more members which required an oath as a prerequisite for membership would have to file a copy of its constitution and a roster of its membership with the Secretary of State. Labor unions and benevolent associations were specifically exempted. Here, if it were passed, would be an even more effective way of unmasking the Klan. Apparently 1925

TABLE 24

House Bill 634
Illinois, 1929
Klan

| | Rural | | | | | Cook | |
	1	*2*	*3*	*Total*	*Urban*	*County*	*Total*
Dem.							
F	3	2	1	6	4	16	26
A	2	2	3	7	3	2	12
O	5	4	2	11	4	9	24
Rep.							
F	1	4	3	8	10	16	34
A	6	3	4	13	6	7	26
O	7	3	5	15	8	6	29
Total							
F	4	6	4	14	14	32	60
A	8	5	7	20	9	9	38
O	12	7	7	26	12	15	53

was not the year for such action in Illinois, however, and the bill was defeated by rural opposition in the house.

During the next few years the issue remained quiescent in the legislature, while the Klan was being splintered by scandal, but it was brought up again in 1929 with results that suggest that the opposition four years earlier had been aroused by the clause that demanded the publication of names. The sponsors

of the legislation circled around that obstacle this time by submitting two bills instead of one. The first required that such
organizations file their constitutions with the secretary of state.
The rural vote was split here, but the bill was passed because of
the solid support it received from Cook County. It was the other
one that ran into serious trouble. It required the registering of
names in each county with the recorder of deeds. This bill
failed to pass because one-third of the house members ab-
stained, and it could not gain the absolute majority needed.

Even well after the public revelations about the Klan, then,
the rural districts put up stiff and partially effective resistance
against Cook County's attempts to erode Klan strength through
public exposure. In addition, a breakdown of the voting on
these measures reveals that Klan-like sentiment was tending to
gather in the Republican party, which was no doubt the counterpart to intensive efforts by the Democrats to recruit the new
immigrants into their party. Nevertheless, while pockets of
Klan strength remained right up to the Wall Street crash, the
movement was on the wane after mid-decade in Illinois and
Iowa.

There are still some things about the Klan that are puzzling.
While it shared much in common with the rural revolt of the
1920s, for instance, it was never a rural movement to the same
degree that prohibitionism was. In fact, its center of strength
in Iowa lay in the capital and largest city, Des Moines. In a
strong effort to capture the machinery of power in that city the
Klan entered the primary elections of 1924 and was defeated.
After the election an anti-Klan editor thought that this setback
would be felt by the Klan throughout the state. "Polk county
[Des Moines] was the hotbed of the Klan," he reported, "and
the Klans looked to that locality for strong support." [41] As it
was, his use of the past tense here turned out to be a bit pre-

mature. The Klan rebounded a year later in the Des Moines school board election, and succeeded in electing the three candidates whom it had endorsed.[42] Thereafter, the Klan faded rapidly from public life in Iowa, but not before Des Moines had been deeply stained by it.

If the Klan blossomed in such places as Des Moines and Rockford, it could not have been, strictly speaking, just another manifestation of rural discontent. And yet, because it was never seriously heard from in the cities like Cedar Rapids and Moline, let alone Chicago, it was obviously not primarily a creature of the cities either. In order to clarify this point it is necessary to distinguish clearly between *motivational* and *operational* factors, and to recognize differences in the timing of changes that were occurring in the Midwest.

The *motivation* of Klansmen grew from the fears and resentments felt by a long-dominant group toward the challenge posed by hordes of pressing outsiders who did not fit into their scheme of things. In this sense the virus was ethnic and cut across urban-rural boundaries to infect many of the smaller cities that were only beginning to feel the impact of large numbers of these newcomers for the first time. On the other hand, the river cities on both borders of Iowa, and many of its inland cities as well, were much more industrialized, and had experienced their own cultural tremors a generation earlier when thousands of natives had lashed out at the heavy influx of Catholics by joining the American Protective Association. Essentially, Des Moines was passing through a similar crisis after the war. It had developed as a center of commerce and government bureaucracy, and its growth had been fed by a steady flow of readily assimilable migrants from among the state's marginal farm families. In recent years, however, this homogeneity had been upset by the arrival of Italians, Negroes, and Jews, and when the Klan blustered onto the scene promising to do something about it, local residents responded.

The basic ethnicity of this conflict, and of much of the cultural revolt in general, shows up also in the persistent enclave of Cook County legislators who voted for prohibition, and against legalized boxing and the anti-Klan bills. These men almost invariably came from the suburbs, which remained largely closed to Jews and Catholics, yet uncomfortably close to them, or from the embattled islands of old-stock strength which remained in the city.[43]

At an *operational* level, however, this intense cultural animosity was most apparent and most effective in the small towns and villages—broadly speaking, in the rural areas—where there was virtually no counterbalance to the upsurge of feeling among old Americans. Public figures in rural areas could voice these feelings because they did not have to fear political reprisal. In the cities, however, politicians were becoming highly sensitive to the increasing self-consciousness of the enormous blocs of new immigrants. Whatever they felt personally, they found it expedient to solicit this bloc vote. If Des Moines and other cities like it stood as exceptions, it was usually because the new immigrant populations were too small or still too inert politically to force the issue in their own interest. The point is that these cities *were* exceptions. Much more typical were such cities as Chicago, Cedar Rapids, and Dubuque, which fought bitterly against this provocative response from an older America. In a functional way, then, ethnic hostilities flowed into the larger stream of cultural conflict which divided the cities from the countryside, and at times threatened to dominate the public affairs of the 1920s.

And still, in spite of the obvious kinship of the Klan to the wider currents of cultural animus, it never came close in Iowa or Illinois to creating the uproar that it did in the neighboring corn-belt state of Indiana. Never did it capture a legislature as it did in Oklahoma, or elect a governor as it did in Oregon. The only statewide election in which it played an important role was in the narrow defeat of Iowa's Senator Brookhart in 1924, and it is probable that Brookhart, who supported LaFollette in the presidential election that year, lost more votes because he angered Republican party regulars, and because Iowa was repudiating the insurgent tradition in the 1920s, than because he was opposed by the Klan. Not one scrap of legislation is traceable to Klan activity, while, on the other hand, both states passed anti-Klan laws. What is really surprising in these states is not that the Klan grew, but that it did not grow into a really large or effective pressure group. One would think that aroused ruralites everywhere would have been eager to support an organization that said what they were thinking, and appeared to have the size, organization, and resources to do something about it.

On the surface, of course, the Klan did share the objectives of the rural uprising. It was against liquor, against immigrants, against gambling, against sexual novelty, and against anyone who was against the Klan. At a more critical level, however, one is hard put to explain its existence at all during these years. After all, the standard legal machinery was being used to cope with all of the evils against which the Klan stood. Nor does it really solve the problem to argue that the significance of the Klan lay in the function that it served as a fraternal lodge in lodge-minded small-town America.[44] The last thing that small-town America needed was another lodge, especially one with such an unsavory reputation as the Klan.

The Klan was not so much attractive for the ends it pursued as for the means it proposed to use in pursuit of those ends, for the one thing the Klan offered that was uniquely its own was extra-legal or even illegal action to compensate for the sluggishness of legal processes in stopping the onrushing forces of the new America. Its very raison d'être was violence or the constant promise of imminent violence. Organizations such as the Masons existed to unite anti-Catholics in fellow feeling, if that is what they wanted; the Elks and the Odd Fellows would give anyone a run for his fraternal money; the Anti-Saloon League was really trying to do something about the liquor problem; and politicians and political processes were proving at that very time their susceptibility to cultural pressures. Only the Klan, however, offered the possibility of emotional release through violence, actual or vicarious.

In a recent sociological overview of the history of prohibitionism, Joseph Gusfield has suggested the concept of "expressive politics" to explain that brand of political behavior which is undertaken for its own sake rather than to change "the distribution of valued objects." [45] Political action here becomes an end in itself; legislation is incidental or even irrelevant. No movement of the era seems better described by this process than the Ku Klux Klan. Prohibitionists at least had a concrete objective which might be realized through concrete political action. Klansmen did not really work toward such ends. Except for the law they passed to outlaw parochial schools in Oregon, and some widely scattered local ordinances, they rarely did anything through normal political channels even when they dominated the machinery of government. Their most broadly shared objective was to lacerate human hides and spill viscera about the countryside. And it is a good bet that the great majority, who never got to experience the thrill of the hunt at first hand, spent a significant part of their fraternal time talking about those who did. Chalmers's observation that "merely belonging

to the Invisible Empire solved many of the Klansman's problems" is more meaningful in this sense than in the context of
fraternal goodwill in which he proposed it.[46]

This orientation toward physical excess is what rural papers
alluded to in their repeated attacks on the Klan as un-American and un-Christian, as a threat to American institutions, and
as undemocratic. Thus, paradoxically, violence becomes the
key to understanding both the limited success and the broad
failure of the Klan in Iowa and Illinois. Instead of capturing a
solid base of support among the tens of thousands of ruralites
there who sympathized with its nativism, the Klan alienated
most of them even before it discredited itself with scandal. It
remained a repository for an extreme, almost pathological, expression of what Leuchtenburg has called "political fundamentalism," a variant that was desperate enough in its frustration to drive itself beyond the pale of acceptability for the run-
of-the-mill nativist.[47]

In the country areas of Illinois and Iowa during these years
there was a vast reservoir of ill-will and hostile actions directed
toward the immigrant-laden cities. The Ku Klux Klan was related to these sentiments in many important ways, but in
others, equally important, it was not so much an expression of
this hostility as a caricature of it.

Ruralites in the Midwest entered the 1920s with clear ideas
about where the world was going wrong and why, but they were
not of one mind about how to correct it. For some of them a
religiously based attempt to smother modernism by suppressing
Darwinism seemed to be the answer. Others found the pulpit
too tame, and sought the answer in terror. The antievolu-
tionists, however, met with apathy while the Klansmen encountered hostility and resistance. Neither came close to unit-
ing the rural areas against the cities.

That job was accomplished by issues that avoided the bramble of Protestant sectarianism and the fine points of laws against arson and murder. The drive for prohibition and the opposition to boxing and horse racing grew directly from rural images of the city, but among them there was a difference. It was the cities that made issues of boxing and racing, and their persistence ultimately paid off. The farmers and villagers did not yield gracefully, of course. If fact, they did not yield at all on boxing in Iowa, they remained divided over it in Illinois even as it was legalized, and most of them fought against horse racing to the end. The difference was not so much in what they felt about these issues as in how far they were willing to go to back up their feelings. At that, they might have continued effectively to block racing and boxing out of Illinois if they had not been bought off with fat dividends and the assurance that these "sports" would be confined to the cities. Prohibition, however, was not for sale because it was *the* rural cause, the one nationwide symbol of rural opposition to everything that was wrong in America. It lost some rural support—crucial support—during the decade, but for other reasons.

NOTES

1. *Chicago Tribune,* January 16, 1919.
2. Ibid., April 2, 1919. This particular ballot was divided by sex.
3. It is worth noting, though, that the rural districts and smaller cities together did not supply enough votes in the legislature to ratify the amendment. Without the "handful" of defectors in Cook County, Illinois would have rejected prohibition. See the methodological appendix for an explanation of the abbreviations in these tables.
4. Illinois, General Assembly, *Debates of the House of Representatives, 1919;* see pp. 506 ff. for the entire speech. This was the last year for which Illinois published its legislative debates (hereafter cited as *Illinois House Debates, 1919*).

5. *Galena* (Illinois) *Gazette,* January 27, 1921.

6. Ibid.

7. *Virginia* (Illinois) *Republican-Gazette,* December 23, 1921.

8. Their attempt to outlaw drinking itself had been quashed in the senate two years earlier.

9. The Volstead Act defined any beverage as intoxicating that contained at least one-half of one percent alcohol by volume.

10. *Iowa Conference of the Methodist Episcopal Church, Minutes of 1927.* This statement was part of the Report of the Committee on Temperance.

11. *Ames* (Iowa) *Daily Tribune,* April 16, 1927.

12. *Illinois Conference of the Methodist Episcopal Church, Minutes of 1921.*

13. *Monticello* (Iowa) *Express,* June 30, 1921.

14. Ibid., August 18, 1927.

15. Ibid., November 17, 1927. The *Monticello* (Iowa) *Express* complained that the fight films had only first been confiscated in Iowa after having been shown in Des Moines, "the headquarters of law enforcement."

16. *Ames* (Iowa) *Daily Tribune,* March 4, 1927. It hardly seems fortuitous that the voice of organized temperance sentiment should have aligned itself actively against professional boxing.

17. A similar division appeared in 1921 when the Illinois House sought to outlaw religious libel. The more comfortable farmers favored the bill by a majority of more than six to one, while those at the bottom of the heap in that bitter depression year split about evenly on it. The poorer farmers thus appeared much less willing to take legal action against public anti-Semitism and anti-Catholicism than were the richer ones.

18. The best account of the trial and certain of its implications is Ray Ginger's *Six Days or Forever?* (Boston, 1958). Ginger, borrowing freely from the concepts of anthropology, concluded that the affair was an expression of southern sectionalism, a "joint commitment to a transcendent cause" by a semiclosed society now feeling itself unwillingly pried open by the encroaching forces of a hostile and alien civilization. See also Lawrence W. Levine, *Defender of the Faith,* pp. 324–355.

19. *Monticello* (Iowa) *Express,* February 9, 1922.

20. Ibid., January 18, 1923.

21. *Knoxville Journal,* July 2, 1925.

22. *Davis County* (Iowa) *Republican,* July 21, 1925; *Carrollton* (Illinois) *Patriot,* June 11, 1925; *Carmi* (Illinois) *Tribune-Times,* June 18, 1925.

23. *Fremont County* (Iowa) *Herald,* June 18, 1925.

24. *Virginia* (Illinois) *Republican-Gazette,* July 10, 1925.

25. *Bardolph* (Illinois) *News,* July 2 and July 9, 1925.

26. *Galena* (Illinois) *Gazette,* May 28, 1925.

27. The *Census of Religious Bodies* made no distinction between fundamentalists and modernists within such denominations as Methodism and Presbyterianism, or between fundamentalism in the towns and on the

farms *within* the rural districts. It did suggest that many of the purely fundamentalist *sects* were disproportionately rural, but not all fundamentalists—perhaps not even most of them—were confined to these sects. Talks with people at the Garrett Theological Seminary and at the School of Religion of the University of Chicago revealed a widespread "feeling" that both sectarian and denominational fundamentalism characterized farmers far more than townsmen, but did not turn up evidence to support the impression. The denominations themselves all felt that this was a matter of "individual conscience" and kept no records on the matter.

28. The information for the following paragraphs was drawn from the published minutes of the Iowa Conference of the Methodist Episcopal Church, the Iowa Baptist Convention, and the Illinois Conference of the Methodist Episcopal Church. I must emphasize that my explanation is intended only as a hypothesis. Affirmation, modification, or rejection of it awaits a separate study of the relationship between structure and theology in Protestant sects and denominations at the time.

29. *Iowa Conference of the Methodist Episcopal Church, Minutes of 1928.* Two years earlier the Presbyterians of central Iowa had been petitioned by a church journal to join the fight against modernism. The request was directed to an obscure committee which promptly dismissed it and buried the issue.

30. The most comprehensive study of the Klan to date is David Chalmers's *Hooded Americanism.*

31. *Galena* (Illinois) *Gazette,* November 1, 1923.

32. *Bardolph* (Illinois) *News,* June 11, 1925.

33. *Oblong* (Illinois) *Oracle,* June 20, 1924.

34. See, for instance, the *Monticello* (Iowa) *Express* during the spring of 1924, *passim.*

35. *O'Brien County* (Iowa) *Bell,* December 21, 1921.

36. *Iowa Union Farmer,* October 17, 1923.

37. *Northwest Iowa Conference of the Methodist Episcopal Church, Minutes of 1922.*

38. *Rock Rapids* (Iowa) *Reporter,* March 27 and June 19, 1924.

39. Paul Angle, *Bloody Williamson* (New York, 1952). See also Chalmers, *Hooded Americanism,* pp. 184–189.

40. *Ames* (Iowa) *Daily Tribune,* February 15, 1923. The identity of these Klansmen was not revealed by the editor.

41. *Monticello* (Iowa) *Express,* June 12, 1924.

42. *Des Moines Register,* March 10, 1925.

43. Although the state legislative districts of Chicago were not necessarily coterminous with ward boundaries, it was still possible to estimate their ethnic composition by a very cautious comparison of census data with the street boundaries of the districts.

44. Chalmers, *Hooded Americanism,* p. 115.

45. Joseph Gusfield, *Symbolic Crusade,* p. 19.

46. Chalmers, *Hooded Americanism,* p. 115.

47. This still does not explain the explosive success of the Klan in Indiana, which after all probably did not have a much larger proportion of pathological extremists than Illinois and Iowa. The solution to this problem awaits a comparative study which examines the differences among state Klans, as well as the similarities.

5

Economic Conflict

It is not difficult to understand how some recent historians, peering back through the dismal depression of the 1930s, might be blinded to the day-to-day economic problems of corn-belt farmers by the dazzling cultural controversies of the 1920s. Certainly compared to other eras—to the flaming rural revolt of the 1890s or to the Farm Holiday and tenant farmer movements of the 1930s—the rural discontent of the 1920s was flatly undramatic. What is misleading here is the assumption that the absence of towering reform movements and far-reaching farm legislation in Washington is proof that farmers were not in bad shape. It is not necessary to demonstrate that they were writhing at the nether edge of malnutrition to point out that they were in trouble. If they were no longer the source of great economic reform movements it is because they were working out new techniques with limited means and ends to ameliorate their problems at the national level, and because they were being backed increasingly into a defensive position in state politics. It is not because their problems were illusory.

Crudely speaking, the aim of farmers was to cut as large a piece of the economic pie for themselves as possible. In practice this could mean increasing their income, hence the great hopes invested in the McNary-Haugen plan. But it could also mean cutting their expenditures, and it was toward this end that they concentrated their actions in the state capitals. In particular there were three related areas of economic pressure that ruralites hoped to relieve. One of these was the growth of state bureaucracies with ominous new expenditures. A second was the demand for costly new roads to serve a rapidly expanding automobile culture. The third, which grew directly from the other two, was the need for higher taxes. The complex inter-relationship of these factors, and the political conflicts in which they were framed, absorbed far more time and attention in the legislatures of Iowa and Illinois during the 1920s than did cultural animosities.

The issue of bureaucratic expansion was foreshadowed in a bill brought before the Illinois legislature in 1919. Presaging the various welfare measures that would flow before state and nation in the following generation, this one proposed a retirement pension for judges who had served at least twenty-four years on the bench. Perhaps it was because judges occupy an almost hallowed niche in American society that the measure eased through the house with room to spare. In more concrete terms, however, the judges owed special thanks to the Cook County delegation whose nearly unanimous support provided the votes necessary to put the bill over the top. The hallowed position of judges carried less weight with the rural legislators, nearly half of whom sought to block the measure.

A related type of public expenditure that aroused many of the farm representatives involved the salaries of public officials. For the most part, these salaries had lagged well behind the inflationary tendencies of a war economy, and were proving woefully inadequate to cope with postwar needs and wants. Time after time during the 1920s attempts were made to raise the pay levels of these officials, and time after time the resistance was centered in the rural areas.

TABLE 25
House Bill 31
Illinois, 1919
Pension Judges

	Rural				Urban	Cook County	Total
	1	*2*	*3*	*Total*			
Dem.							
F	1	6	4	11	3	26	40
A	8	3	0	11	2	0	13
O	2	2	2	6	2	2	10
Rep.							
F	4	7	5	16	11	21	48
A	8	8	4	20	5	3	28
O	1	1	3	5	4	5	14
Total							
F	5	13	9	27	14	47	88
A	16	11	4	31	7	3	41
O	3	3	5	11	6	7	24

To the casual observer there appears often to be a pettiness in this obstructionism that almost beggars understanding. To be sure, the better-paid public officials who held important positions might be asked to bide their time until conditions were sunnier. But when farmers tried to deny the drones of government—court clerks, prison guards, election judges, and the like,

who were sadly underpaid—it seemed like pure spite. Actually
it was more complicated than that. Commenting on precisely
such a situation, Dante Pierce, editor of the *Iowa Homestead*,
discussed a defeated proposal to raise the pay of the enrolling
clerk of the Iowa House by two dollars per day:

> It is true that $2.00 a day is not a large sum for the state . . . to
> debate over, but the dispute involved something more than that.
> In a 100-day session it means $200.00, and if the salary were once
> fixed at that figure, it would never go back. . . . But aside from
> that, there is a question of psychology involved—it is the psy-
> chology that when legislators become careless in small matters, it
> develops a state of mind that is likely to make them indifferent in
> larger ones.[1]

So there were two reasons for the stubborn opposition in
many of the rural areas. First of all, a few dollars per day multiplied by hundreds, perhaps thousands, of eager hands, meant
trouble. More important, once exceptions were made in little
cases, they would be unavoidable in large ones. If farmers were
to ride out hard times, they would have to resist *all* demands for
increased public paychecks. Why should they deepen their own
anguish so that others might live more comfortably?

The issue came up regularly in state legislatures during the
decade, and as regularly was opposed by some measure of
rural resistance. In Iowa, the house approved pay raises for
bank examiners and minor officials, supreme court judges and
other lesser public employees. In each instance, the opposition
was concentrated in rural areas, but proved inadequate to with-
stand these pressures. On the other hand, rural reluctance was
able to block pay increases to district court judges until 1929,
and to sheriffs, prison officials, and election judges. As a rule,
whenever rural feelings were divided, strong urban support was

enough to sweep such matters through. However, solid opposition from rural legislators was, in the nature of things, sufficient to overcome any amount of urban enthusiasm.

TABLE 26
House File 210
Iowa, 1927
Raise Salary
Minor Officials

	Rural					
	1	*2*	*3*	Total	Urban	Total
F	10	17	8	35	21	56
A	11	13	16	40	1	41
O	1	3	3	7	4	11

TABLE 27
Senate File 328
Iowa, 1925
Raise Salary
Supreme Court Justices

	Rural					
	1	*2*	*3*	Total	Urban	Total
F	11	15	15	41	17	58
A	11	20	12	43	4	47
O	1	0	0	1	2	3

The same pressures were operating in Illinois at the time. In 1921, a measure to make the jobs of local government commissioners more remunerative narrowly passed in the house over rural opposition. Only a solid front of support from Cook County saved the bill. Two years later, the house proposed to

TABLE 28
House File 208
Iowa, 1927
Raise Salary
Minor Officials
(County Officers of Large Urban Counties)

	Rural					
	1	*2*	*3*	*Total*	*Urban*	*Total*
F	12	17	9	38	21	59
A	6	10	8	24	4	28
O	4	6	10	20	1	21

TABLE 29
Senate File 360
Iowa, 1921
Raise Salary
Judges (District Court)

	Rural					
	1	*2*	*3*	*Total*	*Urban*	*Total*
F	6	13	3	22	17	39
A	17	22	23	62	6	68
O	0	0	1	1	0	1

TABLE 30
House File 166
Iowa, 1925
Raise Salary
Penal Officials

| | Rural | | | | | |
	1	*2*	*3*	*Total*	*Urban*	*Total*
F	3	3	4	10	9	19
A	18	28	21	67	11	78
O	2	4	2	8	3	11

TABLE 31
House File 209
Iowa, 1927
Raise Salary
Minor Officials
(Election Officials)

| | Rural | | | | | |
	1	*2*	*3*	*Total*	*Urban*	*Total*
F	6	8	8	22	16	38
A	15	18	15	48	4	52
O	1	7	4	12	6	18

establish a committee of legislators to investigate the prospects for standardizing the salaries of all state employees. Obviously, if such a plan were implemented, it would tend to raise the lower salary levels rather than lower the top ones. As usual, the farmers stood to pay for it, and as usual many of them opposed

TABLE 32
House Bill 605
Illinois, 1921
Raise Salary
Minor Officials

| | *Rural* | | | | | *Cook* | |
	1	*2*	*3*	*Total*	*Urban*	*County*	*Total*
Dem.							
F	0	2	2	4	1	23	28
A	5	5	4	14	4	0	18
O	3	2	0	5	2	2	9
Rep.							
F	7	5	5	17	11	24	52
A	4	3	6	13	5	1	19
O	4	6	4	14	4	7	25
Total							
F	7	7	7	21	12	47	80
A	9	8	10	27	9	1	37
O	7	8	4	19	6	9	34

the measure. Much the same results were evident during that session in attempts to raise the pay of the judges and to double the lieutenant governor's pay, and in later attempts to boost the salaries of the clerk of the supreme court, county judges, state's attorneys, and general assessor. Early in the decade, the

TABLE 33
House Bill 407
Illinois, 1923
Salary Commission

| | Rural | | | | | Cook | |
	1	*2*	*3*	*Total*	*Urban*	*County*	*Total*
Dem.							
F	1	3	2	6	2	15	23
A	9	6	2	17	3	3	23
O	3	1	2	6	3	10	19
Rep.							
F	6	10	12	28	14	22	64
A	1	2	0	3	0	0	3
O	4	2	3	9	5	7	21
Total							
F	7	13	14	34	16	37	87
A	10	8	2	20	3	3	26
O	7	3	5	15	8	17	40

TABLE 34
Senate Bill 367
Illinois, 1923
Pay of Judges

| | Rural | | | | | Cook | |
	1	*2*	*3*	*Total*	*Urban*	*County*	*Total*
Dem.							
F	6	3	3	12	5	28	45
A	4	6	2	12	1	0	13
O	3	2	1	6	2	0	8
Rep.							
F	2	3	3	8	9	26	43
A	7	9	12	28	7	1	36
O	2	1	0	3	2	2	7
Total							
F	8	6	6	20	14	54	88
A	11	15	14	40	8	1	49
O	5	3	1	9	4	2	15

TABLE 35
Senate Bill 72
Illinois, 1923
Raise Salary
Lieutenant Governor

| | Rural | | | | | Cook | |
	1	*2*	*3*	*Total*	*Urban*	*County*	*Total*
Dem.							
F	1	2	3	6	4	23	33
A	8	7	0	15	3	0	18
O	4	2	3	9	1	5	15
Rep.							
F	5	8	8	21	9	20	50
A	4	2	5	11	4	2	17
O	2	3	2	7	5	7	19
Total							
F	6	10	11	27	13	43	83
A	12	9	5	26	7	2	35
O	6	5	5	16	6	12	34

TABLE 36
House Bill 681
Illinois, 1925
Raise Salary
Clerk of Supreme Court

| | Rural | | | | | Cook | |
	1	*2*	*3*	*Total*	*Urban*	*County*	*Total*
Dem.							
F	0	2	0	2	3	12	17
A	8	4	3	15	2	1	18
O	3	3	2	8	2	13	23
Rep.							
F	0	5	9	14	12	17	43
A	9	6	4	19	3	3	25
O	4	3	3	10	5	11	26
Total							
F	0	7	9	16	15	29	60
A	17	10	7	34	5	4	43
O	7	6	5	18	7	24	49

TABLE 37
Senate Bill 479
Illinois, 1925
Raise Salary
County Judges

| | Rural | | | | | Cook | |
	1	*2*	*3*	*Total*	*Urban*	*County*	*Total*
Dem.							
F	3	4	2	9	7	23	39
A	6	3	1	10	0	0	10
O	2	2	2	6	0	3	9
Rep.							
F	4	7	12	23	14	21	58
A	8	6	2	16	5	1	22
O	1	1	2	4	1	9	14
Total							
F	7	11	14	32	21	44	97
A	14	9	3	26	5	1	32
O	3	3	4	10	1	12	23

TABLE 38
Senate Bill 68
Illinois, 1927
Raise Salary
State's Attorneys

	Rural				Urban	Cook County	Total
	1	*2*	*3*	*Total*			
Dem.							
F	2	3	1	6	7	24	37
A	6	3	3	12	0	0	12
O	3	2	1	6	2	4	12
Rep.							
F	3	4	6	13	16	19	48
A	9	5	4	18	9	2	29
O	1	1	2	4	2	8	14
Total							
F	5	7	7	19	23	43	85
A	15	8	7	30	9	2	41
O	4	3	3	10	4	12	26

antispending faction even attempted to block a bill designed to increase the mileage allowance of the legislators themselves. This bill, as was the case with almost all the others in Illinois, passed in spite of considerable rural resistance.

TABLE 39
House Bill 125
Illinois, 1929
Raise Salary
Governmental Assessor

| | Rural | | | | | Cook | |
	1	*2*	*3*	*Total*	*Urban*	*County*	*Total*
Dem.							
F	2	1	1	4	7	23	34
A	7	7	4	18	2	0	20
O	1	0	1	2	2	4	8
Rep.							
F	7	2	0	9	13	21	43
A	5	7	11	23	7	4	34
O	2	1	1	4	4	4	12
Total							
F	9	3	1	13	20	44	77
A	12	14	15	41	9	4	54
O	3	1	2	6	6	8	20

A different type of expenditure grew from the expansion of regulatory commissions during the 1920s. Ostensibly intended to supervise various trades and professions in the public interest, the way in which these proposals were framed suggests that public needs were only one consideration among many.

The idea of regulatory commissions was, of course, not a

new one, and had deeply involved a variety of pressure groups
for many years. In their attempts, for instance, to gain a measure of control over the rates they paid railroads to haul freight,
farmers and merchants had combined to press for the enactment of the Granger laws and finally the Interstate Commerce

TABLE 40
House Bill 825
Illinois, 1921
Mileage Allowance

| | Rural | | | | | Cook | |
	1	*2*	*3*	*Total*	*Urban*	*County*	*Total*
Dem.							
F	2	1	1	4	4	17	25
A	5	8	3	16	2	0	18
O	1	0	2	3	1	8	12
Rep.							
F	6	6	10	22	15	26	63
A	7	6	3	16	4	2	22
O	2	2	2	6	1	4	11
Total							
F	8	7	11	26	19	43	88
A	12	14	6	32	6	2	40
O	3	2	4	9	2	12	23

Act of 1887. Their continued efforts in this direction also
played a key role in the rate legislation early in the century.
The ideal of regulatory commissions was greatly expanded after
the turn of the century in Wisconsin and Iowa, and spread to
other states as well. The proliferation of these commissions in
ensuing decades has not yet been fully explained, but the

animating impulse appears to be a result more of interest-
group pressures than of enlightened leadership moving to protect the public from unimaginable abuses and dangers. Leadership in Illinois and Iowa during the 1920s was not always
enlightened in the same sense that Robert LaFollette was at an
earlier time as governor of Wisconsin; yet the commission idea
continued to grow.

The public, of course, might truly benefit if state regulation
compelled barbers to conform to prescribed professional standards and hygienic conditions, but so too might the barbers
themselves by eliminating marginal, often spare-time, competi-
tors who would find it difficult to continue in business because
of costly sanitation regulations.

On the other hand, these measures threatened to strike
with disproportionate severity at the rural areas that were often
too sparsely settled to support full-time professional plumbers,
for example, and where consequently plumbing was done by
the local handyman, or by a friend, or simply by oneself. Even
if state regulation did not impose itself on local customs at first,
there was no telling what might happen later on once the prece-
dent had been set. It was a bit like that two-dollar pay increase:
the initial bite might not hurt much, but the "psychology" of
relaxed vigilance could lead ultimately to unnecessary grief.
And not the least of the problem would be the higher government costs that would inevitably result from the larger bureaucracy that would be needed to administer the programs. To
allay such fears, the proponents of regulation often took pre-
cautions to specify that the regulating commissioners would be
unpaid, drawn frequently from the legislature itself and from
respected members of the profession or trade involved. But the
skeptics knew that there were no guarantees against filling these
positions with paid bureaucrats in the future, as had happened

in the past. Furthermore, commissions meant paperwork, and paperwork meant clerks and typists who did not commonly demonstrate their public-spiritedness by working for nothing. Here again, the two-dollar-a-day syndrome caused ruralites to balk.

Thus, there were several different kinds of interests tugging and hauling at the commission idea in the 1920s. Health officials and doctors sought to protect the public by raising the standards of nurses' training; real estate salesmen would benefit from limiting their numbers by examinations and regulations; architects might of course pad their wallets by blocking out amateurs, but they would also fulfill a commitment to high professional standards. At the same time, part-time operators were understandably resentful at the possibility of diminished income, while farmers and villagers were wary of the implications of regulation and alarmed at the prospective costs.

Both states considered a variety of commission proposals during the 1920s. In the Illinois legislative session of 1919, a bill went before the house which would require the licensing of masons and the inspection of their work. At one level this was a proposal that, if properly enforced, would protect the public from the expense and danger of faulty workmanship. At another, however, it can be viewed as a kind of guild device to limit competition from wildcats and amateurs. Viewed from the farmer's angle of vision, it was just another useless agency digging a hand into his pocket. Rural opposition to the measure proved futile, though, as Chicago and the smaller cities united to push it through in the house.

More or less similar attempts were made in later sessions at Springfield to regulate housing, town planning, and the installation of electrical equipment. There was even a bill introduced that sought to regulate stores that sold ladies' apparel by preventing customers from trying on garments until they were first "covered with sanitary coverings impervious to perspiration under the arm pits." Each of these bills ranged a bloc of farmers against solid urban support, but only in the clash over armpits, which went unregulated to the end of the decade, did rural opposition win out.

TABLE 41

House Bill 684

Illinois, 1919

License Masons

| | Rural | | | | | Cook | |
	1	*2*	*3*	*Total*	*Urban*	*County*	*Total*
Dem.							
F	3	6	2	11	3	21	35
A	2	4	0	6	1	3	10
O	6	1	4	11	3	4	18
Rep.							
F	3	5	6	14	14	17	45
A	7	7	4	18	2	0	20
O	3	4	2	9	4	12	25
Total							
F	6	11	8	25	17	38	80
A	9	11	4	24	3	3	30
O	9	5	6	20	7	16	43

In Iowa, the drive for regulation experienced much tougher going. At various sessions, proposals were made to regulate (or to tighten already existing regulations on) plumbers, bakers, nurses, schoolteachers, real estate brokers, architects, barbers, and "cosmetologists." All of these bills divided rural and urban areas, and many were defeated.

TABLE 42
House Bill 529
Illinois, 1927
Regulate Sale
of Clothing

| | Rural | | | | | Cook | |
	1	2	3	Total	Urban	County	Total
Dem.							
F	3	2	0	5	3	16	24
A	5	3	2	10	4	6	20
O	3	3	3	9	2	6	17
Rep.							
F	2	5	3	10	10	17	37
A	4	4	7	15	6	4	25
O	7	1	2	10	11	8	29
Total							
F	5	7	3	15	13	33	61
A	9	7	9	25	10	10	45
O	10	4	5	19	13	14	46

TABLE 43
Senate File 214
Iowa, 1919
Regulate Plumbing

| | Rural | | | | | |
	1	2	3	Total	Urban	Total
F	9	20	10	39	20	59
A	5	14	9	28	0	28
O	2	9	7	18	3	21

TABLE 44
House File 222
Iowa, 1925
Regulate Plumbing

	Rural					
	1	*2*	*3*	*Total*	*Urban*	*Total*
F	7	11	11	29	16	45
A	12	16	8	36	3	39
O	4	8	8	20	4	24

TABLE 45
Senate File 250
Iowa, 1919
Regulate Bakeries

	Rural					
	1	*2*	*3*	*Total*	*Urban*	*Total*
F	3	7	8	18	10	28
A	12	23	12	47	11	58
O	1	13	6	20	2	22

TABLE 46
House File 835
Iowa, 1921
Certify Nurses

	Rural					
	1	*2*	*3*	*Total*	*Urban*	*Total*
F	6	10	6	22	15	37
A	16	20	19	55	5	60
O	1	5	2	8	3	11

TABLE 47
House File 123
Iowa, 1925
Regulate Real Estate Brokers

	Rural					
	1	*2*	*3*	*Total*	*Urban*	*Total*
F	4	7	2	13	16	29
A	17	24	17	58	5	63
O	2	4	8	14	2	16

TABLE 48
Senate File 25
Iowa, 1925
Regulate Architects

	Rural					
	1	*2*	*3*	*Total*	*Urban*	*Total*
F	5	14	8	27	15	42
A	17	16	17	50	7	57
O	1	5	2	8	1	9

TABLE 49
Senate File 56
Iowa, 1927
Regulate Barbers

	Rural					
	1	*2*	*3*	*Total*	*Urban*	*Total*
F	19	15	15	49	24	73
A	3	14	10	27	0	27
O	0	4	2	6	2	8

The patterns of support and opposition remained much the same throughout. In Illinois, the greatest source of strength behind them was almost invariably Chicago. The opposition varied in strength but never in locus. It appeared regularly in the rural areas, but was rarely strong enough to defeat these bills in the house because Chicago was usually supported by the lesser cities. In Iowa, the centers of support and opposition were much the same. Support came disproportionately from the cities, opposition from the rural areas. Yet the fate of these

TABLE 50

Senate File 158

Iowa, 1927

Regulate Cosmetologists

	Rural					
	1	*2*	*3*	*Total*	*Urban*	*Total*
F	15	17	11	43	20	63
A	6	13	11	30	2	32
O	1	3	5	9	4	13

measures in Iowa was often different, because of the absence of a huge metropolitan bloc interest in the legislature. Iowa's cities were like the smaller cities in Illinois, and like them frequently gave a bit less support to regulation. In addition, Iowa's rural areas were far more militant in their opposition and enjoyed far better representation in the statehouse.

There were also a few very illuminating departures from this pattern of rural obstructionism. When it came to creating bureaucratic agencies to serve their own interests, farmers were almost carefree, ignoring the fact that tax inequities would lay the burden heavily upon themselves. In other words, they

were willing to spend if they were convinced that they would
gain more than they would lose by it. Thus, in Iowa, the manufacture and sale of hog cholera vaccine was brought under
state regulation because of overwhelming rural support which
swamped urban opposition. In Illinois, battle cries of the past

TABLE 51

Senate File 448

Iowa, 1921

Regulate Hog Cholera Vaccine

	Rural					
	1	*2*	*3*	*Total*	*Urban*	*Total*
F	15	22	22	59	9	68
A	7	10	3	20	11	31
O	1	3	0	4	3	7

echoed through the corridors in Springfield as farmers sought
to gain control over Chicago's vitally important marketing
facilities. One downstate representative to the constitutional
convention curtly opposed urban home-rule because farmers
had interests in Chicago which they wanted to protect.[2] They
had been trying for years, for instance, to regulate the stockyards. During the decade the Illinois Agricultural Association
tried to rally farm support for key measures to curb Chicago's
influence over farm income. Defending its support for a bill to
regulate the grain exchange in 1927, the Association asserted
that "there is no reason why the Chicago Board of Trade
should not be subjected to the same supervision as are banks,
public utilities, and insurance companies."[3] In the same session, the Association pushed a public warehousing bill.[4] The
sad truth, however, was that these bills—for the most part un-

finished business from as far back as the Granger era—never even made a dent in Illinois. Either they were buried in committee or killed on a first or second reading in the house. By 1929, the farmers had no more control over the grain pit and the stockyards than they had had in 1919.

TABLE 52

House File 568
Iowa, 1923
Regulate Amusement
Places

	Rural					
	1	*2*	*3*	*Total*	*Urban*	*Total*
F	15	23	18	56	7	63
A	6	11	8	25	16	41
O	2	1	1	4	0	4

Rural tolerance for the "right kind" of bureaucratic expansionism was not limited to mere pecuniary aggrandizement either. Farmers were willing to pay for cultural gains as well, and when it came to appropriating funds for cultural restrictionism their purse strings loosened considerably. In Illinois, their generosity spilled over in favor of an elaborate system to detect violations of the state's liquor laws, and for a state commission to manipulate this system. Iowa ruralites supported a bill to toughen the liquor laws and to expand the machinery for punishing violators. They were also enthusiastic about a bill that stipulated that city and county boards of public welfare were to function in a "supervisory" capacity to regulate theaters, dance halls, and roadhouses. The primary consideration for a permit was to be the probable impact of such places on "good government, peace and order, vice and immorality." The cities were willing to brave the risks of these contaminating influences, and voted solidly against the bill. Not so the ruralites, however. Again overlooking what it would cost them, they rallied behind the bill and saw it comfortably through the house.

TABLE 53
Senate Bill 303
Illinois, 1919
Maximum Hours for Women

| | Rural | | | | | Cook | |
	1	*2*	*3*	*Total*	*Urban*	*County*	*Total*
Dem.							
F	9	7	4	20	5	23	48
A	2	3	1	6	1	0	7
O	0	1	1	2	1	5	8
Rep.							
F	9	12	5	26	12	15	53
A	3	2	6	11	7	2	20
O	1	2	1	4	1	12	17
Total							
F	18	19	9	46	17	38	101
A	5	5	7	17	8	2	27
O	1	3	2	6	2	17	25

Some of labor's difficulties during the 1920s were also mirrored in the legislatures, and they too affected economic conditions in the countryside. Of particular importance to the unions were their attempts to provide, or extend, maximum hours legislation for women. In Illinois, which already had a ten-hour law on the books, trade unions decided to press for an eight-hour maximum in 1919 and immediately met with stout resistance from small-town merchants, who led the opposition throughout the decade. One member of the house pointed out that these merchants had to remain open until ten o'clock on Saturday nights in order to survive on the business they did with farmers from the surrounding area. If this bill were to pass, he continued, they would be forced to double shift, their payroll would increase, and their very livelihood would then be jeopardized.[5] Because earlier Supreme Court decisions had decreed that such legislation was justifiable only where long hours constituted a health hazard, the sponsors of the bill had couched their arguments in these terms. They were met, however, with uncomfortable reminders that country stores were not sweatshops or factories, that indeed the girls who worked in them were in the habit of bringing their knitting and "fancy work" along to keep themselves occupied as they visited from store to store.[6] Still, the opposition in the house, vociferous though it was, was not strong enough to worry the bill. It was in the senate that it was stymied.

When it was next seriously considered four years later, the hours bill was toned down because labor was willing to compromise in order to weaken the opposition. This time the bill called for only a nine-hour maximum. Again it passed the house, although this time it lost some support in the smaller cities and the rural areas. Once again it was lost in the senate and the issue remained unresolved. Doggedly, labor returned to the fray again in 1925, this time reverting to its demands for an eight-hour limit. The tide, which had begun to run against the unions two years before, now engulfed them completely, and the bill did not even get out of the house. In 1927, the unions, growing frantic, tried with a bill in each chamber, which enabled the mounting opposition to defeat labor twice instead of only once.

Opposition to the bill in 1919 had been weak and diffuse. Labor was still basking in the warm afterglow of the nation's military victory, for which it could claim its own measure of praise, and it was sharing as well in the dizzying general pros-

TABLE 54
House Bill 88
Illinois, 1923
Maximum Hours
for Women

| | Rural | | | | | Cook | |
	1	*2*	*3*	*Total*	*Urban*	*County*	*Total*
Dem.							
F	7	6	5	18	3	24	45
A	6	4	1	11	5	1	17
O	0	0	0	0	0	3	3
Rep.							
F	6	7	3	16	8	20	44
A	5	7	12	24	10	5	39
O	0	0	0	0	1	4	5
Total							
F	13	13	8	34	11	44	89
A	11	11	13	35	15	6	56
O	0	0	0	0	1	7	8

perity that had grown out of the war. Farmers, at the apogee of two decades of fairly regular economic ascent, could afford to harken back to their nineteenth-century ideological flirtations with labor and were not prone to deny some respite for women. Among the Chicago delegates, support had been widespread

TABLE 55
House Bill 90
Illinois, 1925
Maximum Hours
for Women

	Rural				Urban	Cook County	Total
	1	*2*	*3*	*Total*			
Dem.							
F	4	3	2	9	4	24	37
A	5	4	2	11	2	0	13
O	2	2	1	5	1	2	8
Rep.							
F	7	7	1	15	7	15	37
A	6	6	12	24	11	9	44
O	0	1	3	4	2	7	13
Total							
F	11	10	3	24	11	39	74
A	11	10	14	35	13	9	57
O	2	3	4	9	3	9	21

TABLE 56
House Bill 61
Illinois, 1927
Maximum Hours for Women

| | Rural | | | | | Cook | |
	1	*2*	*3*	*Total*	*Urban*	*County*	*Total*
Dem.							
F	4	3	3	10	4	19	33
A	7	5	2	14	4	2	20
O	0	0	0	0	1	7	8
Rep.							
F	6	5	3	14	11	15	40
A	7	5	8	20	13	12	45
O	0	0	1	1	3	2	6
Total							
F	10	8	6	24	15	34	73
A	14	10	10	34	17	14	65
O	0	0	1	1	4	9	14

and bipartisan. For years, both parties in that heavily industrialized city had vied for the labor vote, and neither one
showed any inclination to desert it the year before a presidential election.

TABLE 57
Senate Bill 97
Illinois, 1927
Maximum Hours for Women

| | Rural | | | | | Cook | |
	1	2	3	Total	Urban	County	Total
Dem.							
F	3	3	2	8	4	18	30
A	6	4	1	11	3	1	15
O	2	1	2	5	2	9	16
Rep.							
F	5	6	3	14	11	14	39
A	7	4	8	19	11	11	41
O	1	0	1	2	5	4	11
Total							
F	8	9	5	22	15	32	69
A	13	8	9	30	14	12	56
O	3	1	3	7	7	13	27

By the time the bill came up for reconsideration in 1923,
conditions had changed drastically. For one thing, by supporting a broad wave of strikes after the armistice, trade unions
scarcely endeared themselves to farmers and villagers. For another, farmers, crushed by the price collapse of 1920–1921, were
quick to charge off a share of their misfortune to the insatiable
demands of labor. Any reservoirs of goodwill that survived

among ruralites in 1919 rapidly evaporated during the 1920s. Through the rest of the decade, rural representatives lined up more and more solidly against lowering maximum hours for women.

If labor still entertained hopes for passage by mid-decade they were dashed when the Republican party in Chicago began to feel that it could thrive without competing for the union vote. Only two Cook County Republicans had dared to vote against the bill in 1919. Eight years later, twelve of them did. By 1929, whether by design or default, the Democrats had emerged clearly as the party of labor in Chicago.

TABLE 58
House File 437
Iowa, 1919
Maximum Hours for Women

| | Rural | | | | | |
	1	*2*	*3*	*Total*	*Urban*	*Total*
F	5	25	14	44	19	63
A	8	12	8	28	0	28
O	3	6	4	13	4	17

Thus, to their dismay, labor leaders saw the friendly coalition of 1919 replaced by an alliance that bristled with hostility a few years later. In a striking way, this shift helps to illustrate the mournful fortunes of labor during the 1920s, and to foreshadow one of the significant political struggles in the years to come.

In Iowa too, unions attempted to fix hours for women at a maximum of nine per day. In 1919, they succeeded in steering their bill through the house over mild rural opposition, only to see it buried in the senate. Thereafter support for the bill waned, and labor's diligent efforts to revive it failed.

In fact, by 1921, the unions of Iowa found themselves fighting desperately to prevent an antilabor bill which would have paralyzed them. This measure proposed to place a number of key industries, including mining, public utilities, and transport, within the police powers of the state. Strikes and lockouts in these industries, and strikes of state employees, were to be forbidden. Instead, disputes between labor and management

TABLE 59

House File 272

Iowa, 1921

Anti-Labor

| | Rural | | | | | |
	1	*2*	*3*	*Total*	*Urban*	*Total*
F	7	17	16	40	4	44
A	15	16	10	41	18	59
O	1	2	1	4	1	5

were to be arbitrated by a panel of three judges appointed by the governor. The bill was camouflaged in rigidly neutral language, but there was no doubt that its intent was to hobble labor. Unions, asserting that the bill was an attempt to impress laborers into "industrial slavery," bent every effort to defeat it.[7] And in the debates before the final vote, its sponsor dissolved all doubt by justifying it as an antistrike weapon.[8] Only the determined opposition of urban delegates and the poorer farmers prevented this bill from becoming law. Such were the fortunes of labor during the 1920s.

Here is further evidence that rural parsimony was not rooted in a Jeffersonian distaste for big government, as some apologists have claimed, any more than urban extravagance was especially related to an idealistic commitment to progress. The fact was that all of these measures were related in one way or another to pressures growing out of technological change. How one voted on them was ordinarily a function of whether they were tailored to fit his interests, *as he defined his interests.* If many farmers ranged themselves in the antispending blocs, it was because most of the spending was in the interest of the cities. They opposed it because they were unhappy about picking up the check for what looked to them like an urban feast. But they did not oppose spending on principle, and they did not oppose bigness on principle.

As long as real property remained the heart of the tax base in both states, it was not likely that farmers and villagers would change their miserly demeanor on these urban-oriented measures. But what might their attitude have been if city dwellers, and not themselves, were saddled with the burden of taxation to pay for these governmental innovations? This is not simply a rhetorical question, because ruralites heaved mightily to change the method—and ultimately the distribution—of taxation, and managed to touch off some of the most heated struggles in the legislatures in the 1920s.

Perhaps there had been a time when the system of property taxation was not nearly so regressive, a time when most people were landowning farmers, and land constituted the major source of wealth. But that era had long since passed into history. By the end of the war, farmers were no longer the major element in the population, but only one among numerous others. By then, much of the wealth was being harvested by industrialists and merchants in the expanding cities. These groups, along with the growing numbers of laborers, were urging their needs more and more insistently upon the legislatures, and each time they succeeded it cost the farmers money. Rural-ites knew that their best hope for escaping the squeeze lay in changing the source from which tax revenues were drawn. If they could manage this, they might then bend a bit to the pressures for fatter state budgets.

TABLE 60
Senate Bill 385
Illinois, 1919
Re: Assessment of
Property

| | Rural | | | | | Cook | |
	1	*2*	*3*	*Total*	*Urban*	*County*	*Total*
Dem.							
F	0	1	0	1	0	26	27
A	11	10	5	26	6	1	33
O	0	0	1	1	1	1	3
Rep.							
F	1	6	5	12	6	27	45
A	10	9	7	26	14	0	40
O	2	1	0	3	0	2	5
Total							
F	1	7	5	13	6	53	72
A	21	19	12	52	20	1	73
O	2	1	1	4	1	3	8

The urban areas saw the problem in different terms. While they did not pay proportionately as heavy taxes as the farmers, neither did they derive anywhere near the share of state reve-nues due them according to their percentage of the population.

The cities found themselves ill-equipped to cope with the acute problems of advanced industrialization in a system of political apportionment that robbed them of legislative vitality. They needed more money to meet the challenge of technological change, yet they were not likely to get enough of it without a reorganization of the entire political structures of the states. The hue and cry over taxation thus inevitably became entangled in the fight for political reform, and became more and more a wedge dividing farms and cities in the postwar years.[9]

In Illinois, the conflict was already mature by 1919, when the Cook County delegates introduced into the senate two bills aimed at increasing revenues without changing the existing tax base. One of these measures proposed to increase the valuation of property from the prevailing one-third of the assessed value to one-half. Thus, a man who owned property assessed at $30,000 would henceforth pay taxes on $15,000 instead of on $10,000. When the bill first came to a vote, it produced one of the sharpest rural-urban splits of the entire decade. Of the fifty-four Cook County delegates who voted (only three were absent), all but one of them supported the measure. This time, though, the metropolitan landslide was not enough to overcome the relentless opposition of the smaller cities, where the ratio of home-owners to apartment-dwellers was much higher than in Chicago, and of the farm areas. This was, in fact, one of the rare times during the decade when rural opposition was sufficiently unified to overcome a bloc vote in Cook County. And even this proved not enough in the long run, for the bill was soon called up to another vote, and this time it squeaked through, not over strong opposition—there was not a dissenting vote now—but because nearly half the representatives abstained, allowing the bill to pass with a bare majority. The peculiar disappearance of rural opposition here was probably due to some log-rolling maneuver, since the abstentions cut across party lines.

The other tax measure was intended to soften the impact of the valuation bill by reducing taxes levied for purely county purposes by one-third. The measure carried the house easily

TABLE 61

Senate Bill 554
Illinois, 1919
Re: Assessment
of Property

| | Rural | | | | | Cook | |
	1	2	3	Total	Urban	County	Total
Dem.							
F	1	5	0	6	2	26	34
A	4	2	4	10	4	0	14
O	6	4	2	12	1	2	15
Rep.							
F	6	11	7	24	12	24	60
A	5	3	3	11	2	0	13
O	2	2	2	6	6	5	17
Total							
F	7	16	7	30	14	50	94
A	9	5	7	21	6	0	27
O	8	6	4	18	7	7	32

over a small, tough core of rural opposition. Taken together, these bills imposed a major defeat upon the farmers, for not only did they force a painful addition to his tax burden, but even the concession of lower county taxes was a mixed blessing, since it tended further to centralize control over spending in

Springfield by cutting into county prerogatives. Coming as it did at the outset of the decade, this legislation provided a framework for the fight ahead and awaited only the collapse of farm prices to set a match to the powder.

In 1921, the question was held off while the broader issue of constitutional reform was being thrashed out in both states, but by the time the legislatures met again two years later the constitutional reform drives had failed, and both sides were compelled to prepare for action in the legislatures once again. By early spring, the fight was on in earnest. Farmers in both states, suffering from a sharp decline in income, mobilized behind proposals calling for that old friend of agrarian radicals, the income tax.

TABLE 62

House File 458

Iowa, 1923

Income Tax

	Rural					
	1	*2*	*3*	*Total*	*Urban*	*Total*
F	11	19	19	49	5	54
A	10	13	6	29	12	41
O	2	3	2	7	6	13

In Iowa, the tax was to run from 1 percent on the minimum taxable income of $1,500 ($2,500 for a married couple) up to a maximum of 10 percent on all income above $9,000. The measure was to apply to both personal and corporation incomes, but since relatively few working-class families, and for that matter not too many farmers, earned the $50 per week necessary to qualify them, the bill was obviously aimed primarily at the middle class of the cities and at corporation wealth. The proponents of the Iowa bill argued that it would pour $12 million into the state's coffers annually, an amount which would allow the legislature to shrink property taxes almost to the vanishing point.

TABLE 63

House Bill 483

Illinois, 1923

Income Tax

| | *Rural* | | | | | *Cook* | |
	1	*2*	*3*	*Total*	*Urban*	*County*	*Total*
Dem.							
F	9	3	2	14	1	0	15
A	2	5	3	10	4	24	38
O	2	3	1	6	3	4	13
Rep.							
F	5	5	9	19	8	4	31
A	4	3	3	10	8	20	38
O	2	5	3	10	3	5	18
Total							
F	14	8	11	33	9	4	46
A	6	8	6	20	12	44	76
O	4	8	4	16	6	9	31

In Illinois, where much stiffer resistance could be expected from urban businessmen, the farmers introduced a more modest proposal. The first $1,000 of income was to be exempt from taxation ($2,500 for a married couple); after that the tax would increase very gradually from 1 percent on incomes under $10,000 to a maximum of 3 percent on incomes above $50,000.

Like its counterpart in Iowa, the Illinois measure would tax corporations as well as individuals.

The advocates of the income tax were not strong enough yet in 1923 to reach their objective, and the bills were beaten down in both states. In Illinois, with farmers wavering in their support of the tax, solid opposition from Cook County defeated it. In Iowa, however, the income tax measure failed by only one vote, and gave promise of better things to come for the farmers.

TABLE 64
House File 45
Iowa, 1925
Income Tax

| | Rural | | | | | |
	1	*2*	*3*	*Total*	*Urban*	*Total*
F	13	14	11	38	1	39
A	10	21	16	47	22	69
O	0	0	0	0	0	0

The issue remained dormant in the following session of the Illinois General Assembly, but it was revived again in Iowa. This time its supporters, seeking to mollify the urbanites, tamed their demands so that the law would graduate the tax only up to a maximum of 6 percent on all incomes over $5,000. At the same time, however, the exemption was cut from $1,500 to $1,000, which would make its effect felt by a much greater number of low-income people in the state. Some measure of the relief that it was expected to afford property-owners is found in the prediction that it would provide the state with an additional $5 or $6 million in revenue, and allow property taxes to be cut by more than three mills.[10]

The interests supporting and opposing the tax quickly took shape and proceeded to bring what pressures they could to bear on the legislature. The Iowa Farmers' Union, supported by the Iowa Federation of Labor, the mine workers, and the railroad brotherhoods, petitioned the legislature to pass the bill, arguing that only the wealthy opposed the income tax. At the same time, the trade unions in Cedar Rapids actively opposed the bill, while the Farm Bureau appears to have remained aloof, so that neither organized workers nor organized farmers were able to present a united front.[11] Merchants and manufacturers marshaled their strength in the face of such faltering support,[12] and the bill was smashed by a union of nearly all the urban delegates with a majority of the farm legislators.

TABLE 65
House File 9
Iowa, 1927
Income Tax

			Rural			
		1	*2*	*3*	*Total*	*Urban*	*Total*
F	12	21	21	54	2	56
A	10	11	6	27	22	49
O	0	1	0	1	2	3

By the middle of the decade, the conflicting factions had built a deadlock of serious proportions. Fiscal needs in both states were mounting, but nobody was willing to pay for them. Obviously such a situation could not continue forever. In Iowa, the first signs of a breakthrough appeared in 1927, with the Farm Bureau finally coming out strongly for the income tax measure.[13] With this powerful organization swinging its weight alongside the weaker Farmers' Union, the rural legislators re-

versed their 1925 position, going for the bill by a two-to-one
majority over bloc opposition from the cities. Successful in
the house, the bill was, however, rejected in the senate, and had
to be revived for another try in 1929, when it encountered the
same fate it had met two years earlier; the house, led by the
rural delegates, passed it; the senate killed it.

TABLE 66
House File 117
Iowa, 1929
Income Tax

	Rural					
	1	*2*	*3*	*Total*	*Urban*	*Total*
F	14	21	20	55	4	59
A	6	11	7	24	22	46
O	2	1	0	3	0	3

After a decade of beating down the income tax, Iowa's urbanites attempted to turn the tables in 1929 by raising the debt
limit for road construction, a maneuver which ultimately
would hit very hard at property-owners. Previously, no county
could mortgage itself beyond 3 percent of the value of its taxable property. A house measure sought to raise that to 5 percent, and then hedged the possibility of defeat on the bill by
introducing a milder one in the senate which set 4½ percent
as the limit. The ambitious house bill was rejected in a clear
urban-rural division, but the senate measure lured enough rural
votes for it to pass. Thus Iowa's farmers, in spite of their
weighty majority in the house, were unable to put over their
cherished income tax, and had no alternative by the end of the
decade but to give ground before the pressures of the times by
increasing their own taxes.

Meanwhile, the advocates of tax revision in Illinois changed tactics after their severe reversal of 1923. The legislature in 1925 proposed to establish the income tax by a constitutional amendment which was to go before the voters for ratification at the next general election. The Illinois Agricultural Association, previously reluctant to throw all its weight behind the income tax, now mobilized its impressive organizational apparatus to persuade farmers to vote for the amendment. As the

TABLE 67

House File 464

Iowa, 1929

Increase County Debt Limit

	Rural					
	1	*2*	*3*	*Total*	*Urban*	*Total*
F	13	10	7	30	20	50
A	8	22	20	50	4	54
O	1	1	0	2	2	4

election approached, the Association had some reason to hope for victory, because it had been able to summon a sturdy and diverse cluster of organizations to support the tax. Joining with them were the Illinois Federation of Labor, Bankers' Association, Federation of Women's Clubs, League of Women Voters, State Teachers' Association, and Association of Real Estate Boards. The Illinois Manufacturers' Association and the Chamber of Commerce appeared to be fighting a lonely battle against such a broad coalition.[14] With bankers and real estate men joining hands with laborers, farmers, and reformers, and with businessmen badly split, the fortunes of property-owners appeared to be looking up.

And yet, in what the IAA interpreted as a clash of rural and urban interests, the income tax was easily defeated at the polls. In Cook County, there were too many abstentions, and on such proposals an abstention is the same as a negative vote. On the other hand, "in 20 well-organized farm bureau communities 65 per cent voted for, 19 per cent against, and 16 per cent didn't vote on the amendment. . . ." [15] Meanwhile, a survey taken by the Illinois Chamber of Commerce indicated that 75 percent of its members who voted stood solidly against the amendment. For the Illinois Agricultural Association this was enough to conclude that "merchants and businessmen as a class probably think little and know less about tax matters than almost any other groups." [16]

TABLE 68
Senate File 480
Iowa, 1929
Tax

	Rural					
	1	*2*	*3*	*Total*	*Urban*	*Total*
F	14	20	7	41	22	63
A	6	13	18	37	3	40
O	2	0	2	4	1	5

Apart from the fact that the statement is intrinsically ridiculous, it suggests a fallacious analysis of the matter at hand. There simply were not enough "merchants and businessmen" around to defeat the measure without support from other factions. Indeed Chicagoans, who were renters for the most part, had every reason to leave well enough alone. Even if they were to escape an income tax now, there was always the possibility that it might trap them in the future. Most of them paid no taxes as it was and they saw no reason to change things, even if their labor union or teachers' organization thought differently. Thus, the vote on the income tax amendment only proved what ruralites had feared a few years before: a referendum was a statewide headcount, and on any issue which divided farmers and city people they were bound to lose because there were more urban than rural heads to count.

TABLE 69
Senate Bill 446
Illinois, 1927
Property Assessment

| | Rural | | | | | Cook | |
	1	*2*	*3*	*Total*	*Urban*	*County*	*Total*
Dem.							
F	2	1	1	4	1	23	28
A	8	7	4	19	8	1	28
O	1	0	0	1	0	4	5
Rep.							
F	6	4	3	13	15	27	55
A	7	6	7	20	12	1	33
O	0	0	2	2	0	1	3
Total							
F	8	5	4	17	16	50	83
A	15	13	11	39	20	2	61
O	1	0	2	3	0	5	8

By mid-decade the situation was becoming desperate. Farmers were strong enough to frustrate the most extravagant demands of the cities, but not strong enough to pass the draining costs of modern life off on the urbanites through an income tax. All the while, they were being eaten alive in small bites.

When the 1927 legislature convened, each side acted to solve the problem in its own favor. Running true to form, the farmers called for a tax on incomes, but their bill was killed in the Chicago-dominated revenue committee "without the courtesy of a hearing." [17] A similar bill, originating in the senate, did

TABLE 70
Bloc I
Illinois, 1927
Re: Taxes

| | Rural | | | | | Cook | |
	1	*2*	*3*	*Total*	*Urban*	*County*	*Total*
Dem.							
F	3	0	1	4	1	23	28
A	8	7	4	19	6	1	26
O	0	1	0	1	2	4	7
Rep.							
F	10	8	4	22	16	26	64
A	2	2	6	10	8	1	19
O	1	0	2	3	3	2	8
Total							
F	13	8	5	26	17	49	92
A	10	9	10	29	14	2	45
O	1	1	2	4	5	6	15

get out of committee, but an attempt to call it up to a hearing on the house floor was defeated, and rural hopes for a state income tax once again were turned aside by the political muscles which Chicago, in its more disingenuous moments, claimed not to have.

The Cook County faction, having again checked the farmers,

then set about to enact a tax program of its own, and proceeded to plunge the legislature into a tumult and the farmers into despair. The aim of the plan was to double the debt limit of a county without changing the rate of taxation. This neat trick was to be turned first by raising property taxes from the current 50 percent of assessed value to 100 percent, and then by cutting all specific tax levies (in more than one hundred separate bills) in half. On the surface, the scheme would thus simply require property owners to pay half as much taxes on twice as much property and would leave them, for all practical purposes, unaffected by the change. Needless to say, it was not as harmless as that. The real heart of the issue was that a county's bonding power—the legal maximum to which it could go into debt—was pegged to the valuation of property. Currently this limit stood at 5 percent of the assessed valuation. If the property in a county was assessed at $10 million, then it could incur a maximum bonded debt of $500,000. Now the Chicagoans were proposing to double the valuation of property, which in one stroke would double the amount to which a county could legally go into debt, and this is what threw farmers into spasms of anger. Of course the urbanites might blandly say, "After all, you farmers don't *have* to go more deeply into debt if you don't want to. Simply don't spend any money." But the cities were not the only places having financial problems. Many of the small towns and villages in rural counties found themselves in a similar situation, if on a somewhat less grand scale. If the farmers yielded to the siren song of county option now, they were almost certain sooner or later to fall victims to it. And once they succumbed to the pressures for higher debts the only way out would be to raise their taxes once again.

The opposition of farmers to this plan suggests a curious parallel to the underlying assumption of their position on pro-

hibition, an assumption which held that the only way to surmount certain problems was to keep them outside the law altogether. Now they were implying that the only way to avoid
higher taxes was to keep them outside the law too. The cities,
absorbed in their own pressing needs, were proposing permis-
sive legislation that would allow each county to decide for itself whether it had to raise taxes. But the farmers displayed a
lack of confidence in the strength of their own individualism,
or perhaps it was just a realization of the dimensions of their
dilemma. In any case, they obviously placed more stock in
constraint by legal compulsion than in self-restraint to keep
their financial problems from getting completely out of hand.

Before long, the plan was in trouble in the legislature, and it
began to look as if only some extraordinary parliamentary
maneuvering would save it. In 1927, however, Chicago was in
a good position to see its wishes through. For one thing, a Republican governor, beholden not only to farmers for his office,
but to urbanites as well, was evidently able to "persuade" a
large number of downstaters to translate their party identity
with Chicago Republicans into votes.[18] Still, it is unlikely that
the fraternal feelings of political brethren were enough to
swing ruralites behind this fearful measure. Fortunately for
Chicago, it had a bargaining wedge with which to pry loose
rural votes, for in this same session the farmers were seeking a
gasoline tax, and might have been drawn into supporting the
Chicago plan with the promise of a log-rolling exchange.[19] And
finally, rural unity was shattered when the Cook County delegation agreed to exempt the rest of the state from the bill by
reducing the debt limit outside of Cook County to 2½ percent.
So in the end the bill had turned simply into a measure to grant
greater spending authority to Cook County. Farmers would be
free from worry about higher taxes. Or would they? The rub, as

the *Chicago Tribune* pointed out, was that the Illinois Supreme Court would almost certainly rule the plan unconstitutional because of its unequal taxing provisions, and thus subject the farmers once again to the relentless drive for higher taxes.[20] And so, even after all the political blackjacking and horse-trading and compromising, a hard core of rural delegates, mostly opposition Democrats, held out bitterly against the program. It was no use. Bipartisan support in Chicago and astute political maneuvering had welded together a force which rode them mercilessly into the ground.

After ten years of struggling to reverse the flow of higher taxes, the farmers of Illinois and Iowa found themselves in more trouble than ever. Repeatedly they had attempted to overcome their plight by enacting an income tax law, and just as regularly they had been repulsed by determined opposition from the cities, and by telling defections from within their own ranks. The situation was made even worse by their inability to hold the line in the tax system that existed. The rapid growth of government created a voracious appetite and the farmers were being forced to feed it. In the long run, they proved unable either to prevent crippling increases in public expenditures or rising property taxes, and were relegated to the humiliating role of obstructionist harassment in a prolonged retreat.

By all odds the most complicated issue of the decade, and the one that most clearly brought out the various needs of the rural areas, was the matter of road construction.

The introduction by Henry Ford of cheap, mass-produced automobiles shortly before the war had brought a new device of commerce and pleasure within the reach of millions in a time of rapidly growing prosperity. Almost immediately congress acted to facilitate the spread of automobiles with legisla-

lation to supply federal funds to the states on a matching basis
to encourage road building. The intrusion of the war prevented this program from developing as rapidly as had been
hoped, so that by 1919, when there were nearly 6 million cars
in the nation, most of the roads were still those that survived
from the horse-and-wagon era. Seasonal muds and ruts dis-
couraged all but the most intrepid explorers from venturing out
beyond the city limits on a Sunday.

In addition to the pressures emanating from the mass consumption of leisure time, various economic interest groups were
intrigued by the auto's possibilities as well. The automobile industry was already becoming formidable, the construction industry was developing a deep interest in road building, and
as the decade matured, the rising trucking industry hastened
into the fray. Even farmers saw an opportunity to pave their
own roads to fortune by easing the flow of rural commerce.

The interest of farmers in the right kind of road program was
clear and ordinarily straightforward: it would help them transport their crops from farm to market quickly and cheaply, and
would leave them less dependent upon the caprices of the midwestern climate. Perhaps in their less forthright moments the
farm-oriented journals might assert that farm-to-market roads
would be a blessing to the urban consumers,[21] but it was clear
that their primary concern was that farmers "would not have to
rely on a good [i.e., dry] road in order to market his grain during the summer . . . subjecting himself to the other fellow's
price." [22]

Even among farmers, however, there was no general agreement as to precisely what constituted a good road system. Most
of them envisioned a latticework of small roads funneling into
the cities, but after that their views diverged considerably. For
one thing, they could not agree upon whether to link them-

selves to the smaller cities or the larger ones. For another, they
were unable to agree upon a suitable material for construction.
The conflict over dirt, gravel, macadam, and concrete was important since the nature of the material would be a major factor in fixing the costs of the program. For several years the
poorer farmers argued that dirt roads, provided that they were
well graded and adequately drained, would be sufficient; the
more affluent farm areas, however, were not content to settle
for dirt roads, which would only bog them down in the muck
of spring and autumn. Instead, their efforts were directed either
toward gravel roads or toward some kind of paving.[23]

Even regional topography played a role in the discussion.
In the far southwestern corner of Iowa, where farmers were
not as deeply depressed as in some other parts of the state, they
opposed major construction programs because the very hilly
terrain there would send the costs of building soaring no matter
what kind of material was used. As long as townships and
counties were asked to shoulder part of the costs along with
the state and federal governments, they could be expected to
fight all state-directed construction programs.

Urban representatives, for their part, serving altogether different interests, steadily opposed the diversion of funds into
farm-to-market roads. As far as they were concerned, the only
reasonable approach was to pour most of the money into a system of primary highways, fewer in number than the farmers'
roads, but more costly to build and maintain. Obviously these
roads were not proposed with the farmers' economic problems
in the forefront, but as links tying city to city and state to state.
In part, these primary roads would cater to the leisure-time
demands of urban residents—"joy-riding," the farmers called
it derisively—and in part they would serve to attract out-of-
state tourists, few of whom, once drawn to Iowa or Illinois,

were expected to spend much time marveling at the wonders
of the pastoral landscape, but were more likely to gravitate toward the less elevating and more costly entertainment that
awaited them in the cities.

TABLE 71

House File 548

Iowa, 1919

Highway Construction

	Rural					
	1	*2*	*3*	*Total*	*Urban*	*Total*
F	6	27	20	53	18	71
A	10	16	6	32	4	36
O	0	0	0	0	1	1

Of equal importance to the question of whose pockets were
to be lined by the new roads was the vexing problem of whose
were to be emptied to pay for them. Here, quite naturally, the
issue of taxation was injected. Ideally, the farmers would have
wanted roads tailored to their own needs, but financed by the
urbanites, just as the city dwellers cast about for ways of com-
pelling the farmers to foot the bill for a system of concrete primary highways. If the farmers were to have their way, construction would be financed by a gasoline and license tax, the
burden of which would fall on the cities, which is where most
of the cars were owned.[24] The urbanites, however, were hopeful that the funds would come from the usual source—property—which would remove the burden to the rural areas.

On the surface, then, the issue was simple enough. It was
merely a question of who was going to get what kind of roads,
and who was going to pay for them. However, considering that

there were three kinds of taxes proposed, four kinds of building materials available, three types of administrative bodies suggested, and an almost infinite number of potential construction sites, the options for the politics of road building appeared to be almost limitless.

The question was already creating a stir in Iowa immediately after the war with a measure to finance a system of minor roads by taxing adjacent real estate. The bill met some rural opposition, but because it did not tip off what lay ahead it passed easily enough.

TABLE 72
House File 424
Iowa, 1921
Roads

	Rural					
	1	*2*	*3*	*Total*	*Urban*	*Total*
F	11	10	10	31	3	34
A	11	24	16	51	18	69
O	1	1	1	3	2	5

The cleavage among farmers grew wider during the next few years. In the 1921 session of the Iowa legislature the dirt farmers pressed a demand to abolish the State Highway Commission. An administrative agency, the Commission catered to the Farm Bureau and the cities by centralizing planning on a statewide basis, and by implementing its plans with hard roads and a liberal number of primary highways. Its taste proved to be much too rich for the struggling dirt farmers, so they proposed to replace it with a state engineer, and to divert the administration of its funds from the state to the county level.[25] It was a bold bid to reverse the trend toward centralization and return control to the grass roots, but it was effectively smothered in the legislature. Failing here, the dirt farmers next tried to outflank the Commission by calling for a biennial referendum on proposals to abandon road paving. The implications of this bill were almost too horrid for the hard-roads faction to contemplate, for if it were enacted it would virtually destroy whatever efficiency accrued from the long-range planned programs of the Commission. Once again, the dirt-roads advocates were defeated by an alliance of hard-road farmers and urbanites.

Although the legislative guns remained muffled in Illinois, it was becoming clear that the IAA was dissatisfied with the slow progress of hard roads in the state. Seeking to dramatize the urgency of the matter, and to stimulate more responsive consideration in the general assembly, the IAA enthusiastically described an exhibit at the State Fair in Springfield, a diorama entitled *The Farmer's Road to Market,* which graphically displayed the farmer's problems in marketing his crops. The exhibit showed a road (duly labeled "bad roads") leading from a farm to a railroad station, where the rural plight was symbolized by a sign reading "car shortage." A small electric train, meanwhile, was winding its way over the surrounding countryside, through the towns of Gluts, Bulls, and Bears, and past signs that warned, "Danger, market flood ahead." [26] Lest this particular exhibit be too divorced from dollars-and-cents realities, another one nearby spelled out the effects of bad roads, freight-car shortages, and the hazards of the stock and grain markets. This exhibit was centered around a wagon load of corn from which ribbons radiated out to various articles which served to dramatize the decline in rural purchasing power during the past seven years. Thus,

On the 1914 side there were six pairs of shoes as compared with three on the other side, an eighteen inch walking plow as compared with a little nine inch, one horse plow on the other, and a dummy fully clothed with a wool suit, shirt, collar and tie, stood on the 1914 side, as compared with a dummy standing in a barrel with nothing but a coat on, on the 1921 side.[27]

The message was certainly not lost either on the farmers who had seen it in Springfield, or on the less fortunate who had to settle for reading about it. The year had been a crushing one for crop prices, and farmers were being told that the problem grew from the uncertainties of marketing. Among the most acute of these hazards were the state's roads, poor and unreliable as they were. The solution was a simple one: pave them.

By 1923, the probing and parrying were finished. The combatants had revealed themselves in a few preliminary skirmishes, and some of the potential alliances had already been formed and tested. Now the fight began in earnest in both states. In Illinois, a monumental bill was introduced to construct a statewide system of hard roads which was to be financed by a $100 million bond issue. The state was to appropriate the taxes to discharge the annual 4 percent interest on the bonds. The IAA had done its job well. Not only had it convinced farmers of the need for farm-to-market roads, but it had lobbied successfully to make sure that this kind of road would dominate the new program. Thus with only a handful of dissenting votes, rural delegates voted for the bill even though it looked as if their constituents might ultimately have to pay for them through higher taxes. Cook County delegates, ordinarily the stoutest supporters of large-scale road programs, were con-

fronted with highly distasteful alternatives. Either they could
vote for a program designed with the farmer's interests upper-
most, or they could vote against it and end up with no program
at all. In the end they divided their votes evenly between these
alternatives and thus provided enough votes to push the bill
through.

TABLE 73
Senate Bill 376
Illinois, 1923
Road Building

| | Rural | | | | | Cook | |
	1	*2*	*3*	*Total*	*Urban*	*County*	*Total*
Dem.							
F	13	9	4	26	5	13	44
A	0	0	2	2	2	11	15
O	0	2	0	2	1	4	7
Rep.							
F	10	11	11	32	12	12	56
A	1	2	4	7	6	15	28
O	0	0	0	0	0	2	2
Total							
F	23	20	15	58	17	25	100
A	1	2	6	9	8	26	43
O	0	2	0	2	1	6	9

While Illinois was passing its major piece of road legislation
for the 1920s, the Iowa legislature was bitterly split over its
own important proposals. At hand was a bill to levy a gasoline
tax of two cents per gallon, which alone was enough to arouse
the cities. The crux of the issue, however, involved how the

money was to be spent. The senate wanted a fifty-fifty split between primary and secondary roads, but house advocates were demanding that all revenues be poured into secondary roads. According to urbanites, this would "take two and a half millions of dollars out of the pockets of city motor car users and spend it entirely upon highways that those city drivers never use." [28] When the shoe was on the other foot it hurt awfully. Finally a compromise was struck which sent two-thirds of the funds into secondary roads and the remainder into the construction of two cross-state primary highways. The state's larger cities were livid but helpless to stop the program.

TABLE 74
Senate File 273
Iowa, 1923
Gas Tax

	Rural					
	1	*2*	*3*	*Total*	*Urban*	*Total*
F	11	27	17	55	8	63
A	11	8	10	29	15	44
O	1	0	0	1	0	1

The Iowa roads struggle was carried over into the 1925 session of the legislature as the "good-roads" faction pressed to continue the program of paving Iowa's highways. By this time, however, most of the roads in the northern part of the state were already paved or graveled, and the ardor of the more prosperous farmers cooled considerably at the prospect of paying to pave the roads of the poorer farmers to the south. Simultaneously, the dirt farmers experienced a miraculous conversion and became "progressives" on the issue.[29] In March, the

Farm Bureau, which represented the more affluent farmers, reported on a statewide referendum among its members, and the report was a bad omen for good roads. Over 80 percent favored a gas tax and partial decentralization of control to the counties, and over 90 percent favored an equal division of gasoline tax funds among primary, county, and township roads, and opposed a suggested $85 million road bond issue.[30]

TABLE 75
Senate File 159 II
Iowa, 1925
Highways

	Rural					
	1	*2*	*3*	*Total*	*Urban*	*Total*
F	8	20	9	37	20	57
A	14	15	18	47	3	50
O	1	0	0	1	0	1

The big fight in the legislature that year involved a bill to coordinate the state's road plan with the federal aid program in order to further the construction of primary roads. In the past, such a bill would have been bitterly contested by the dirt farmers because of its centralizing implications and potentially high costs. Yet if the costs could be apportioned "properly" then centralization would be extremely attractive to them. They knew that it was their own counties which most desperately needed road work, and that the Highway Commission would plan accordingly. The more affluent farmers knew it also, which is why they turned against the bill. By the end of February, a large group of farmers from the southern counties arrived in Des Moines to lobby for the measure, and joined with the urban counties to urge it through the house.[31] Six weeks later this coalition won a fierce struggle to amend the bill so that funds would not be provided on an area basis, but on a "cost of improvement" basis, which made the measure acceptable in the southwestern corner of the state where hilly terrain would send construction costs shooting upward.[32] At the same time, a gasoline tax of two cents per gallon was passed. The revenues were to be split equally among primary, county, and township roads, which was the price that urban delegates had to pay for any road legislation at all in this session.

This political realignment was strengthened during the 1927 session of the legislature. Once again, it was the Highway Commission that divided the house. Until 1927, the Commission had held an ambiguous role in the state's road program. It had preserved its powers to plan and coordinate highways within the limits prescribed by the legislature, but it had been seriously hampered from effective long-range planning because control over funds had been left, for the most part, in the hands of county boards of supervisors. There was nothing to prevent a county from simply terminating a road at its border by refusing the funds to continue it,[33] which is not the most efficient way to run a program. Previously, farmers in the poorer counties had felt that these county prerogatives were imperative if they were to survive bitter times and rising taxes. Now it was these same counties that were to receive the bulk of the aid from the new programs,[34] and the wealthier counties which would help to foot the bill with the gasoline tax. As one editor put it, "Now that northwestern Iowa is given the privilege of helping southern Iowa get out of the mud, the boys down there are wildly enthusiastic over creating permanent roads."[35] He might have added that the boys in northwestern Iowa were less than wildly enthusiastic about lending a hand.

The final vote on the bill demonstrated perfectly the extent of the realignment. For every delegate from the wealthier counties who supported it there were six who opposed it. Against the coalition of poorer farmers and urban delegates, however, their opposition was inadequate to block the bill. The instability of the alliance was then shown immediately when an

TABLE 76
Senate File 104
Iowa, 1927
Primary Roads
Centralization

	Rural					
	1	*2*	*3*	*Total*	*Urban*	*Total*
F	14	17	4	35	23	58
A	8	14	23	45	3	48
O	0	2	0	2	0	2

attempt was made to help finance the new program by boosting the gasoline tax by a penny. At once the older coalition of northerners and urbanites was reactivated and the bill rejected.

By this time, the gasoline tax had become a major issue in Illinois as well. Fully aware that most of the cars in the state were in the cities, and especially in Chicago, the IAA lobbied for a two-cent gasoline tax tailored to the farmer's interests. The bill would exempt gasoline used for agricultural purposes, would split the revenue evenly between state (primary roads) and county (secondary roads) agencies, and would empower the counties to design their own secondary-road network. This last provision, as the IAA put it, would "remove state politics from the selection" of secondary roads.[36] Shrewdly assessing the issue

for what it was, the IAA pointed out that the measure ob-
literated partisan political lines completely in what was trans-
parently a fight between rural interests and the large cities.[37]
Indeed, the vote did polarize the Chicago-rural differences, and
the scale was tipped only when the smaller cities showed their
preference for a gasoline tax over higher property taxes, and
voted with the farmers to pass the bill.

TABLE 77
House File 481
Iowa, 1927
Gas Tax

	Rural					
	1	*2*	*3*	*Total*	*Urban*	*Total*
F	12	14	4	30	1	31
A	10	18	23	51	24	75
O	0	0	0	0	1	1

Two years later, the battle was resumed with a proposal to
increase the gas tax by another penny. Again, the IAA favored
an even split between the state and the counties, but was willing finally to compromise on one-third for the counties and
two-thirds for the state.[38] Thus they cleared the way for the
Republican-dominated state and city machines to herd together
enough urban strength to pass the bill. On the issue of the
gasoline tax, farmers, rich and poor alike, were welded firmly
together. Against them and their small-city allies, Cook County
opposition stood alone in defeat.

Iowans at this time, with the gas-tax issue already settled,
turned their attention to a major road-bond issue, such as the
one Illinois had passed a few years earlier, and such as the Iowa

TABLE 78
House Bill 499
Illinois, 1927
Gas Tax

	Rural				Urban	Cook County	Total
	1	*2*	*3*	*Total*			
Dem.							
F	11	7	3	21	4	2	27
A	0	1	2	3	3	23	29
O	0	0	0	0	2	3	5
Rep.							
F	12	10	9	31	21	3	55
A	0	0	1	1	6	22	29
O	1	0	2	3	0	4	7
Total							
F	23	17	12	52	25	5	82
A	0	1	3	4	9	45	58
O	1	0	2	3	2	7	12

Farm Bureau had cautioned against during the preceding legislative session. However, a special session of the 1927 legislature
had passed a $100 million road-bond issue in Iowa. Soon there-
after the act was challenged in the courts, and the supreme
court of the state only finally handed down its decision negating
the bond issue in early March of 1929. With the legislative ses-

TABLE 79
Senate Bill 85
Illinois, 1929
Gas Tax

| | Rural | | | | | Cook | |
	1	*2*	*3*	*Total*	*Urban*	*County*	*Total*
Dem.							
F	9	7	4	20	8	0	28
A	1	1	2	4	3	24	31
O	0	0	0	0	0	3	3
Rep.							
F	14	10	10	34	20	13	67
A	0	0	0	0	3	15	18
O	0	0	2	2	1	1	4
Total							
F	23	17	14	54	28	13	95
A	1	1	2	4	6	39	49
O	0	0	2	2	1	4	7

sion already in full swing, the delegates were plunged into
feverish activity to repair the damage. So diligent were their
efforts that they were rewarded with not one, but two proposals
to relieve the situation. One of these sought to limit the maximum indebtedness to $60 million, and to finance the measure

with the sale of anticipatory warrants on the revenues expected from the roads in the future. The other measure more ambitiously proposed to restore the lamented $100 million bond issue by a constitutional amendment, which thus would render judicial review irrelevant. While proponents of the more modest bill argued that there was no basic incompatibility between their measure and the constitutional amendment, the $40 million difference between the two suggests otherwise, as indeed does the difference in the support received by the two proposals, which again brought together the poorer counties and urbanites. Actually both bills passed the house. The cheaper one was supported strongly by the northern rural counties and drew barely enough support from other factions to edge it through. At the same time, their sharp opposition to the proposed amendment was impotent before the solid support it received from the cities and the southern counties.

TABLE 80

House File 360

Iowa, 1929

$60 Million Road Bond

	Rural				Urban	Total
	1	*2*	*3*	*Total*		
F	11	19	18	48	7	55
A	10	13	8	31	19	50
O	1	1	1	3	0	3

The struggle over roads in Iowa was further complicated by two other proposals before the legislature in 1929. One of these would have permitted counties to increase the limit of their bonded indebtedness for building and maintaining primary

roads within their own borders. Previously limited to a maximum of 3 percent, the counties would now be allowed to increase their indebtedness to 5 percent for road building. The
cities were heartily in favor of this proposal, arguing that those
counties which opposed incurring additional debts were not
constrained, after all, to improve their roads. Most of the rural
legislators shied away from the bill, however, reluctant to commit themselves to the probability of such a high debt burden
in the future. The senate, meanwhile, had introduced an alternative proposal that would hold the debt ceiling to 4.5 percent.
This compromise again attracted the poorer farmers into the
urban camp to pass the bill.

TABLE 81

HJR 6

Iowa, 1929

$100 Million Road-Bond Issue

	Rural					
	1	*2*	*3*	*Total*	*Urban*	*Total*
F	17	19	7	43	21	64
A	4	13	20	37	3	40
O	1	1	0	2	2	4

A final bill was intended to deal with the problem of secondary roads, where the struggle between farmer and city dweller
could be fought out on the most immediate level. Administration of the secondary roads had previously rested in the hands
of township governments, which is to say that they had been
controlled almost completely by farmers. The new measure
would have transferred the administration of these roads from
the townships to the county governments where the weight of

the cities could be brought to bear more effectively. The farmers countered this attempt by the cities to grab a larger share
of road allocations by tacking an additional penny onto the
gasoline tax, raising it from three to four cents, but in con-
ceding this point the urbanites won an amendment that would
have turned over 30 percent of the revenue gained from the
added tax to the cities for road construction and maintenance
within their own boundaries. The jockeying for position was
intricate, a concession to one side eliciting an immediate coun-
ter-demand from the other. It came perhaps as something of an
anticlimax, after so much maneuvering, when the lieutenant
governor nullified the gasoline tax on a "point of order." [39] Left
with only the original bill to vote on, many of the farmers withdrew their support, and it failed to pass by the narrowest of
margins.

The various contests over roads had begun harmlessly
enough after the war, but had soon grown into major battles.
Viewed from any angle this was a bread-and-butter struggle
over the spending and collecting of dollars and cents. Even the
shifting alliances which constantly expanded and centralized
the road programs were expressed in the baldest economic
terms. That is why conflicting farm groups exchanged positions
in the middle of the decade. Actually, in spite of what appeared
to be a complete reversal of form, they were being perfectly
consistent. When the issues changed they changed their votes,
but their basic interest remained firm throughout.

Except that it brought the competing economic factions into
finer focus, the roads issue was not in any basic way different
from the other areas of economic conflict. When it served the
ends of a group of farmers to support or oppose a bill, they did
so with almost mechanical predictability. If they could not
unite with other farmers and villagers in a common agricultural

position it was because ruralites did not all have the same eco-nomic interests. As a result, their political energies were poorly integrated and frequently unsuccessful. Worse still, their efforts were often further diluted in the more urbanized farm districts by the political pressures emanating from the nearby towns, whose interests were not necessarily coterminous with those of the farmers.

By the end of the 1920s, with prosperity spreading into the countryside, and with the bitterly divisive issues of cultural conflict somewhat eased, the problems of economic control were coming almost to the point of consuming the legislatures.

NOTES

1. *Iowa Homestead*, February 3, 1921.
2. Illinois, *Proceedings of the Constitutional Convention of the State of Illinois*, p. 146.
3. *IAA Record*, May, 1927.
4. Ibid., June, 1927.
5. *Illinois House Debates*, 1919, pp. 762–763.
6. Ibid., pp. 766–768.
7. *Des Moines Register*, January 13, 1921.
8. Ibid., March 10, 1921.
9. The struggles for political reform will be taken up in the next chapter.
10. *Monticello* (Iowa) *Express*, February 5, 1925.
11. *Ames* (Iowa) *Daily Tribune*, March 17, 1925; *Des Moines Register*, March 17, 1925.
12. Ibid.
13. *Monticello* (Iowa) *Express*, March 24, 1927.
14. *IAA Record*, November, 1926.
15. Ibid., December, 1926.
16. Ibid.
17. *IAA Record*, August, 1927.
18. *The IAA Record* of August, 1927, alluded angrily to the pressures being exerted by the Republican tandem of Small and Thompson.

19. *Chicago Tribune,* June 24 and June 25, 1927. The *Tribune* asserted that this was the case, but if it was, the Chicago Republicans reneged when it was time for the political payoff. Only three of them voted for the gasoline tax, which, however, would have passed even without their votes. The strength necessary came instead from the Republicans in the smaller cities.

20. *Chicago Tribune,* June 26, 1927.

21. *Bardolph* (Illinois) *News,* March 17, 1921.

22. *Carmi* (Illinois) *Tribune-Times,* October 13, 1921.

23. The *Bardolph* (Illinois) *News* was certain that hard roads were a luxury that would cater mostly to tourists, and argued this position constantly early in the decade. In Iowa, meanwhile, opposition to hard roads was centered in the Farmer's Union and located in the southern part of the state. By the end of the 1920s these dirt farmers were drawing their share of ridicule from the farmers who had already paved. See the *Knoxville* (Iowa) *Journal,* January 10, 1929.

24. *Carmi* (Illinois) *Tribune-Times,* March 28, 1929.

25. *Ames* (Iowa) *Daily Tribune,* March 23, 1921. The plan had been introduced two years earlier, but had been killed in the senate without coming to a vote in the house.

26. *Illinois Agricultural Association Newsletter,* August 25, 1921.

27. Ibid.

28. *Ames* (Iowa) *Daily Tribune,* April 4, 1923.

29. Ibid., April 1, 1925.

30. Ibid., March 16, 1925.

31. *Monticello* (Iowa) *Express,* February 26, 1925.

32. *Ames* (Iowa) *Daily Tribune,* April 1, 1925; and *Des Moines Register,* April 9, 1925.

33. *Des Moines Register,* February 27, 1927.

34. Ibid. See also the *Iowa Homestead.* The *Homestead* had been a hard-line advocate of "county option" early in the decade, but had also undergone a conversion by 1927.

35. *Storm Lake Pilot-Tribune,* quoted in the *Monticello Express,* March 18, 1926.

36. *IAA Record,* July, 1927.

37. Ibid.

38. Ibid., June, 1929.

39. *Des Moines Register,* March 28, 1929.

6

The Struggle for Control

THE struggle for political control in Illinois and Iowa was directly related to the issues of cultural and economic conflict, for whoever was best able to manipulate the political process would be most likely to gratify his other wishes. As things stood at the end of the war, farmers were in a good position to dominate politics. Legislative districts had been drawn up years earlier when the populations of both states had been heavily rural. Since that time, the population shift to the cities, without accompanying reapportionment, had left the rural areas grossly overrepresented, and gave them a distinct advantage in the legislature.

To overcome this weakness, the cities had two courses of action open to them. The first, which was basically a matter of tactics, required splitting the ruralites into factions over specific issues and then drawing one of these factions into an alliance against the other. The structure of politics in both states was such that this method provided urbanites with their best opportunities. On a year-to-year basis it proved to be their most effective weapon. At best, however, it was an unreliable weapon which misfired too often for comfort. Consequently, the cities pursued a second course of action, one that was strategic in scope and much bolder because it sought nothing less than a complete reconstruction of the political process. If they succeeded, they would be freed of the need to fish for rural support; if not, they would have lost nothing in the attempt.

Preparations for the fray in Illinois were made shortly after the end of the war when the initiative and referendum were included on the ballot at a special election whose main purpose was to choose the delegates to a forthcoming constitutional convention. Although the results of the voting on these measures would not be binding, the convention might nevertheless be expected to look upon them with more than transient interest. As a result, the initiative and referendum were taken in all seriousness.

Each of these measures was designed to serve a different function. With the initiative, the voters could circumvent a sluggish legislature by amassing a specified number of signatures on a petition, and then submitting a piece of legislation to the voters at large. The referendum, on the other hand, was meant to be a popular check upon too active a legislature by sending certain kinds of laws—especially tax and appropriations bills—to the electorate for ratification.

The advocates of these proposals had some very effective propaganda weapons at their disposal. For decades, the initiative and referendum had been the rallying cries of embattled farmers in their struggles to wrest political control from railroad-dominated legislatures. These measures had accumulated a positive symbolic charge in the countryside which might now be utilized by a new generation of reformers from the cities. In addition, the initiative and referendum had implications that struck deep to the very core of nineteenth-century democratic ideology. They owed their existence to an argument that claimed that legislative politics had become corrupted, a closed province where powerful groups acted to preserve their special economic interests against the public welfare. In other words, the form of democracy had been used to thwart the practice of democracy. The initiative and referendum had been devised to allow popular pressures to circumvent this legislative obstacle. They were thus seen as the means of restoring a lost democracy. This had been the heart of the rural argument against railroads and manufacturers in the late nineteenth century. Ironically, it was the same argument that was now being directed against the farmers by a latter-day group of legislative underprivileged, the cities, and it was the farmers who were forced to defend themselves now by urging caution against the dangers of too much democracy.

One of the most persistent among the many rural critics of direct democracy suggested that it was the liquor interests and radicals, as well as big-city reformers trying to unload urban problems onto rural shoulders, who were supporting the initiative and referendum.[1] Surely it was unthinkable to allow these elements, which stood opposed to everything sacred in democracy, to demand the initiative and referendum in the name of democracy. As a warning against false prophets, this editor pointed to the states where the initiative and referendum had been adopted, and had "become the tools of the rag tag and riff raff elements. . . ." Direct participation in government did not represent democracy, but "democracy run mad," and the growing preponderance of cities in the Illinois population foretold of rough times ahead for farmers if the measures ever became law.[2]

If his readers doubted him before the election, they had good

reason to believe him after the returns were in. The initiative
and referendum received a comfortable majority, and they did
so because of the urban areas of the state. As he saw it, the
measures had carried because ward bosses were able to line up
the "Chicago slums [and] the areas tinctured with bolshevism
and I.W.W.-ism. . . ." [3] In fact, it was not as simple as that.
Cook County did provide the margin of victory with a two-
thirds majority, but the other urban areas also voted strongly
in favor of the proposals. Meanwhile, the rural areas, reluctant
to cede power to the cities, voted almost two-to-one against
direct democracy.[4]

TABLE 82

Vote on Initiative and Referendum
(November 4, 1919)
(Illinois)

Area	Yes	Percentage	No	Percentage
All Rural	8,286	28.7	20,953	71.3
1–25 Percent Urban	12,246	33.9	23,913	66.1
25–50 Percent Urban	36,747	42.3	50,102	57.7
Rural	57,279	37.6	94,968	62.4
Urban	51,805	57.6	38,143	42.4
Cook County	148,646	66.5	76,267	33.5

In the storm that developed over this question, only the Illinois Agricultural Association remained temperate in its straightforward plea for the farmer to protect his economic interests
by voting against the measures. The true depths of the farmers'
fears were plumbed by other segments of the country press. Bolshevism was already a reality in Russia. In the trial of a wave
of strikes at the time, there seemed to be no guarantee that it

would not come to the United States as well. With disruptive Socialists, Communists, and Wobblies, and the special menace of the liquor interests and the new immigrants who supported them, one could not be too cautious. So far the traditional bulwarks of politics and society had dammed up these turbulent currents, if only imperfectly. If direct democracy were to become a reality, the dam would crumble and the old America would be swept away by the floods of change. The farmer's militant opposition to direct democracy was designed to prevent this, and was only smart politics.

Of one thing the farmers could be sure: armed with the encouraging results of this plebiscite, urbanites were sure to press for its inclusion in the constitution that would come out of Springfield. Things were different at the convention, however, because the farmer had his trusted ally—malapportionment—working for him there. The delegates to the convention were chosen in the same way as delegates to the legislature, except that each district sent only two members to the convention. Thus, the ratio of rural to urban delegates remained unchanged, which meant that the rural districts held the whip.

Conflict over the initiative and referendum broke out almost as soon as the convention met. Once again, Chicago and the smaller cities sought to redress what they felt to be the state's political imbalance. In the debates over direct democracy, Charles Merriam, though not a delegate to the convention, was brought in to speak on behalf of Cook County. Merriam, onetime alderman in Chicago, and a political scientist by training and profession, spoke loftily of the democratic implications of the initiative and referendum, and rather bitterly of the way in which the general assembly had snubbed various popular mandates endorsing them in the past. The most recent of these, he reminded his audience, had been in the very election that had chosen the members of this convention.[5] He was suggesting that the delegates could not honestly ignore the wish of a majority of the voters of the state.

The rural areas saw things in a very different light. They brought in Clifford Gregory, editor of the *Prairie Farmer,* to speak for them. Gregory pointed out that the majority for these measures had been culled from Cook County and that the farmers wanted nothing to do with direct legislation, as they had demonstrated in the election. In many of the purely rural districts, there had been "hardly more votes in favor of the proposition than fingers on one hand." [6] He was disarmingly candid in admitting that farmers opposed direct democracy because they were a minority in the population, and could not expect to control legislation by this means. If such a proposal became law, he asserted, the farmers would be forced to contribute to a "defense fund," and they desired profoundly to avoid this for obvious reasons. Facing up to those who pointed out that the initiative and referendum had first been advanced by farmers of the Illinois Grange in an earlier era, and that farmers to the west still sought the measures, Gregory answered with further candor that the situations were not comparable at all:

> Those states have an agricultural population that is greatly in the majority. They do not have the large City of Chicago, and Cook county, with its three and one-half millions, almost half the population to be contended with. We do have that to contend with and we are afraid of it.[7]

To Gregory's arguments, J. O. Thompson, secretary of the Illinois Agricultural Association, added that farmers saw no need for these measures since they had always had pretty good luck in the legislature. In addition, he pointed out that the problems involved in securing the required 100,000 signatures would be much more difficult in rural Illinois than in Chicago.[8]

What it all boiled down to was that democracy had nothing to do with the issue at hand. Only where the farmers were themselves assured of a working and workable majority—as they were in North Dakota, and as they had once been in Illinois—was direct democracy attractive. Under present conditions in Illinois, however, it was "democracy run mad." What was at issue here was not an ideological position, but bald power, and the farm spokesmen were startlingly blunt in saying so. Ruralites understood full well that in a power struggle with the cities they had nothing to gain from the initiative and referendum, and plenty to lose. The cities might as well have handed them ropes and asked them to concur in a democratic vote for mass suicide. Once again, the cities were to be frustrated in their efforts to bring majority power into their hands. The convention voted down the initiative and referendum.

One of the fearsome possibilities of direct legislation, as farmers saw it, was urban control over rural affairs. This they were understandably reluctant to grant. At the same time, however, the existing structure of state politics did place an inordinate degree of control over cities in rural hands. As political entities, the cities were creatures of the state government. They had to turn to the legislature for permission to administer almost all of their affairs. In recent years, the complexities and rapidity of change in a technological era had profoundly affected the cities. Finding the haphazard approach of legislative politics inadequate, and encountering maddening opposition from unresponsive ruralites at every turn, the cities, led by Chicago, had long since been arguing for greater autonomy in their own affairs. "Home rule," they called it. If the state would only grant them home rule, they would not have to go before the legislature every two years like mendicants begging for the barest crumbs of subsistence. They would be able to serve their own needs, and would also release the legislature for consideration of other pressing needs.

Once again, it was the widely respected Charles Merriam who was enlisted to inform the convention of the reasonableness of urban demands. Among other things, he reminded the delegates that with home rule Chicago would be able to change its form of government to the commission-manager plan. To a group of ruralites for whom the name of Bill Thompson was alone enough to discredit the mayoral system, the commission-manager system might sound very refreshing, and Merriam knew it. Beyond this he emphasized that home rule would allow Chicago to eliminate the irrational duplication of offices that existed between city and state, and, above all, that it would allow Chicago to levy its own taxes.[9]

Although many of the downstate spokesmen sounded solicitous of Chicago's needs and assured Merriam that they were, as one of them put it, "very anxious to favor granting Chicago all possible power of home rule that may be consistent with good government . . ." they really felt that the present system gave Chicago all the freedom it needed. What they were really saying, of course, was that any extension of power to Chicago would not be consistent with good government.[10]

There was something profoundly unconvincing about the ruralites when they were spooning out the soothing syrup of reassurance. Every time they made one of these quasi-promises it trailed off in a clause that undermined the fond hopes that had just been raised. There were always some more outspoken ones among them, however—men like Representative Fifer— who grew impatient with indirection, and blurted out their feelings in a way that quickly got to the heart of the matter. According to Fifer, farmers had a deep involvement in some of the affairs of Chicago. To cite only a few, he mentioned the grain warehouses and the stockyards. For years they had been trying to regulate these businesses, but they had not yet succeeded because they had not been able to muster the necessary majority in the legislature. With such important considerations still pending it would be foolhardy for the farmer, he maintained, to let go altogether.[11]

The issue was resolved to the complete dissatisfaction of the cities when the convention passed a home-rule clause that was fangless. Most important, it forbade them to levy taxes or borrow money without express authorization from the legislature. In the future, as in the past, the cities would have to come to Springfield with palms outstretched for whatever handouts fell their way.

Having been checked in their efforts to include direct democracy and meaningful home rule in the new constitution, the Chicago delegates funneled all of their energy into one last drive. If the legislature were reapportioned to reflect Chicago's true percentage of the population, and if provisions could be made for similar adjustments in the future, then the defeats on the other issues would be softened immeasurably. Chicago would be able to meet its needs by dominating the legislature. The solution was not perfect, but it would certainly be an improvement over the situation that prevailed. Naturally, the farmers were aware of this also, and the ensuing struggle over reapportionment became one of the bitterest of the session.

Consistently the rural representatives refused to recognize the majoritarian concept of democracy as a legitimate basis for negotiation. One of them, Representative Barr, who was always offering to take away from Chicago in his second sentence what he had promised in the first, assured Chicagoans that the people must be fairly represented, but then warned them that no one community, however populous, must ever be allowed to dominate the legislature.[12] Another, in whose breast the passions of the recent war still burned, vowed that he would "bitterly oppose any attempt to turn over to the sixth German city in the world the government of the state of Illinois." [13] Apparently called to task for such a supreme political blunder, he returned to speak the next day and proceeded to compound the error by assuring everyone that he had certainly had no intention of impugning the loyalty of Chicagoans in any way. What he had had in mind was that Chicago contained large foreign populations. He had meant to say only that, but instead the phrase, "the sixth German city," had "slipped off" his tongue.[14] The statement was greeted with a stony silence from the Cook County delegates, who apparently found small grounds for rejoicing in the correction.

The demands and accusations and disclaimers continued for round after round of speeches, and as skins wore thin the tone grew more acrimonious. From a rural county far to the south of Chicago came Representative Schuyler to say that farmers did not really mind the fact that Chicago had grown wealthy from the arbitrary prices set there on the farmer's grain. "We are content to live the simple life," he said, "to look upon the golden grain as it grows . . . to sit by the flaming fireside. . . . We are content to live by the sweat of our face." Then, setting his contentment aside for the moment, he concluded bitterly that "we refuse to be ruled by any claimed superiority of plutocracy." [15] The peroration was greeted by a burst of applause from the floor of the convention.

As far as Chicagoans were concerned, they had been listening to a lot of evasive circumlocutions, and they were tiring of it. Finally, Representative McEwen accused the downstaters of hiding behind spurious arguments. What they really had in mind in their opposition to Chicago were the kinds of people who lived there:

> You say you have got a half million Jews in Chicago in your vote; you say you have got a couple of hundred thousand Poles; you have got one hundred thousand or more . . . of the black men, and so on down the line, and you say that they are not Americans, they are not in sympathy with American institutions.[16]

If this is what ruralites had in mind, as no doubt it was in part, they refused to be smoked out into the open on the issue. Although there were enough vague references to "differences in population" or "foreign population" to reveal their feelings, the downstaters avoided any direct or explicit attacks on Chicago's immigrant population.

For the most part, rural opposition was argued in terms of an unwillingness to allow one group or one area to control politics in the state of Illinois. If any area contained nearly half of the state's population, or if it incorporated a great diversity of groups and interests, that was of no consequence. In the farmer's eyes, Chicago constituted a monolithic interest because it opposed what he wanted, and wanted what he opposed. Chicago was meaningful to the farmer not in terms of its intrinsic complexities, but in terms of the threat it posed to his hopes. In this sense it becomes almost useless to argue that what the farmer was *really* afraid of was the immigrant, or the laborer, the plutocrat, or the crooked politician. He was afraid of them all because they were Chicago. When Representative Fifer set the problem between Chicago and downstate in an almost cosmic framework, he came as close as anyone to articulating the intensity of rural feelings on the matter. After paying his obligations to the usual homilies which contrasted a "home-loving and home-staying" rural population with the shifting urban types, he got down to cases:

> In every instance, if you will read your records, in which a free people have lost their liberties it has been a country that was dominated by large cities, congested communities without a single solitary exception. . . .
>
> Now, I have this to say, I have this warning to proclaim to my fellow-members, that when this great land of ours is dominated and controlled politically by the great cities of this country, the time will have come when some Gibbon can begin his first chapter on the decline and fall of the great American republic.[17]

And so it went, on and on. Cook County delegates accused the Anti-Saloon League of conspiring behind the scenes to block needed legislation, such as reapportionment; downstate delegates paused briefly to deny such calumnies before charging forth with menacing pictures of Chicago as a "spectacle of crime, of vice, of degradation, the ruin of men, women and children. . . ." But when it was all over, when both sides had exhausted their supply of verbal brickbats, the issue was settled in the only way that it could be settled, as everyone must have known it would be. To be sure, the constitution was to include a new method of apportionment, but it still only granted one-third of the house seats to Chicago, and the provision for future adjustments made sure that Chicago would continue to have only about a third of the seats as long as the new constitution remained in effect. Everything had changed; nothing had changed.

If it had only been for such issues as home rule, the initiative and referendum, and reapportionment, the farmers needn't have made the journey to Springfield. In fact, there might never have been a convention if these had been the only matters at hand. But farmers had not come simply to make life miserable for urban representatives. They had come to write a constitution that would solve their own most urgent problem. That problem was taxation, and over it raged another fierce contest at the convention.

Most of the tax revenues in Illinois were drawn from real property, or "tangible property" as it was called. Tangible property was land, and the farmer was the major landowner in the state, which meant inevitably that he was also the major taxpayer in the state. Nothing delighted farmers more than the prospect that someone else would pay most of the taxes, and as far as they were concerned that is what the convention was all about in the first place. What they had in mind was to shift the burden of taxes to one form or another of intangible property, which might mean the interest from stocks, bonds, and loans, or simply wages and salaries. However, this was easier said than done. The farmer, after all, was unable to hide his property. A piece of land was there for all to see, including the tax assessor. Bankers and securities holders, however, found it easier to conceal their "property," and thus to evade the taxes that might be levied on it. In the past, the best hope for landowners had been somehow to lower the estimated value of their property. As Representative Fifer pointed out, there had thus developed a race over the years:

> . . . a footrace between the owners of intangible property and the owners of real estate to get away from this heavy burden of taxation; and the owners of intangible property have been the fleetest runners, until today real estate is paying eighty per cent of the taxes. . . .[18]

The issue under discussion at that moment was the controversial majority report of the Committee on Taxation,
which was proposing that a distinction be made between tangible and intangible property, that intangible property be
classified according to what kind it was, and finally that all
property be taxed on an ad valorem basis, i.e., according to its
value rather than its income.

The majority report was obviously written by Cook County,
or at least in such a way that Cook County would find it easy
to live with. It is not surprising then that farmers saw in it a
plot designed to keep them in precisely the kind of tax bond-
age from which they were trying to escape. Once a distinction
had been made between types of property, they pointed out,
immense pressures would be brought to bear on the legislature
to tax intangible property at a lower rate than real property.
It was bad enough that intangible personal property, such as a
business, was paying only 20 percent of the state's taxes, said
Fifer, but it was downright unfair that other intangible property, such as money out on loan, was paying only 7 percent of
the total.[19] What the farmers had in mind was a system that
would lump all categories of property together, so that banks,
for instance, might not escape taxation, and then to levy a tax
on the *income* of all property, whether from interest, profits,
wages, or land. This was the substance of a minority report submitted by the committee. If enacted, the minority report would
allow property-owners to deduct the usual land tax from their
income tax, and would thus place the burden of taxes relatively
more on the cities and less on the farms.

One of the urban spokesmen tried to calm the ruralites by
reminding them disingenuously that the majority report did
not *require* classification of property, but only *permitted* it
if the legislature should choose to make such a distinction in

the future. After all, he continued, even if the farmers had their way and taxed the banks, it would not be the banks who would pay the tax ultimately, since they would simply pass along the costs of higher taxes to the borrowers. In the final analysis, the lenders would remain untouched by an income tax, and businessmen and farmers would be made to carry the load.[20]

In spite of all of the arguments and pressures generated by the urbanites on this issue, the mission of the farmers was clear. They had come to the convention to lighten their tax burden. To accomplish this they had decided upon an income tax, and they were determined to write a constitution that included it. When the cities had worn themselves down fighting, that is exactly what they did.

Once they had rid themselves of the tax issue, the ruralites could turn to other matters almost as pressing. Economic relief by itself, after all, was not enough when the moral decay of the cities was reaching crisis proportions. With the nation racing to hell in a motorcar, delay could be fatal. Still, caution was in order because the most likely antidote for moral poison, as they saw it, was religion, and the injection of religion into public life could easily arouse the interest of the courts, which was something they would rather avoid. The proponents of official morality were going to have to tread lightly on this issue. They thought that they saw a way out in a measure that would permit nondenominational Bible reading, without comment, in the public schools. They believed that such neutral phrasing would not offend religious groups, and they were confident that it would hold the courts off at a safe distance. As soon as they entered their proposal, however, religious minorities were up in arms. Rural supporters of the clause could not understand why Catholics and Jews were raising such a fuss. The measure did not compel Bible reading, but only permitted it; it made no distinctions between Old and New Testaments, nor any among the different versions of the Bible. A Catholic teacher would be free to read from the Douay Version, or a Jew from the Old Testament only.[21] Nobody need feel neglected or offended. That at least was the theory behind the clause.

The *feelings* behind it were something else again. One of the ruralites, for instance, demanded it on the grounds that there was a need "in this great Christian State and Christian country [for] a form of instruction to the youth of this state that will give them a basis of Christian morality. . . ." [22] That was it, of course—the almost unconscious assumption that there was only one kind of morality to be learned from only one kind of religion. Another downstater was even more outspoken:

> All Christians read the Bible for their inspiration, and this is a Christian country. It was settled by Christians. It was developed mainly by Christians, and Christianity is, in spite of all that anybody can say, the religion of the United States of America and the religion of the State of Illinois.[23]

It is understandable that Jews felt somewhat neglected by such statements, but then they were only a small minority of the population, as one delegate pointed out, and far from a helpless one. As everyone knew, he said, Jews were endowed with more brains at birth than other groups and were generally "equipped by the Deity with the ability to look after themselves in every place on earth, except perhaps Scotland." [24] And in the constitutional convention, he might have added.

This was not simply a case of Christians against Jews, however; it was a case of some kinds of Protestants against all contenders. One of the delegates allowed himself to be carried to indiscretion when he bellowed angrily that the Bible, "the inspiration of all Christians," was "the only book on earth" excluded from the public schools. The crying need of the convention now was to determine "whether the Christians alone, *and more particularly the Protestant Christians,* shall be discriminated against or not. . . ." [25]

The crux of Chicago's opposition to the Bible-reading clause—and the opposition included German Lutherans as well as Catholics and Jews—revolved around two points. First of all, there was a fear that religious warpage would be the consequence of having predominantly Protestant schoolteachers reading from the King James Version of the Bible. Secondly, and related to this fear, was the inescapable probability that the issue would be injected into local politics.[26] And if religion ever became an overt political football, minority religions would have good reason to tremble in a nation where they preserved their religious autonomy on sufferance from a Protestant majority.

At bottom, then, this brief clause contained the destructive potential for a modern holy war which minority groups were in a poor position to win precisely because they were minorities. They fought to keep the subject out of the constitution, but they did not have the strength to prevail. Not only did the rural areas have religion and morality on their side, but, more important, they had apportionment working for them also. The outcome was a constitution framed to include this provision to safeguard the children of the state and to set it back on the road to righteousness.

What the voters of Illinois were given to accept or reject finally was a rural document that was intended to realize the farmer's dream of lower taxes and purer morals, and to frustrate any attempt by the cities to alter the power structure of the state. The provision for legislative reapportionment would guarantee that Chicago would remain hobbled for as long as the constitution remained in effect. Direct democracy was out. There was a home-rule provision, but it was sterilized by a codicil that denied Chicago the right to tax itself. And finally, after blocking each of Chicago's moves to escape, the down-staters ended the game by checkmating the cities with a Bible-reading clause and with the income tax.

As the time for ratification approached, the Illinois Agricultural Association repeatedly urged its members to vote for the constitution, primarily because of the income tax. The need for a large turnout was paramount because of Chicago's deep hostility to the document.[27]

There was a large turnout all right, but it was all in the towns and cities. The only counties that returned a plurality for the constitution were those which did not have an urban area in them. Elsewhere it was slaughtered. It was rebuffed in the rural counties that had urban areas in them, and it was battered in the urban counties. In Cook County, an astonishing 95 percent of the voters spurned it. Casting about for an explanation to the debacle, the Illinois Agricultural Association could do nothing better than come up with the truth. Its *Newsletter* stated:

> The mining communities of southern Illinois returned a large majority against the constitution. Practically all of the industrial and manufacturing towns of the state voted "no." . . . The income tax provision, it is believed, is one of the provisions which brought out a large town and city vote against the constitution. The Bible reading clause is declared to have turned many against the document.[28]

So it all ended exactly where it had begun. It had taken two years of fierce debates, and tens of thousands of dollars of the taxpayers' money (falling disproportionately on farmers, of course) to determine that the business of the state would limp along just as it had, with the cities underrepresented and the farmers overtaxed.

Of constitutional conventions that succeed we hear much. They catch the historian's fancy quite naturally because of the dramatic manner in which they alter politics and illuminate social and economic change. Reputations have been made, and are still being made, by studying the United States Constitution, and by studying its students. The constitution-making of new states entering the Union, and of old ones adapting to new circumstances, has been fair game for historians, and rightly so. The less dramatic examples of constitutions that were written but rejected, however, have been starved for attention. They occupy a place in historical knowledge roughly similar to that of unsuccessful vice-presidential candidates, and with much less justification. To be sure, the failure of a constitution to get itself adopted leaves things pretty much as they were. Yet it is the genius of these documents, no less than of those which were later ratified, that they floodlight "things as they were" in a way that the ordinary course of politics rarely does. The conventions chosen to write them pick and choose the basic issues, almost ruthlessly casting aside the lesser ones. For a brief moment they intensify the hopes and frustrations of contesting factions. The kind of struggle that broke out in Springfield over the initiative and referendum was almost primeval in its political purity. Legislative sessions ordinarily haggle over such questions as when to hold political primaries, or what percentage of the primary vote a candidate needs in order to become his party's nominee. These are, of course, im-

portant questions. In many senses the compromises over such
details make the stuff of legislative history. But when a constitutional convention discusses the initiative, contesting factions are drawn nakedly into the open, for this is not a question of compromising the disparity of a few percentage points.
It is a question of fundamentally opposed commitments. The
argument at Springfield was not over how many signatures
were needed to initiate a piece of legislation. It was more basic
because one side demanded all and the other conceded nothing. If there was a neutral ground on which to meet and compromise, they could not or would not find it. So it was also with
the income tax. The argument was not over how high the
income tax should be, but whether there should be one at all.

Perhaps the most urgent consideration of a constitutional
convention is the feeling that it is a now-or-never affair. For
a legislature there is always the next biennium, and the one
after that, and those that trail off beyond the horizon of the
future. They can manipulate; they can maneuver; they can roll
political logs. In short, they can compromise, knowing that next
time they might get a little more. For the makers of a constitution there is no tomorrow. Whatever concessions they make today might have to stand for generations. They might never regain what they have conceded for the sake of compromise. And
there is always the nagging doubt that they might be getting
the worst of the bargain; they might be giving away too much
and receiving too little in exchange. If they make this mistake
they stand to harm themselves permanently.

It is possible that the way in which this question is handled
is what makes some constitutions acceptable and others not.
After all, the problems confronting the Illinois convention
were certainly no more difficult than those at Philadelphia in
the 1780s. The difference was that the constitution-makers in
Philadelphia were able to strike compromises that proved ac-

ceptable and workable, while those in Springfield refused even
to consider meaningful compromises. Two-thirds of the delegates represented downstate Illinois. Most of them had come
to Springfield to preserve the interests of the rural areas against
urban intrusions. So as one after another of the major issues
were brought before the convention they were decided in favor
of the rural areas. The give-and-take of debate was present, but
it was the only give-and-take of the sessions. Reciprocity and
compromise did not follow.

TABLE 83

Vote to Ratify Constitution

(December 12, 1922)

(Illinois)

Area	Yes	Percentage	No	Percentage
All Rural	26,242	51.3	24,951	48.7
1–25 Percent Urban	28,032	38.6	44,637	61.4
25–50 Percent Urban	57,984	29.8	136,634	70.2
	112,258	35.2	206,222	64.8
Urban	44,266	20.3	173,965	79.7
Cook County	27,874	4.9	541,206	95.1

What the voters of the state were given to ratify or reject was
a document that made few concessions to the shifting socio-
economic realities of the times. And in the one major exception—the income tax—where an attempt was made seriously to
adapt to changing circumstances, it was Chicago that proved
to be inflexible and incapable of compromise.

When the constitution was presented to the voters for ratification, the time for compromise was past. It was not fed to
them clause by clause. They could either swallow it whole or

not at all. When an issue is submitted to a polarized electorate, it is effectively decided by the side that can marshal the most votes. The distribution of Illinois populations, and indeed the very nature of urban politics, predetermined that the constitution would be rejected. Many were disappointed, but somehow nobody seemed very surprised.

In Illinois, the attempt at constitutional reform ended in futility. A parallel development in Iowa concluded in a complete fiasco. According to the Iowa constitution, the voters of that state are to vote once every decade on whether or not they wish to call a constitutional convention. The only time in the twentieth century when a majority decided in favor of such a convention was in 1920. It was left to the legislature to decide when and under what circumstances the convention would meet, but most assuredly that was all it was authorized to decide. If all went well, the convention would probably meet early in 1922. Certainly that appears to have been the expectation of nearly everyone when the matter was settled at the polls. Indications were that most of the major farm and labor organizations of the state, including the Farm Bureau, had favored the convention originally.[29] But something went drastically wrong. Between the time the legislature first convened and the time it finally adjourned, its position turned around completely. Early in the session, preparations were being made to implement the mandate of the voters; when it was drawing to a close, however, the lawmakers flatly refused to provide the necessary money or machinery. At best, they acted in a very cavalier fashion; at worst, their actions were unconstitutional. In either case the clearly expressed wish of a majority of the voters had been blatantly ignored. Much of the press was curiously obscure in discussing the affair, but it appears very much as if the convention died stillborn because the farmers of the state wanted it that way.

One glimpse of the issue was provided in the final meeting of the house prior to adjournment. It was a stormy session in which the efforts of a handful of delegates to bring the convention bill back to life on the house floor were beaten back. Leading the pro-convention faction was Forsling of Sioux City, one of Iowa's largest cities. Forsling's bitter tirade against those who were denying the will of the people accomplished nothing, and all hopes for the convention died with the end of the legislative session.[30]

In a postmortem, the *Des Moines Register* listed several reasons for the decision. Many of the lawmakers feared, said the *Register,* that a new constitution would permit women to sit in future legislatures. While such an explanation cannot be ruled out in the strongly traditional rural areas of Iowa, it certainly appears to be a pallid reason for such a controversial action. More to the point was the *Register*'s assertion that many legislators feared that constitutional changes would necessitate a costly revision of the code. In the context of Iowa farm difficulties at this time, a reason such as this makes much more sense. When one considers that many farmers in the same legislature opposed a two-dollar-per-day pay increase for the enrolling clerk of the house, a raise that would amount to something like $200 annually for the taxpayers, the costs of a code revision take on serious implications.

The bluntest analysis of the maneuvering that undermined the convention appeared in the *Iowa Homestead* shortly after the adjournment of the session. According to the *Homestead,* the voters had been duped by the Iowa Farm Bureau in the first place. At the behest of the Bureau most farmers had voted for the convention, said the *Homestead,* but once the legislature had gotten under way they had come to realize that the Bureau "had failed to reveal any real need for a revision." [31] Of course, the *Homestead*'s explanation was hardly impartial, since it was an outspoken foe of the Farm Bureau. Nevertheless, this journal made sense, especially when it suggested that the anticipated cost of the convention—between $250,000 and $500,000— was prohibitive.[32] At the trough of a farm depression, in a legislature that had fought to hold the line against even petty appropriations, a few hundred thousands of dollars could not be laughed away. And finally, there was a growing realization among farmers, according to the *Homestead,* that the convention was not being called solely for themselves. "Every selfish interest . . . would have its representatives on hand to influence . . . the safeguards of the people against exploitation, and the result might be more disastrous than beneficial. . . ." [33] The convention, in other words, might open a Pandora's box of horrors at a time when farmers already had enough trouble.

Before the decade had barely swung under way, both Iowa and Illinois very nearly rewrote their constitutions, yet in the end neither one did. In one case, it was because the farmers were too aggressive, in the other, because they were too timid. In many senses, these drives for constitutional revision were the culmination of problems that had long been developing in the Midwest. That neither of these states was able to solve its problems by revision reflects the bitterness of the deadlock that had grown. As a consequence, documents that had been attuned originally to the tempo of the waltz were forced to adapt to the pace of the Charleston. Dislocation was inevitable.

Of course, political conflict did not suddenly terminate. Skirmishes often broke out which reflected the discontent of both sides. In the Illinois general assembly session immediately following the constitutional debacle, for instance, a home rule measure of sorts was enrolled which was aimed at giving the cities, and especially Chicago, the right to tax, license, and

regulate a number of businesses. The bill passed over tepid
rural opposition. It did little to fill the long-range needs of
Chicago, but it was a small step in the direction of home rule.
Otherwise, the fight for political reform lay in abeyance for the
rest of the decade, while the legislature of Illinois immersed
itself in economic and cultural issues.

TABLE 84
House Bill 655
Illinois, 1923
Some Home Rule

| | Rural | | | | | Cook | |
	1	*2*	*3*	*Total*	*Urban*	*County*	*Total*
Dem.							
F	11	7	6	24	2	28	54
A	1	3	0	4	4	0	8
O	1	1	0	2	2	0	4
Rep.							
F	2	2	4	8	7	17	32
A	9	10	10	29	11	8	48
O	0	1	1	2	0	4	6
Total							
F	13	9	10	32	9	45	86
A	10	13	10	33	15	8	56
O	1	2	1	4	2	4	10

The drive for political reform in Iowa also flagged after the
convention was killed. In 1925, a bill to reapportion the senate
came before the house. One of the Des Moines delegates tried
to amend the bill so that the nine largest (urban) counties
would have additional representation. The amendment was

beaten badly, but only because the cities were outnumbered
badly. With only two dissenting votes, they voted en bloc for
the amendment, while the rural counties voted almost as solidly
against it.[34]

TABLE 85
Senate Joint Resolution I
Iowa, 1925
Reapportion Senate

	Rural					
	1	*2*	*3*	*Total*	*Urban*	*Total*
F	5	3	1	9	21	30
A	14	28	25	67	2	69
O	4	4	1	9	0	9

More serious was a measure before the house in 1927 to
trim the powers of the cities in primary elections. As the law
stood, a candidate needed a 35 percent plurality in a primary
election to win his party's nomination. Some years earlier, one
of the rural delegates had pointed out that the difficulty with
this procedure was that the system lent itself to control by a
well-organized minority.[35] The well-organized minority, of
course, was the urban vote. The nature of urban machine politics and the physical proximity of urban voters to the polls
placed farmers at a considerable disadvantage in the primaries.
As long as the law required such a large plurality it was unlikely that they would be able to control them. The 1927 bill
aimed to solve the problem by allowing *any* plurality to suf-
fice. The bill passed the house in spite of urban opposition, but
was defeated in the senate. Two years later, the farmers dealt
with the problem in a slightly more devious fashion. Now they

proposed that whenever nobody received the requisite plurality the choice would be made between the two top vote-getters
by a convention of the party. So it was that farmers, who in an
earlier era had demanded the direct primary to democratize
Iowa politics, now found themselves looking for a way out of
the consequences of the democracy that they had brought to
the state.

TABLE 86

House File 53
Iowa, 1927
Primary Elections

	Rural					
	1	*2*	*3*	*Total*	*Urban*	*Total*
F	13	18	21	52	9	61
A	8	13	6	27	15	42
O	1	2	0	3	2	5

TABLE 87

House File 85
Iowa, 1929
Nominating Conventions

	Rural					
	1	*2*	*3*	*Total*	*Urban*	*Total*
F	15	19	14	48	9	57
A	6	9	11	26	15	41
O	1	5	2	8	2	10

There were a few attempts during the 1920s to patch away
at the political structures of Iowa and Illinois, but they lacked
the fire of the constitutional battles. For all practical purposes

the decade ended with the same balance of political forces that had begun it. Unknowingly, the residents, rural and urban alike, drew closer to a horrendous economic crisis with governments that were plainly not suited to the weighty problems of industrial depression.

NOTES

1. *Carrollton* (Illinois) *Patriot,* October 30, 1919.

2. Ibid.

3. Ibid., November 13, 1919.

4. Illinois, *Blue Book of the State of Illinois, 1919–1920.* Even the degree of urbanization in a rural county affected the outcome. The more rural the county, the stronger its opposition to direct democracy.

5. Illinois, *Proceedings of the Constitutional Convention of the State of Illinois,* p. 317.

6. Ibid.

7. Ibid.

8. Ibid., pp. 759–760.

9. Ibid., pp. 799–801.

10. Ibid., p. 146.

11. Ibid.

12. Ibid., p. 1615.

13. Ibid., pp. 1615–1616.

14. Ibid., p. 1665.

15. Ibid., p. 1625.

16. Ibid., p. 1699.

17. Ibid., pp. 1721–1723.

18. Ibid., pp. 2182–2183.

19. Ibid., pp. 2083; 2115–2116.

20. Ibid., pp. 2123–2124.

21. Ibid.; see, for instance, the speeches by Rinaker, pp. 3568–3569, and Carlstrom, pp. 3572–3573.

22. Ibid., p. 3569.

23. Ibid., p. 3601.

24. Ibid., p. 3603.

25. Ibid., p. 3601; italics added.

26. Ibid., p. 3611 and passim, pp. 3566 ff.

27. *IAA Newsletter,* October, 1922.

28. Ibid., December 14, 1922.

29. *Ames Daily Tribune,* November 1, 1920, and *Iowa City Press-Citizen,* November 6, 1920.

30. *Ames Daily Tribune,* April 9, 1921. Opposition to the bill was uniformly heavy among all classes of rural delegates. Support was disproportionately high among the urban representatives.

31. *Iowa Homestead,* April 21, 1921.

32. Ibid.

33. Ibid.

34. A disproportionate share of the few rural votes for this amendment came from the poorest counties, while the most affluent ones opposed it almost without exception.

35. Representative Fred Himebaugh, as reported in the *Ames Daily Tribune,* February 20, 1923.

7

Bright Lights and
Simple Living

I

IN his inaugural address of January, 1929, Governor John
Hamill of Iowa told the citizens of his state that the nation
must "return to the simple living and high thinking of another
day if we are not to journey the path of luxurious living leading to the same inevitable decay that awaited other nations
drunk with material success." He pointed out that "self-help-
fulness" was the most certain road to success. "On this bit of
homely wisdom," he said, "the farmers need no instruction. No
class surpasses them in industry, self-reliance and the general
understanding of their business." [1]

The decade was drawing to a close and with it an era. Hamill
spoke briefly of the possibility of an imminent economic crisis,
but he assured his audience that it could be ended quickly by
"the release of three billions in construction contracts by public and quasi-public authority. . . ." [2] Still, it was unlikely that
such drastic action would be necessary, he continued. Instead,
the best preview of the future was to be seen in a summary of
the recent past, and when the governor spoke in these terms he

abandoned the languorous cadence of country joys for the crisp staccato of dollars-and-cents realities:

> Our assessed valuation of $539,737,596 in 1900 has grown more than eight fold to a total of $4,407,649,584 in 1928. Sometimes we become impatient that the growth has not been faster and yet this is surely a consistent gain. This retrospect should renew our faith in our state and reassure us that Iowa is moving steadily forward in material development.[3]

In his address to the legislature, Hamill unwittingly drew a sharp portrayal of the divided mentality of his rural constituents. When they spoke of what they were and what their world was like, they spoke in terms of ideal modes of human behavior such as industriousness, self-reliance, and simple living. For decades, these ideals had been foundation stones in the structure of rural values. However, when they turned their attention to gaining a livelihood, they spoke without embarrassment of assessed valuation and total economic growth. In one breath they flayed the false gods of materialism and in the next they sang hallelujah to them.

Clearly, farmers were troubled during the 1920s. After years of almost uninterrupted economic expansion capped by the delicious prosperity of the war years, they had tumbled steeply into the depression that inaugurated the new decade. Complacency turned quickly into bewilderment and then anger as farmers tried to explain to themselves what had happened. In the years that followed, as it became clear that agriculture lagged far behind the rest of the economy, and as bureaucratic expansionism strained an antiquated tax system, rural rancor deepened. Farmers were trapped in a situation which discriminated against them and in favor of the cities. On top of that, the cities were now even bidding to replace them as the symbols of the nation's greatness.

Ruralites were not inclined to accept their predicament stoically. In order to fight it, they fell back to their strongholds in the state legislatures, because they knew that there, if anywhere, lay their best hopes to restore their purses and their prestige to the levels of happier days. True, in Illinois they did not have a majority in the house, but even with Chicagoans occupying every third seat their prospects were bright as long as they could hold their own lines fast and pick up a scattering of votes from other factions. Across the river in Iowa, rural delegates controlled 75 percent of the house. As long as they maintained reasonable discipline among themselves they would be able to work their will in the state, passing the legislation they needed and smothering the bills that displeased them.

In view of the distribution of political power, what is surprising is their failure to control legislation in either state.[4] Time after time, they were set against Chicago on economic issues in the Illinois house, and in two cases out of every three they lost because they could not enlist the support of the smaller cities. To add to their distress, a wide majority of these bills were initiated by Cook County, and were designed in one way or another to shift the balance of economic power from downstate to Chicago. Chicago's victories in these matters were dependent in part upon support from the smaller cities, which were suffering from miniature doses of the same maladies that were hobbling the lakefront metropolis. The basic political alignment in Illinois over economic issues, then, was not simply Chicago against the rest of the state; it was the cities against the rural areas, with the cities usually emerging triumphant.

The frustration of Illinois farmers over these controversies was nowhere better demonstrated than in their fight to push through an income tax. Never were they able to muster the legislative strength to enact such a law. Only in the constitutional convention were they powerful enough and united enough to realize their wishes on this matter, and then their hopes were dashed by the overpowering urban rejection of the constitution at the polls.

Bit by bit, farmers were losing their grip on economic affairs in Illinois. As they saw it, they were being cruelly exploited by urban demands, and if they were able to salvage anything it was only because the senate was more mindful of their wishes than the house. The cities, for their part, were equally certain that they were being victimized, blocked at every crucial turn by the blind reaction and ruthless greed of rural tyranny.

The same general situation prevailed in Iowa, though it is more dimly seen because of the tremendous preponderance of agrarians in the legislature. Over half the bills of an economic nature were the creatures of the cities and received powerful support from them. Moreover, the cities won the contests over these bills 75 percent of the time because farmers were unable to present a united front of opposition. On the other economic measures, when the cities were able to draw together in opposition they were able to defeat about half the bills. Not quite as many of the economic measures reflected urban demands as in Illinois, and the Iowa cities did not win as many of the pitched battles as the cities in Illinois did. This meant, however, only that the tides of change flowed more slowly in Iowa. It is doubtful that farmers there were much cheered by the knowledge that they would be inundated at a later date when their state too became more heavily urbanized.

The successes that cities enjoyed on these measures grew largely from the fact that they voted together whereas the ruralites were divided. Even in grossly malapportioned Iowa

the urban areas were able to triumph on many issues by splitting the farmers along the fault of natural economic differences, and then lining up with one group against the other. An
excellent case in point was the highway controversy. Early in
the decade the more prosperous farmers of Iowa agreed with
the urban drive for "good roads" and joined with the cities in
a coalition that overrode dirt-farmer opposition. Then after
the prosperous rural areas had built all the roads they wanted,
they did some hard rethinking about the matter. They realized
that they, along with the cities, owned most of the cars in the
state, and that consequently the new gasoline tax would fall
more heavily on them than on the poorer farmers in the southern counties. Since new highway construction was to be financed in part by the revenues from this tax, they knew therefore that they were going to be paying for someone else's roads
in the future. At that point, they were awakened to the wisdom
of economy in government, and turned against any serious extension of the state's highway system. Simultaneously, however,
the dirt farmers were converted to the cause of good roads and
approached it with a happy abandon that contrasted sharply
with their erstwhile penny-pinching. And why not, after all,
now that the gas tax made it possible for them to have good
roads which would be financed by the generosity of city people
and the more affluent farmers? "Progressiveness," as the good-
roads commitment was called by its partisans, was cheap at
those prices. It was this prospect of cut-rate highways that transformed yesterday's reactionaries into today's visionaries. The
cities, meanwhile, which had an unchanging interest in good
roads throughout the state, maintained a consistently "progressive" posture, and in the end gained much more than they surrendered, even though they had to concede the gas tax to do it.

Peering hastily at this controversy through the propaganda

that surrounded it, one might conclude simply that a forward-looking group of good-roads advocates was gradually able to persuade conservatives of the need for better highways. Such an appraisal, however, obscures more than it explains. The issues behind the rhetoric were clear. When any of the diverse economic blocs were convinced that they would reap material benefits from the program, they supported it. Whenever they were sure that they would pay more into the program than they would draw out of it, they opposed it. It is a basic political equation.

By astute management of their political affairs the cities were able to show surprising strength in the legislatures, but this is not to say that they had anything like a blank check to direct economic affairs. They were, after all, involved in a delicate legislative situation in which success hinged upon their ability to keep ruralites divided. If their demands had grown excessive they would have alienated allies whom they could not afford to lose. In Iowa, for instance, they had to tread lightly on the roads issue and concede more secondary roads than served their own immediate interests. Had they held firm for more primary highways and fewer farm-to-market roads, they would almost surely have found themselves facing a solid wall of rural opposition which they could never hope to surmount. Undoubtedly it was much the same on other economic controversies. If the urban areas won most of them, it was because their demands were more modest than their yearnings.[5] What resulted was a series of compromises that left all parties with residual feelings of dissatisfaction. The cities felt that they were made to feed on a few vagrant crumbs when their metabolism required a far richer diet. As far as the farmers were concerned, they were being eaten alive by the voracious appetites of the cities. Oddly enough, it is possible that they were both right.

The point, however, is not that one faction or the other had justice on its side, but that the total flow of economic legislation was away from the farmers and toward the cities. To the extent that the cities succeeded, they did so because they were able to make political capital out of economic cleavages among the farmers, and in Illinois also because executive politics worked in their favor. Republican governors throughout the decade were dependent upon the support of the Thompson machine in Chicago and were willing to secure it when they had to by pressuring key rural votes into supporting urban demands in the legislature. That was how Chicago was able to impose its crippling tax program upon the farmers in 1927.

The needs of these states were closing in on the farmers. Salaries of public officials were rising; new pension programs were established and old ones augmented; new highways added huge new costs to state governments; increased teacher salaries and school consolidation added to the burden at the local level. In every way the cities, large and small, were clamoring for more and more money. Without a system of income taxes to relieve them, farmers were being asked to pay for most of this at a time when there were fewer and fewer of them to tax. Put simply, farmers felt that they were paying higher taxes than ever for expenditures that were primarily to the benefit of the cities. Put simply again, they were correct.

It is possible that they could have handled the situation with more political tact, of course. They might have lightened their tax burden if they had been willing to grant home rule to the cities as a quid pro quo. But then the farmers had other interests in urban affairs, as they openly admitted during the Illinois constitutional convention, and home rule might have destroyed their opportunity to ply those interests. In the end they were badly gored on both horns of a political dilemma. They wanted tax relief desperately, and at the same time they wanted to control vital urban affairs. In order to get tax relief they needed urban support in the legislature, but they would never win it without making major concessions on something like home rule. Ultimately their decision, by default rather than design, was to try to have their way on both issues. As a result they got their way on neither. Their tax load was worse in 1929 than it had been ten years earlier, and their victory over home rule was a hollow one since it did not enable them to regulate the grain exchanges and stockyards of Chicago to their satisfaction. Ironically, the political system which seemed to favor them so strongly actually damaged them because their opponents knew better how to exploit it than they did.

The economic condition of many farmers was wretched enough by itself, but finances were only part of their plight, for now their traditional cultural dominance in America was being threatened as well. In a sense, they felt this cultural menace far more uniformly than they did the economic pressures. There were many categories of farmers, large and small, from relatively comfortable to sorely impoverished. With cultural matters there were few such internal differences. Overwhelmingly the ruralites shared an Anglo-Saxon Protestant heritage and a common addiction to country living. Their heritage and their experiences estranged them from the cities, and because of their cultural unity they were able, for a while at least, to act effectively in pursuit of their cultural goals.

Thus in Illinois, where it was imperative for three out of every four rural legislators to vote together in order to impose their wishes on the state, the farmers usually expressed this degree of cohesiveness on cultural issues, but rarely did on economic matters. In Iowa, only two-thirds of the rural delegates had to vote together to override urban opposition, yet even there they had much more trouble on economic than on cultural issues. On less than half of the economic bills were they able to muster this degree of unity, while they were able to hold together on all but one of the cultural bills.

Among the urbanites in the legislature quite a different picture prevailed. For one thing, because they were fewer in number than their adversaries, they needed even greater solidarity to get what they wanted. Ordinarily they could not tolerate more than one in five defecting from their ranks in Illinois without expecting serious problems. On economic issues, the Cook County delegation achieved this high degree of cohesion almost every time. The exceptions were all highway bills where party differences played an unusually important role. Nor is this picture changed in any important way when the smaller cities are considered for an overall urban view. The urban areas still held together on most economic issues, the major point of variance coming again over road bills, where the smaller cities deserted Chicago to vote with the farmers. Otherwise, Chicago and the lesser cities voted together in a remarkable display of legislative unity against the rural areas. On cultural items, the Cook County group held fast, suggesting that here too there was a distinctive Chicago point of view. On these issues, however, many of the smaller cities deserted to the rural camp so that no common urban interest emerged.

In Iowa, where even urban unanimity was no guarantee to legislative success, the cities achieved 80 percent cohesiveness on more than two-thirds of the economic issues. However, on cultural bills, Iowa's cities only once held together to this extent.

Thus, there were striking differences among the various groups over the kinds of issues that united and divided them. The cities in both states, feeling a common bond of economic interests, acted in unison on money matters, while the farmers fell to squabbling among themselves. Where farmers did agree was over cultural matters, which is precisely where the ties of urban unity were broken. The thread of consistency that united these groups in nearly all cases was the political clarity with which they expressed their interests, once they had defined them. If ruralites agreed on cultural matters and disagreed on economics, it simply reflected the cultural homogeneity and economic diversity that characterized the country districts. If later in the decade their enthusiasm for cultural controversy dimmed, it was because many of them were no longer so certain of their commitments. Conversely, the cities could unite over economic issues because they were afflicted with generally similar economic problems, but their united front fell apart on cultural matters because such places as Des Moines, Rockford, Elgin, and the North Shore suburbs did not conform to the same ethnic patterns as Chicago, Cedar Rapids, Dubuque, and Davenport.

In short, the bitter conflicts between rural and urban areas did not simply polarize two monolithic interest groups. Instead they involved shifting coalitions of groups with grossly different economic capacities and needs, and differences as well, as the decade lengthened, in the direction and strength of their convictions about the kind of world they wanted.

Legislative roll-call analysis is a tedious process, but it is useful for answering certain kinds of historical questions. It permits us, for instance, to isolate and identify the issues generated by cultural and economic conflict, and to see how these issues related to one another as well as to other factors. It is in this way that we are able to test something as comprehensive as Hofstadter's model of political behavior. That model, remember, separates roughly into the following elements: (1) cultural issues, which grow from status anxieties, and class issues, which grow from economic problems, are the dominant features of American politics; (2) economic issues prevail during depression periods and commonly lead to a variety of reforms; (3) in prosperous times, because men are relatively free from economic pressures, cultural issues tend to prevail and are characteristically expressed in a variety of irrational pseudo-reforms. According to this hypothesis, issues such as prohibitionism and nativism, which loomed so large in the 1920s, are best understood as an irrational response to declining status among well-off ruralites. It is possible now to comment directly on this line of reasoning.

First of all, the statement about the 1920s is fundamentally flawed because it assumes that farmers were in fairly good shape economically. In fact, they were not. On the contrary, they were in a tight economic squeeze and they fought incessantly to ease the pressure. True, they did not mount a Populistic crusade, but then not many of them were messianic visionaries in the 1930s either, when their economic problems were as serious as they had been during the 1890s. In the past, they had tried to solve their problems by remaking society, and they had failed. Now they were content to work on the specific issues that affected them directly—crop prices, taxation, government spending—and to let the rest of society fend for itself. Because such problems as taxing and spending were still very close to home, they were fought out urgently and constantly in the state legislatures. There is simply no evidence to indicate either that farmers had few economic problems, or that they were at all placid about the ones they had.

Still, many ruralites did feel status insecurities before the new kinds of people and new style of life centered in the cities, and there is no denying that they met the challenge by reasserting their own life style in a set of issues that were of supreme importance in the legislative affairs of the Midwest. How are we to explain this, if not as a kind of self-indulgent carping that one can afford in good times? It seems to me that the most reasonable explanation is the most obvious one: cultural issues lived a life of their own and flourished on their own terms. They did not ebb and flow with the erratic pulse of crop prices, and they did not vary greatly from the more affluent to the less affluent farm areas. In other words, these cultural issues are not reducible to the price of corn, either directly or inversely.

Finally, there is the assertion that cultural problems are expressed as irrational pseudo-reforms. The statement raises definitional questions, and in any case is hardly susceptible to quantitative testing. In the end, perhaps the matter is anchored in the historian's own values, and can lead at best to a stand-off among historians with different commitments. Still, one is forced to doubt that questions which absorbed the attention of millions of people were unreal, and to balk at dismissing these people as unstable cranks who didn't know what was good for them simply because they supported one side rather than the other. The allocation of status is, to be sure, a subjective phenomenon, but it is a very real one that concerns many people. It ought to follow from this that people who try to regain lost status are probably acting rationally as long as their actions are relevant to the situation, and prohibitionism was relevant to the situation because the dry forces made it so. Surely there was no reason for them to expect, before the fact, that the experiment would be such a shabby failure. What then is irrational about the status discontents of the 1920s, or of the cultural reform efforts that derived from them? Personally, I judge those efforts to have been narrow, bigoted, perhaps immoral, and certainly outrageous, but they were nonetheless real for my outrage, nonetheless rational for my habits, and nonetheless reformist for my values. To ruralites at the time, they were absolutely necessary to preserve a nation they had cherished and, equally important, a nation that had cherished them. That is real enough.

Thus, the model suggested by Hofstadter does not describe certain realities of the 1920s. It is empirically deficient because it relates ruralites to the prosperity of the 1920s, instead of excepting them from it, and because of this error the entire model collapses. Status politics cannot be solely the plaything of prosperous people, because the people who urged cultural reforms were not prosperous. What remains is that cultural issues *were* important, and that rural people *did* press them. Historians of an earlier era missed this because they were swaddled by economic preconceptions. The status historians were cutting through these strictures until they ran afoul of their own more subtle economic biases, which allowed them to ordain that economic issues are real and economic motives rational, while status issues are unreal and status impulses irrational.[6]

II

And yet, if the thrust behind cultural reformism was essentially rational, there were still some contradictions among the reformers that are vaguely unsettling. This sense of unease is probably due to the fact that the historian has not yet developed the critical tools to analyze cultural problems, as he has for the issues of economic conflict. How does one explain, for example, the strain of hypocrisy that ran through the cultural crusade? Klansmen were willing to mutilate and murder on behalf of absolute sexual purity and Christian standards of morality and honesty, yet were themselves caught with embarrassing frequency in assorted fiscal and carnal irregularities, to put it charitably. Villagers and farmers, who saw no good in ritualized, supervised fighting for profit, saw no harm in the no-holds-barred skull-cracking that often brightened Saturday nights in the small towns. Ruralites could hardly wait to bet into the bottomless pits of the carnival shell games that passed through annually to fleece them, or to gamble against the more promising odds at county-fair trotting races, and yet they opposed legalized horse racing around Chicago on the grounds that gambling was sinful. And of course the rural penchant for occasional alcoholic binges is folklore in the countryside, although, as Will Rogers observed, farmers could be counted on to vote dry as long as they could stagger to the polls on election day.

Of course, in one sense this only indicates that ruralites were no less frail than most other human beings. The important difference is that most other human beings at the time were not trying to act as arbiters of a national morality which they themselves might violate with alacrity.

Obviously not all farmers drank and not all Klansmen raped and robbed. But even if the farmers who voted dry were not the same farmers who drank, and the ones who opposed horse racing were not the same ones who gambled, there was still an ambivalence among the very purest of them that undercut all their moralizing, for the great majority applied a double standard to judge the behavior that took place around them. The drinking and gambling of the cities drew roars of protest from the countryside, yet when the same shameful deeds were observed in the rural areas themselves there was scarcely a whimper of indignation. It is difficult to escape the feeling that immoral behavior was less important to ruralites than the kinds of people who behaved immorally.

An explanation for this puzzling behavior has been suggested in Joseph Gusfield's study of prohibitionism. Gusfield argues that Prohibition was actually the symbol for an entire system of values. When that symbol was written into local and state laws, its opponents became criminals; when it was written into the Constitution, they became the lowest kind of pariahs—they were subversives, un-Americans. In this way, ruralites could enhance their status by claiming a special relationship to the fundamental law of the land.[7] Of course not all prohibitionists were ruralites, and no doubt status problems were not the only source of motivation. However, the main thrust for the movement came from farm families and townspeople who were ridden by status difficulties. That was the irreducible core of the movement. It is inconceivable that Prohibition could have survived their indifference for a moment.

Broadened to the entire rural uprising, this hypothesis resolves contradictions which otherwise are not readily understood. In prohibitionism, immigration restrictionism, and the Klan, where rural Americans went on the offensive, and in the fights against legalized boxing and horse racing, where they were forced onto the defensive, the crusaders were bent on defining and legalizing norms of Americanism with which they could identify themselves and exclude outsiders. How one lived his life was really less important than where he lived it; *the enactment of laws was more important than the observation of laws.*

As useful as this explanation is, it offers basically a static analysis of the problem and thus fails to raise the uniquely historical questions. Why did the conflict assume crisis proportions precisely when it did? After all, many of the specific issues of the controversy had been festering for decades, but while they had often set the tone for local politics and had determined the outcome of many elections, they did not really coalesce and drive the nation into hostile camps until after World War I. Even more puzzling, why did the movement rapidly lose momentum after mid-decade, long before a general depression turned the nation's attention to other matters? Legislative analysis helps us to raise these questions, but the framework for answering them must come from deeper historical perspectives.

For years, American farmers had been walking a narrow line between their values, which led them in one direction, and their material appetites, which pulled them in another. Their values committed them to the natural, the simple, and the serene; they exalted the independence of rural life and the primacy of things spiritual; they condemned the city as the source of all evil. Yet from the beginning, farmers had been as eager as anyone in their dash for the great untapped wealth of the new continent. They had speculated in land for profit, and when they had farmed it they had exploited it mercilessly for the quick riches that it promised. They had been perfectly willing to use the government in their quest, and they had proven as resourceful as others in manipulating power when they were able to grasp it. Above all, they had been enthusiastic about the technological innovations that were revolutionizing agricultural production and distribution during the nineteenth century. Early in the railroad era, farmers had even seen the iron horse as a means of increasing their income by bringing them into contact with national and world markets through the burgeoning cities. Their ready assimilation of technological change was not an unmixed blessing, however, because it

cut them adrift in the heavy waters of an international economy over which, as they soon learned, they had little control.
After the Civil War, when they discovered that the iron horse
was really a Trojan horse disgorging an army of brutally high
freight rates, it was too late to pull back. In the long run, their
solution to the problems of technological innovation was more
technology.

In the first place then, there was a contradiction between the
farmer's values and his business. It had grown slowly and ir-
regularly, and had become a fact of rural life long before it was
a fact of rural consciousness. By the 1920s, however, awareness
was drawing abreast of realities. Henry Wallace, who always
saw rural problems more incisively than most, described the
situation as a dilemma in which farmers were living torn between two different worlds:

> One is the world of the handicraft period, of the American fron-
> tier. In this world, he objects to limiting production because he
> does not like to see his neighbor hunger. He looks on the farm
> as a home, rather than a business. He hopes for a good living, but
> does not look for any great amount of wealth.
>
> But he lives also in another world, the world of modern busi-
> ness. There he learns that adjusted production is only sound busi-
> ness; that capitalization of earning power in the form of land or
> stock values is the conventional thing with all great industries;
> that shrewd dealing on the market will make up for lack of skill
> in production. . . .
>
> We think it likely that the standards of the handicraft age, to
> which the farmer still clings in part, have more social value than
> our modern business standards. Yet in a clash between the two,
> can the older standards hope to survive? Perhaps they might . . .
> but certainly not until the farmer learns to see far more clearly
> than now the difference between the two worlds of economic
> thought to each of which he now pledges an impossible allegiance.[8]

To be sure, this clash between conflicting standards was older by far than Wallace. What was new was that he and others like him were beginning to see it more and more clearly for what it was and to agonize over its implications.

This growing crisis of awareness was quickened by the fact that technology was taking on a new meaning in rural areas after the war. In the past, technology had related primarily to the problems of farm economics, but it had not seriously dislocated rural values and had barely touched country life at all. Traditional patterns of belief were still intimate with traditional patterns of living. Now, in the consumer-oriented ethos of the postwar world, technology promised finally to transform the very substance of country living.

For this reason, the fight for better rural roads was justified not simply as a means of getting the farmer's crops to market quickly and regularly, but also as a means of cutting through rural desolation and often simply as a symbol of the "progress" that was essential if the rural districts were to catch up with the cities.[9] But roads were only one means of extending rural horizons. The modern miracles of the young electronics industry were also given a hearty welcome in the countryside almost as soon as the war was over. One Iowa editor enthusiastically proclaimed that "since the better class of country towns have adopted paving and erected modern theater buildings for the motion film there is little left for the cities to offer. . . ." [10] Throughout the decade, other country editors extolled the advantages of the new way of life, citing every modern convenience that was breaking through the loneliness of rural life, warmly greeting the telephone, the automobile, and the radio, and looking forward to the electrification of farm homes.

Even the Methodist and Baptist churches began to yield to the rural rush toward divertissement. Early in the decade, they had stood firmly against the licentiousness rampant in movies, but after the film industry inaugurated its specious effort at self-censorship in 1922, the churches reached a modus vivendi with them. Prior to this time, many of the denominations had called for "public control of the Motion Picture business"; afterward they were generally content to plead for movie houses to help observe the "American sabbath" by staying closed on Sundays.[11] Meanwhile, Hollywood's movies continued to grow more and more lurid. By changing the cry from "Never!" to "Never on Sunday!" the churches made themselves appear more worried about competition than corruption.

By the end of the war, farmers were no longer walking the line between their values and their material commitments; they had crossed it, they had made their choice. Every time they bought an urban-manufactured radio they made their choice, and every time they tuned it in to a broadcast from Chicago they confirmed it; every time they bought an automobile manufactured in Detroit or a fantasy manufactured in Hollywood they made a choice; and whenever they left the humdrum of the farm for a weekend of excitement in Chicago, St. Louis, or Kansas City—or even permitted themselves such a dream—they made the choice.

The choice had dark implications, however, for in making it, farmers were denying their cherished values. At this juncture perhaps they should have cast their old values aside for new ones. But values, unlike the humans who conceive them, rarely roll over and die when their time is up. They have a way of hanging on grimly long after the conditions which nurtured them have changed. It is not an easy thing to abandon the beliefs of a lifetime, especially when those beliefs have been invested with an almost sacred authority by generations of ancestors and polemicists. The pressures to do so are likely to lead to violent eruptions, even when those pressures are self-generated.

Something like that had been happening in the decades before the war. Ruralites had been trying for years to preserve the old values intact while they assimilated the fruits of the new technology. It was not an easy feat because technology was forcing them to graft the old values onto changing realities for which they were ill-adapted. Thus, long before the war, technology had transformed the commercial context of rural America drastically, and yet farmers continued to praise the simple virtues of the individual freeholder of another era.

The movement to enshrine rural values has roots deep into the nineteenth century, but in its modern form it probably dates from the 1890s with the founding of the Anti-Saloon League. More than anything else, however, what intensified this development from a series of localized tremors into a national earthquake was the war. War propaganda matched the impulses of the prohibitionists perfectly. It allowed them to identify their cause with patriotism and to discredit their enemies, the German brewers. At a time when sauerkraut was suspect, this was of no small importance. Even more basic, the war was won largely through industrial mobilization, and it accelerated rural change by organizing the farmer's energies, subsidizing his efforts, further mechanizing his enterprise, and in general sealing his fate in a service occupation for urban industrial manpower.

Worse still, there was no respite from the heavy pressures of change after the war. It was then that the harsh dissonance of the automobile disrupted the simple harmonies of the countryside; it was then, with many farmers beginning to vacation in Long Beach or the Colorado Rockies while their children were away at college, that the rural family began to pull apart; and it was after the war, when ruralites began to enjoy the sweet savor of Hollywood's synthetic confections, that they inadvertently raised questions about the meaning of rural virtues.

It was precisely at that time, when many of the old values were losing relevance to rural life, that the farmer's hostility for the cities broke all restraints and exploded into a holy mission. The crisis developed just when ruralites were becoming conscious of the direction in which their choice was carrying them. Unwilling at first to surrender to the larger meaning of that choice, they mounted an assault against the new urban America, as if the smoke and sounds of battle would hide their shame from the enemy and, more important, from themselves.

Such a tension between ideals and actions could not have lasted indefinitely. Before long there was evidence of confusion in rural thought and behavior. It showed in the ambivalence of churchmen toward secular behavior and in the timidity with which they expressed their position—or lack of it—on important theological issues; it was even revealed in the rhetoric they adopted to discuss the problems of evangelical Protestantism. Agrarian confusion showed also in some of the methods utilized by the Farm Bureau, especially in the movies that dramatized the extracurricular pleasures of modern college life and described the tribulations of jazz-mad farm girls who recognized the error of their ways just in time to return to the fireside—and presumably also to the radios, movies, and automobiles that were reassuringly near at hand.

Nowhere did changing rural living patterns show up more clearly than in the advertisements in the rural press during the decade.[12] Immediately after the war most of this advertising was aimed at selling dry and hard goods in local stores, or livestock at auction, chick mash, farm equipment, and such patent medicines as "Gold Medal Harlem Oil" ("A man is as old as his organs. . . . Keep your vital organs healthy with Gold Medal Harlem Oil Capsules"), Bulgarian Blood Tea (guaranteed to "flush the kidneys" and "purify the blood") and that answer to a thirsty farmer's hoarse prayer, *Pe-ru-na*. Occasional small ads for Edison phonographs, Dodge cars, or the local motion picture house did not impinge upon the essential rural tone of the advertising. By mid-decade, however, chick mash and patent medicines were falling into the shadows of ads urging farmers to take railroad excursions to the West and even to Mexico City, and selling six or seven different kinds of automobiles, washing machines, and typewriters. Movie ads, which had been tiny inserts in 1921, were commonly occupying a quarter of a page, describing the feats of Rod LaRocque in *The Cruise of the Jasper B* ("Ah, what battles and ardent wooing!") and Clara Bow in *It*. By 1929, ruralites were offered a wide choice of automobiles, refrigerators, washing machines, automatic toasters, waffle irons, and grill-griddles, radios, phonographs, and movies, hotel weekends in every city in the Midwest, resorts in Palm Beach, sleds for the kiddies, Camel cigarettes for the men, beauty parlors for the ladies, and Florsheim shoes for all the family. Before the war many of these items and services had not even existed, and those that did were usually numbered among the privileges or vices of the well-heeled classes in the cities. Now they were being laid out—on easy terms—before the farmer and he found them irresistible.

Before long, the confusion began to show among the country editors, who were trying desperately to grasp, along with their readers, what was happening to their world. One of them wondered "why a sane man cannot take a good car, fall in love with it, water it, groom it, house it, feed it and care for it like he would a good horse. . . ." [13] instead of treating it as a weapon loaded for murder or suicide. Another Iowa editor confessed his bewilderment in an amusing commentary which took on an unintended poignancy:

> Speaking of the unrest all over the world, we don't doubt it, being full of it ourself [sic], to the extent that we don't know whether we are coming or going. We no sooner dodge an auto than a motorcycle hits us from, and in, the rear. . . . Between Socialistic and Bolshevistic schemes, uplift dreams, sex hygienics, progressive militant suffragettes . . . long-haired men and short-haired women with more wheels in their head [sic] than a Waterbury watch . . . movies displanting the church, shimmying, short skirts . . . with Hearst press running morally and intellectually naked thro [sic] the public brush with red ink and yellow journalism, Orientals rasing one kind of hell and all Europe another, a plain, old-fashioned scribe like this one doesn't know where he is at or whether he will have to dodge into an incubator with the chicks tomorrow or eat baled hay ground up in a . . . coffee machine and delivered next day by wireless. . . . A few years ago we knew a whole lot and now we don't know straight up.[14]

Pouring out of this perplexed soul, in spite of the intended humor, was a virtual stream of consciousness which revealed all of the ruralite's commitments to, and fears about, a mechanized world. Yet here is exactly the point—that in spite of their fears ruralites were becoming more and more committed to the trappings of a technological civilization, to incubators for the chicks, to automatic coffee grinders, radios, autos, and motorcycles. It might have dazed them, but it didn't stop them.

By mid-decade the cultural grievances of the countryside were beginning to recede because they were slowly being drained of substance. Many ruralites no longer felt quite the same depth of commitment either to the old society or against the new one. They might continue to speak of hearth and home and family and individualism as the components of a way of life unique to the countryside, and as the source of the nation's greatness, but the home was becoming little more than a base of operations, family ties were coming unstrung, and individualism hurt them economically. In the organizational measures they took to mitigate the economic impact of their individualism, farmers were becoming indistinguishable from urban businessmen, whom they despised, and urban laborers, whom they feared. The growing awareness of all this worked to undermine the old commitments.

In an earlier era, when rural life had been supreme, the farmer might have been the architect of a new society, and the trailblazer who carried it across a continent. Now, however, that society was crumbling under the corrosive influence of another kind of civilization, a mode of social organization framed and directed by the wonders of technology and the rigors of economic rationalization, and cut from the pattern of urban America. The farmer's efforts to resist were fierce but in the end futile, because he found much more in the new way of life that attracted him than repelled him. Once he began to enjoy this tender embrace with the new society he could no longer really attack it with quite the same unqualified conviction.

This did not happen all at once of course. It did not begin in 1919 and it did not end in 1929. Rural hostilities against the cities had been building since early in the industrial era and they persist today. The 1920s, however, served as a pivotal era in the process. It was at the end of the war that these feelings were blown up to crisis proportions, and it was later in the same decade that they began to subside. Not all of the cultural sourness had been dispelled by any means, but just enough of it had been neutralized to begin the transformation from a coherent national crusade into a jumble of local skirmishes.[15] After repeal, prohibition in Illinois was fought out on the precinct level where it disintegrated as a symbol before the abrasions of hundreds of local issues. Such oldstock bastions as Evanston might remain dry, as befits the national headquarters of the Women's Christian Temperance Union, but it hardly mattered as long as Chicago lay conveniently close at hand. In Iowa, the rural areas struck a hollow compromise by banning the sale of liquor in bars, and imposing their wish on the rest of the state until the 1960's when they too succumbed to the pressures of urbanization. The Klan had generated some localized excitement, but the glamour faded quickly and the hooded order withdrew to the South where its underlying racism found more productive soil to manure. Perhaps ruralites were slow to tap new reservoirs of love for immigrants, but they were content with the restriction laws enacted during the 1920s. Meanwhile, they had little heart left for improving the moral tone of the cities. For all practical purposes the crusade ended when they began to pay more attention to the previews of coming attractions at local movie houses that appeared in their local papers than they did to the monotonous liturgy of illusory "victories" in the adjacent columns of temperance news. Except for occasional, largely abortive, outbursts of cultural wrath, what survived in the corn belt to divide the cities from the rural areas were, above all, the ever-present sources of economic conflict.

Farmers were finding a new place for themselves in the fast-changing world of the 1920s, and it was a place in the new world of the cities. The pain of adjustment was almost unbearable at first, but it was fairly brief. They had started the postwar years with hopes high that they could remake the cities in their own image. On the eve of the Great Depression they could look back over the decade and ponder instead the ironic turn of fate that had recast their own world in the mold of urban America.

NOTES

1. Iowa, General Assembly, *Journals of the House of Representatives,* 1929, pp. 62–63.

2. Ibid., p. 81.

3. Ibid., p. 62.

4. The discussion on the following pages is based upon evidence gathered for the chapters on cultural and economic conflict.

5. On innumerable occasions the bills which embodied urban economic demands were either scaled down in committee or amended down on the floor of the house.

6. I have discussed the economic and status historians more fully in Don S. Kirschner's "Conflicts and Politics in the 1920's: Historiography and Prospects," *Mid-America.*

7. Gusfield, *Symbolic Crusade,* see especially pp. 11 and 120.

8. *Wallace's Farmer,* August 14, 1925.

9. *Ames* (Iowa) *Daily Tribune,* August 20, 1923; *Monticello* (Iowa) *Express,* August 7, 1919, quoting the *Mt. Vernon* (Iowa) *Hawkeye.*

10. *Monticello* (Iowa) *Express,* August 7, 1919, quoting the *Mt. Vernon* (Iowa) *Hawkeye.*

11. The decline of church opposition to the movies can be traced in the published minutes of such organizations as the Illinois Conference of the M.E. Church, the Illinois State Baptist Association, the Iowa Annual Conference of the M.E. Church, the Iowa Baptist Convention, and the various county and regional subgroupings of these organizations.

12. The changing nature of rural advertising was pervasive and almost uniformly evident throughout the village press.

13. *Osceola* (Iowa) *Tribune,* May 21, 1925.

14. *O'Brien County* (Iowa) *Bell,* January 25, 1923.

15. It seems to me that the issues raised by Senator McCarthy in the 1950s, and by Senator Goldwater in 1964, were related to the kinds of tensions that existed in the 1920s, but in different ways and with different support. The cities were no longer the targets, nor were farmers particularly the source. On the contrary, the farmers of Iowa and Illinois remained cool to the Wisconsin senator, and translated their fears of a Goldwater victory into a landslide vote for his Democratic opponent.

Methodological Appendix

FOR many historians there is still something exotic about quantification. By now most of them are tolerant perhaps, and will grant that statistics are all right for those with a stomach for that sort of thing. Not all historians are so flexible, however. There are those, for instance, who comprise a kind of methodological ancien régime and judge any departure from orthodoxy as a heresy. At the other extreme, some of the recent converts to quantification appear at times to lose patience with historical problems that cannot be tabulated. In the pursuit of methodological and linguistic purity they run the risk of creating a new orthodoxy, and a very private one at that. For the purpose of communicating with these mutual antagonists, I think it is important that I explain to one group just what I have tried to do, and to the other why I did not do more of it.

Both Richard Hofstadter and William Leuchtenburg have suggested that the rural status discontents of the 1920s were a function of the prosperity of that decade. The empirical basis for this assertion is not apparent, but the argument does contradict what earlier historians had said about farm conditions at the time, and obviously merits another look if Hofstadter's hypothesis is to be tested.

This hypothesis can be verified in one of two ways: (1) one might demonstrate that economic conditions in the rural areas were generally good, and that status issues prevailed there in a general, rather than selective, way; (2) one might demonstrate that some rural areas were much more prosperous than others, and that status issues prevailed disproportionately in these prosperous areas. The discussion of economic conditions in Chapter I was designed to provide a basis for testing both of these propositions.

To examine the first, I gauged long-term conditions in the farm economy of Iowa and Illinois from 1910 (1900 in some cases) to 1930. I used census data on capital value (land, buildings, and machinery) and mortgaged indebtedness, supplementary information on farm income in Iowa,[1] and some very impressionistic evidence on farm taxes. The study was not sophisticated by any means, yet the evidence pointed so heavily and consistently in one direction that it seemed adequate to support the generalization—hardly a novel one—that I submitted. Nevertheless, it became clear quite early in the study that there were considerable differences in the economic conditions of corn belt farmers. They were separated by economic gaps in the good years through 1919, and after the price decline of 1920–1921 they were still separated, although at a generally lower level. Before the second proposition could be tested, and in general before the voting behavior of rural legislators could be explained, these variations had to be pinned down.

In this case it was necessary to collect economic information for every rural legislative district in both states. This was easy enough for Iowa, because census data were given on a county basis, and each county in Iowa was a separate legislative district. In Illinois, however, the rural legislative districts were usually made up of several counties—as many as six or seven—so that it was necessary to devise a fairly elaborate system that would yield average figures for the entire district. In both states I used census data on gross income, value of land, buildings and machinery, and ratio of debt to value, and then measured the information for each legislative district against a statewide average. The districts were then grouped into three categories: (1) those that fell well below the average—the least prosperous; (2) those that were near the average; (3) those that ranged far above the average—the most prosperous.[2] Information from the 1920 census was used to classify districts for the 1919 legislative session, which was the last one before the price break. Those figures, however, represented the peak of a twenty-year rise in farm fortunes, and would clearly not do for the depression-oriented sessions that followed. Instead, the 1930 census was used because it better reflected the conditions of the 1920s—even 1921—without yet being seriously affected by the new crisis that was breaking in agriculture.

What emerged was a kind of scale of rural legislative districts ranked according to their *relative* economic conditions. It might have been possible to make it a little more precise by amassing further information (which exists in abundance), but the purpose of this book is not to analyze the farm economy in depth. What I had was accurate enough, it was workable, and it corresponded remarkably with what is common knowledge about conditions in these states: the southern counties in both were the most depressed, whereas northwestern Iowa and central Illinois were the least depressed. The advantage of the scale was that it placed each legislative district into a specific economic niche.

Because this study deals not only with the politics of hard

times, but with the politics of hard feelings as well, it was necessary to pay considerable attention to the "rural mind." By rural mind I mean the loosely integrated cluster of images, values, and attitudes through which country people perceived and interpreted their world. It was this mentality that fostered so many of the cultural issues of the 1920s.

Typically, it was in the country press that the rural mind was reflected and reinforced. The editors of these village newspapers and farm journals commonly came from the same environment in which they wrote. They met increasing competition from the metropolitan dailies by providing their readers with a full range of local news, and by commenting on national affairs in terms of local views. Week after week they circulated their ideas to small, homogeneous, geographically narrow audiences,[3] and are thus an excellent historical source for the rural mind.

I selected about three dozen of these papers from very small towns in all parts of Iowa and Illinois. In these journals alone, tens of thousands of editorials appeared on every subject imaginable, from hybrid corn and local boosterism to the new literature, theology, and international politics. To my mind, they constitute a much fuller and more representative index to the rural mind than the haphazardly surviving diaries and letters of a handful of farm leaders. The themes I chose to develop were those that were repeated time and again throughout the 1920s. What emerged was a widely shared core of views that defined the rural mind.

Legislative analysis boils down ultimately to finding out who voted how on what kinds of issues. The boiling-down process, however, becomes rather complicated. Hundreds of bills came before each biennial legislative session in the 1920s. Some of them were of slight significance—a legislator doing a small favor for one of his constituents, or perhaps a request to compensate some farmer for minor property damage. Others more ambitiously sought to revise anything from the state's tax structure to its morals. Each time a legislator voted on one of these measures he went on record with a specific opinion on a specific issue. It is with those votes that I am concerned.[4]

The major procedural problem was to decide which bills to include in the study and which ones to omit. Toward this end, a number of criteria were set up. First of all, a two-thirds majority of the total membership of the house had to vote on the bill, in order to limit the study to the more important matters that came up.[5] Second, at least 15 percent of those voting had to vote against the majority, so that meaningful generalizations could be made about the dissident group. Next, all votes that did not split rural and urban areas were eliminated. Occasionally, for example, the legislature would divide along party lines. In those cases, being a Republican was obviously more important than being a farmer. Illuminating in their own right, such bills, however, would contribute little to an understanding of specifically rural problems. Finally, only those bills that were split more sharply, or came up in several sessions, were retained. The tests were more or less arbitrary, but they were not mindless. Their cumulative purpose was to select out only the most important and most durable issues that divided urban and rural areas.

A much more knotty problem, yet one that held priority over all the others, was to decide which areas were urban and which ones rural. At what point and by what magic does a cluster of people become a city? Demographers, farmers, economists, and poets all offer different answers to this question, and there is something to be said for each of them. The Census Bureau was content in 1920 to define an urban area as any

incorporated place with more than 2,500 inhabitants. Now
this has the advantage of being a perfectly precise definition;
yet the researcher must contain his enthusiasm for an imperative that would place Mendota, Illinois, in the same category
as Chicago, an act which no doubt would horrify the residents
of both of those "cities." Recognizing this incongruity, the Bureau acted to refine the "urban" category in 1930 to include
"metropolitan districts." The metropolitan district was a city
and all contiguous populations in which at least 50,000 people
lived in the core city and 100,000 in the entire area. It was the
modern city with its suburbs. Still, although the redefinition
allows us to avoid some gross absurdities, we are left wonder-
ing whether we have changed the game or merely raised the
ante; we have replaced Mendota with Rockford, but Rockford
after all was much closer in size to Mendota than to Chicago,
and for that matter might have been qualitatively different
from both.

In the end it seemed that the major block to using the census definitions was Chicago, since no other city in either state
even remotely approached its size. The most reasonable solution thus was to isolate Chicago (Cook County) as a separate
category, and then use the census criterion of 2,500 people as
the dividing line between rural and urban for the rest of
Illinois and for Iowa. That way, differences between Chicago
and Rockford would show up, and if it turned out that there
were no differences, that too would be valuable information.
Thus, an urban legislative district was defined as one in which
more than half the population lived in towns and cities of
more than 2,500 people; where less than half the population
lived in such areas the district was defined as rural. Actually,
most of the very small towns—those of 4,000 or 5,000 people—
were absorbed either in a solidly rural district or into one

dominated by larger cities. As a result, almost all of the urban districts were much more urban than one might infer from the standard set by the Census Bureau.

	Rural					Cook	
	1	*2*	*3*	*Total*	*Urban*	*County*	*Total*
Dem.							
F	9	6	3	18	2	0	20
A	2	5	2	9	4	28	41
O	0	0	1	1	1	0	2
Rep.							
F	12	15	12	39	10	12	61
A	1	1	0	2	10	16	28
O	0	0	0	0	0	1	1
Total							
F	21	21	15	57	12	12	81
A	3	6	2	11	14	44	69
O	0	0	1	1	1	1	3

It does not seem unreasonable in a political study to pay at least some attention to political parties, although party differences had less impact than one might imagine. During the 1920s, Iowa was essentially a one-party state. Even dissent was normally expressed through the Republican party, as it had been since around the turn of the century. Rarely did the Democrats send more than a handful of men to Des Moines, and those who went voted much as Republicans from similar districts did.[6] Consequently, party affiliation was not included as a variable for Iowa.

In Illinois, the situation was very different. Because of a complicated system of multiple voting that was designed to guarantee minority representation, the usual pattern was for each district to send two of its allotted three members from one party and the third from the other. In only a relatively few districts was one party strong enough to sweep all three seats. Thus, in contrast to their moribund compatriots across the Mississippi, Illinois Democrats functioned as a viable minority of 30 to 40 percent in the legislature, and held the potential to act as a political bludgeon when they united against a divided foe. For this reason, party affiliation was included as a variable in Illinois.

The basic categories for the legislative analysis are rural and urban districts. The rural districts in both states were sub-divided into economic groupings, and for Illinois party affiliation was included as well. The evidence is summarized in the form of tables. The Iowa tables should be clear enough to read without difficulty, but the Illinois tables require some explanation.

The table above describes voting in the Illinois House of Representatives to ratify the Eighteenth Amendment to the Constitution in 1919. "Dem." refers to Democrats, "Rep." to Republicans; "F" represents the votes *for* ratification, "A" the votes *against,* and "O" the number who did not vote. Among the rural votes, those under "1" were from the least prosperous districts, those under "2" were from average districts, and those under "3" were from the most prosperous ones. With the exception of a few representatives from the suburbs, "Cook County" refers to Chicago, and "urban" refers to all other urban districts in the state. The table reveals that Chicago and the rural areas were drastically split on the question of a pro-hibition amendment, while the lesser cities were divided; Re-publicans everywhere were more prohibitionist than Demo-crats, but urban Republicans were far wetter than rural

Republicans; finally, questions of affluence and poverty in the rural areas did not influence voting on the liquor question at all.[7]

A few words ought to be said about some of the variables that were *not* included in the study. Because of the large dimensions of cultural conflict in the 1920s, it might seem appropriate to consider ethnic differences in the rural districts. However, the responses of rural legislators to cultural issues were surprisingly uniform, which should not be surprising since they represented constituencies that were peopled almost entirely by native Americans of northwestern European descent. No study of the large cities, of course, would be valid without careful consideration of this factor, but this is a study of the rural areas, and not of the cities. At best, ethnic differences between rural Germans and rural Dutch, for instance, *might* explain the behavior of the small minority of dissenters from the rural pattern. It is equally possible that these "deviant" votes were simply cast by maverick legislators. In a few instances, party considerations probably played a role. In any case, however, since the rural areas often achieved a kind of consensus on these matters, it seemed more important to explain the consensus than the dissenters from it. Of the few cases where I did look into the question, some appeared to be rooted in ethnic background (German rural areas were less than enthusiastic about Prohibition), while others did not.

Another variable that might have been included is the degree of urbanness in a rural district. In fact, I did break the rural category into three other subgroupings originally: (1) the districts that were entirely rural, i.e., did not have even one town of at least 2,500 people in them; (2) those that were up to 25 percent urban; (3) those that were between 25 and 50 percent urban. I ran every bill of all the sessions in both states through this mill, and in some instances I did turn up some complicated splits within the rural camp. Usually, however, this only added tidbits of nonessential information or chipped away slightly at some of the generalizations without substantially adding to or qualifying information already available in the less complicated "rural" category. And the tables that resulted were ghastly to contemplate.

It seems to me that there is a trap for the unwary or the overcommitted in quantitative methodology. It is attractive because it allows one to answer certain kinds of questions with considerable accuracy, and because occasionally it may even open up vistas that are not readily accessible through the tried and true techniques. The trouble is that the number of possible categories and correlations in legislative analysis is almost limitless. Having made his initial commitment to accuracy, the researcher is apt to feel obligated to test all of them, at which point his methodology threatens to become an end in itself. The reductio ad absurdum of these methodological refinements is to set up a separate category for each legislator. There is no logical reason not to do so. After all, there were 108 representatives in Iowa and each one voted for his own reasons on every bill that came before him. Then why not establish 108 categories and test each one for every social, political, economic, ideological, and psychological variable imaginable, as well as all possible combinations among them? The evidence would be inscrutable, the inferences unfathomable, and the book interminable, but at least nobody could fault our zeal for methodological purity. No, short of pursuing the methodological imperative for its own sake, the problem is to strike some kind of balance between comprehensiveness and comprehensibility, between methodological fundamentalism and human discourse. If that premise is granted, then the problem is to make qualitative judgments about how far to go with quantitative techniques so that data can be analyzed, questions answered, and ideas communicated. That has been my methodological guideline throughout.

NOTES

1. I am not aware of a similar study for Illinois, but it is highly unlikely that farm conditions there were substantially different from those in Iowa.

2. Initially, I tried breaking these into five different groups, but this refinement added little that was not apparent in the threefold division, except perhaps confusion.

3. Such journals as *Wallace's Farmer* and *The Iowa Homestead* addressed audiences that were larger and more widely dispersed but no less rural in their makeup.

4. The legislative process, of course, does not begin and end with the final vote on a measure. Indeed, the course of any bill through a legislature traces a history of its own. From the time it is introduced it is subjected to a variety of pressures, is modified in committee, and amended and re-amended on the floor until the finished product may be only a distant relative of the original. And since discretion is often the better part of political valor, the entire process is likely to remain hidden in a shroud of secrecy. When all is said and done, however, my aim is neither to analyze the legislative process nor to trace the shifts in a legislator's attitudes. It is to record how he finally votes on a bill, since that is the opinion that he will have to carry back to his constituents at the next election.

5. This study has been limited to the house of representatives in each state.

6. Party affiliation was tested as a variable for the 1929 session of the Iowa legislature and proved to be of no great consequence.

7. A few of the tables in Chapters IV and V show a majority of both rural *and* urban voters in favor of the bill. In one sense, of course, such a bill did not divide rural and urban areas, since both favored it. Bills of this nature, however, occasionally enlisted such widely varying *degrees* of support that it is more illuminating to emphasize the disparity than the area of agreement. If one could demonstrate, for instance, that 60 percent of German men, and 98 percent of German women, approved of Hitler's accession to power, one might draw two inferences about German politics in 1933: (1) most German men and most German women approved of Hitler's accession to power; (2) disapproval of Hitler's accession to power came almost entirely from men. Both inferences are legitimate, but they say very different things. Of them, the second clearly would lead to a better understanding of Germany at the time. Similarly, it is of more consequence to note that opposition to legalized horse racing in Illinois came from the rural areas than it is to note that rural and urban delegates both voted in favor of legalized horse racing, although both statements are accurate.

Selected Bibliography

Public Documents

ILLINOIS. *Blue Book of the State of Illinois.* 1919–1929. (Springfield, 1921).

ILLINOIS. *Constitutional Convention Bulletins.* 1920.

ILLINOIS. General Assembly. *Debates of the House of Representatives.* 1919.

ILLINOIS. General Assembly. *Journal of the House of Representatives.* 1919–1929.

ILLINOIS. *Legislative Synopsis and Digest.* 1919–1929.

ILLINOIS. *Proceedings of the Constitutional Convention of the State of Illinois,* 4 vols. 1922.

IOWA. *The Book of Iowa.* 1932.

IOWA. *Code of Iowa, Supplement to 1913.* 1914.

IOWA. *Code of Iowa, Supplemental Supplement to 1915.* 1915.

IOWA. *Code of Iowa, 1919.*

IOWA. *Code of Iowa, 1924.*

IOWA. *Code of Iowa, 1927.*

IOWA. General Assembly. *House Bills and Resolutions, 1919–1929.*

IOWA. General Assembly. *Journals of the House of Representatives. 1919–1929.*

UNITED STATES. BUREAU OF THE CENSUS. *Twelfth Census of the United States: 1900.*

UNITED STATES. BUREAU OF THE CENSUS. *Thirteenth Census of the United States, 1910.*

UNITED STATES. BUREAU OF THE CENSUS. *Fourteenth Census of the United States, 1920.*

UNITED STATES. BUREAU OF THE CENSUS. *Fifteenth Census of the United States, 1930.*

UNITED STATES. BUREAU OF THE CENSUS. *Census of Religious Bodies, 1916.*

UNITED STATES. BUREAU OF THE CENSUS. *Census of Religious Bodies, 1926.*

UNITED STATES. BUREAU OF THE CENSUS. *Census of Religious Bodies, 1936.*

UNITED STATES. DEPARTMENT OF COMMERCE. *Statistical Abstract of the United States, 1943.*

Books

BOWEN, HOWARD. *Iowa Income: 1909–1934.* Iowa City, Iowa: The State University of Iowa Press, 1935.

BURNER, DAVID. *The Politics of Provincialism.* New York: Alfred A. Knopf and Company, 1968.

CHALMERS, DAVID. *Hooded Americanism.* Garden City, N.Y.: Doubleday and Company, 1965.

FEDERAL WRITERS' PROJECT OF THE WORKS PROJECT ADMINISTRATION OF ILLINOIS. *Illinois, A Descriptive and Historical Guide.* Chicago: A. C. McClurg and Company, 1939.

GINGER, RAY. *Six Days or Forever?* Boston: Beacon Press, 1958.

GUSFIELD, JOSEPH. *Symbolic Crusade.* Urbana, Illinois: The University of Illinois Press, 1963.

HICKS, JOHN D. *Republican Ascendancy.* New York: Harper and Brothers, 1960.

HIGHAM, JOHN. *Strangers in the Land.* New Brunswick, N.J.: Rutgers University Press, 1955.

HOFFMAN, FREDERICK. *The 20's.* New York: Colliers Books, 1962.

HOFSTADTER, RICHARD. *The Age of Reform.* New York: Alfred A. Knopf and Company, 1955.

INDUSTRIAL DEVELOPMENT COMMITTEE OF ILLINOIS. *Illinois: Resources, Development, Possibilities.* Chicago: The Illinois Chamber of Commerce, 1930.

LEUCHTENBURG, WILLIAM. *The Perils of Prosperity.* Chicago: The University of Chicago Press. 1958.

LEVINE, LAWRENCE W. *Defender of the Faith.* New York: Oxford University Press, 1965.

LYND, ROBERT S., AND HELEN M. *Middletown.* New York: Harcourt, Brace and Company, 1929.

MENCKEN, H. L. *Prejudices: A Selection.* Selected by James T. Farrell. New York: Vintage Books, 1959.

NEPRASH, JERRY ALVIN. *The Brookhart Campaigns in Iowa, 1920–1926.* New York: Columbia University Press, 1932.

SALOUTOS, THEODORE, AND HICKS, JOHN D. *Agricultural Discontent in the Middle West, 1900–1939.* Madison, Wisconsin: The University of Wisconsin Press, 1951.

SHIDELER, JAMES. *Farm Crisis, 1919–1923.* Berkeley, California: The University of California Press, 1957.

SINCLAIR, ANDREW. *Prohibition, Era of Excess.* Boston: Little, Brown and Company, 1962.

SMITH, HENRY NASH. *Virgin Land.* Cambridge, Mass.: Harvard University Press, 1950.

SOULE, GEORGE. *Prosperity Decade.* New York: Holt, Rinehart and Winston, 1947.

Pamphlets

HICKS, JOHN D. *Normalcy and Reaction.* Published for the Service Center for Teachers of History, The American Historical Association, 1960.

Articles

DERGE, DAVID. "Urban-Rural Conflict: The Case in Illinois." In *Legislative Behavior,* edited by John C. Wahlke, and Heinz Eulau, pp. 218–227. Glencoe, Illinois: The Free Press, 1959.

HOFSTADTER, RICHARD. "The Pseudo-Conservative Revolt." In *The New American Right,* edited by Daniel Bell. New York: Criterion Books, 1955.

————. "Could a Protestant Have Beaten Hoover in 1928?" *The Reporter,* March 17, 1960, pp. 31–33.

JEWELL, MALCOLM E. "Party Voting in American State Legislatures." *The American Political Science Review,* 1955, pp. 773–791.

JOHNSTONE, PAUL H. "Old Ideals Versus New Ideas in Farm Life." Department of Agriculture. In *Farmers in a Changing World, Yearbook of Agriculture, 1940,* pp. 111–170. Washington, D.C.: 1940.

KIRSCHNER, DON S. "Henry A. Wallace as Farm Editor," *American Quarterly,* June, 1965, pp. 187–202.

————. "Conflicts and Politics in the 1920's: Historiography and Prospects." *Mid-American,* October, 1966, pp. 219–233.

LINK, ARTHUR. "What Happened to the Progressive Movement in the 1920's?" *The American Historical Review,* July, 1959, pp. 833–851.

MAC RAE, DUNCAN. "The Relation Between Roll Call Votes and Constituencies." *The American Political Science Review,* 1952, pp. 1046–1055.

MAY, HENRY F. "Shifting Perspectives on the 1920's." *The Mississippi Valley Historical Review,* 1956, pp. 405–427.

NOGGLE, BURL. "The Twenties: A New Historiographical Frontier." *The Journal of American History,* 1966, pp. 299–314.

Newspapers and Periodicals

Alta (Iowa) *Advertiser.* 1922–1928.

Ames (Iowa) *Daily Tribune.* 1919–1929.

Bardolph (Illinois) *News.* 1919–1929.

Buda (Illinois) *Plain Dealer.* 1919–1923.

Bureau (Illinois) *Farmer.* 1927–1928.

Carmi (Illinois) *Tribune-Times.* 1919–1929.

Carrollton (Illinois) *Patriot.* 1919–1929.

Chicago Tribune. 1919–1929.

Clarinda (Iowa) *Herald.* 1919–1929.
Davis County (Iowa) *Republican.* 1919–1929.
Decorah (Iowa) *Public Opinion.* 1921–1927.
Des Moines Register. 1919–1929.
Elkader (Iowa) *Register.* 1919–1929.
Fremont County (Iowa) *Herald.* 1919–1929.
Galena (Illinois) *Gazette.* 1919–1929.
Grayville (Illinois) *Mercury.* 1919–1929.
Hamburg (Iowa) *Reporter.* 1929.
Henry (Illinois) *News-Republican.* 1919–1929.
Illinois Agricultural Association Newsletter. 1919–1923.
Illinois Agricultural Association Record. 1923–1929.
Iowa City Press Citizen. 1919–1921.
Iowa Forum. 1919–1921.
Iowa Homestead. 1919–1929.
Iowa Union Farmer. 1919–1929.
Knoxville (Iowa) *Journal.* 1919–1929.
Monticello (Iowa) *Express.* 1919–1929.
Mount Ayr (Iowa) *Record-News,* 1921.
Oblong (Illinois) *Oracle.* 1919–1929.
O'Brien County (Iowa) *Bell.* 1919–1925.
Osceola (Iowa) *Tribune.* 1921–1925.
Peotone (Illinois) *Vedette.* 1919–1925.
Rock Rapids (Iowa) *Reporter.* 1919–1925.
Rossville (Illinois) *Press.* 1919–1929.
Sac (Iowa) *Sun.* 1921–1925.
Sioux County (Iowa) *Index.* 1921–1928.
Virginia (Illinois) *Republican-Gazette.* 1919–1929.
Wallace's Farmer. 1919–1929.
Watseka (Illinois) *Times.* 1921–1927.
Waukon (Iowa) *Democrat.* 1919–1927.
Wyoming (Illinois) *Post-Herald.* 1921–1927.

Reports

Annual Conference of the Presbytery of Des Moines. *Minutes,* 1921–1927.

Illinois Conference of the Methodist Episcopal Church. *Minutes,* 1919–1929.

Illinois State Baptist Association. *Minutes,* 1919–1929.

Iowa Baptist Convention. *Minutes,* 1919–1929.

Iowa Conference of the Methodist Episcopal Church. *Minutes,* 1920–1929.

Macoupin County (Illinois) Baptist Association. *Minutes,* 1919–1929.

Northwest Iowa Conference of the Methodist Episcopal Church. *Minutes,* 1919–1929.

Southern Illinois Conference of the Methodist Episcopal Church. *Minutes,* 1919–1929.

Index